The Phantom of Scapa Flow

Alexandre Korganoff

The Phantom of Scapa Flow

IAN ALLAN LTD LONDON

First published 1969
English edition 1974

ISBN 0 7110 0504 4

Translated by W. Strachan and
D. M. Strachan

© A. Korganoff, Paris 1969
© English translation, Ian Allan Ltd, 1974

Published by Ian Allan Ltd, Shepperton, Surrey,
and printed in the United Kingdom by
The Garden City Press Limited, Letchworth, Hertfordshire

Contents

To My Mother

Foreword

by Grand Admiral Karl Dönitz

Ich beglückwünsche Herrn Alexandre Korganoff zu seinem
Werk "Le Secret de Scapa Flow". Herr Korganoff hat sein
Buch sehr interessant geschrieben und sich bei seinen Dar-
stellungen stets bemüht, der historischen Wahrheit gerecht
zu werden. So würdigt seine Arbeit auch ausgezeichnet die
tapfere Tat des U-Boot-Kommandanten Günter Prien.

Ich wünsche dem Buch guten Erfolg!

Aumühle, den 21. Juni 1969

I congratulate Mr Alexandre Korganoff on his book *The Phantom of Scapa Flow*.

Mr Korganoff's narrative is most interesting and his presentation throughout shows great objectivity towards historical truth. He thus acknowledges and distinguishes the courageous deed of the U-boat captain, Lieutenant Günther Prien.

I wish the book every success.

Aumühle 21st June 1969

Dönitz

Preface

To describe a former enemy's operation, putting oneself in his place, is not an easy task, when one knows what was at stake during the 1939–45 war and the means the enemy did not hesitate to use.

I began the analysis of this mission in the more general context of the tactical and strategic study of the submarine weapon. The persistent contradictions of the German and British versions prompted me to pursue my investigation.

Here are the facts: During the night of the 13th/14th October 1939 *U-47*, advancing on the surface, penetrated into the naval base of Scapa Flow. Her commanding officer, Oberleutnant Günther Prien, announced that he had sunk the battleship *Royal Oak* and disabled the battle-cruiser *Repulse*. The Admiralty answered laconically that "*Repulse* was at sea".

In any case, Prien's raid on the base, which was considered to be inviolable, brought about serious consequences for the British Navy. Temporarily abandoning Scapa Flow, as it was deemed unsafe, the Home Fleet was falling into the trap set by the Commander of U-boats. Commodore Dönitz had correctly guessed the move of the British ships towards the replacement bases, which were still more vulnerable, and had mined them.

The outcome was almost immediate: on 21st November, in the Firth of Forth, the brand new cruiser *Belfast* struck a magnetic mine which broke her keel: on 4th December in Loch Ewe, the flagship *Nelson* was badly damaged by another mine. The damage to the *Nelson* was carefully kept secret.

Like all feats of arms, the raid by *U-47* had its mysteries and its legends. To discover the truth thirty years later is not easy, rather it is problematical, all the more because on the British side, everything concerning this operation is still under absolute secrecy under the terms of the 'Official Secrets Act'.

Some men, especially among the survivors of the *Royal Oak*, do not believe that the ship was torpedoed and maintain that it was sabotage or an accidental explosion. Others mention a mysterious clockmaker in Kirkwall, a German spy, settled in the Orkneys, who might have guided Prien's submarine. This last version belongs to pure journalistic fantasy. The abandonment of Scapa Flow by the Navy until the base was adequately fortified gives the lie to the theory of sabotage or accidental explosion.

What really happened at Scapa Flow, on the night of the 13th/14th October 1939? Has Prien's success been much more important than is recognised even today? Did he really put out of action two ships of the line when he sank the *Royal Oak* and inflicted damage on a second battleship or battle cruiser? Prien thinks he did. The only two German living eye-witnesses, Petty Officer Dziallas and Leading Seaman Hänsel, who were both on the bridge of *U-47* still assert it with strength and conviction thirty years after the event.

To sink the only battleship present avoids any vindication for the withdrawal from Scapa Flow with five torpedoes still on board. In his war diary[1] Prien justifies this withdrawal at length. It seems difficult to understand why Prien would have invented this second ship. To leave behind a main unit of the enemy's fleet disabled and to come back with torpedoes still unused without having even been detected by the enemy can scarcely be qualified as heroic. But, on the other hand, to sink the only ship of the line in the vicinity and bring back the submarine to her base is a victory without flaw. The line of argument is elementary. The mystery and secrecy maintained for thirty years on this episode by the British authorities contributes to accredit Prien's version of the events.

According to the official British history published in 1954, the commander of *U-47* confused *Repulse*, a battlecruiser of 32,000 tons, one of the biggest ships of the Royal Navy, with *Pegasus*, an old aircraft carrier of 6,900 tons, without scoring a hit on it, either. This is all the more improbable because *Pegasus* had the most distinctive silhouette of the whole British Navy.

The Germans specify that they noticed that the second ship, the one Prien identified as the *Repulse*, had two funnels. *Pegasus* had only one, like a stove-pipe and back aft. The only British ships of the line with two funnels were *Renown*, *Repulse*, *Hood* and the *Iron Duke*. Had the battlecruiser *Renown* already got under way to the South Atlantic in pursuit of the German pocket battleship *Graf Spee*? The Admiralty hates to lie and prefers to resort, if it is necessary, to linguistic acrobatics and, in the case of *Repulse* the answer is laconic: on the night

[1] See Appendix V.

of the 13th/14th October 1939 she was at sea. That is a fact. But in which state? There remain *Hood* and *Iron Duke*. The latter really was at Scapa Flow, but where? *Hood* was photographed there by a German reconnaissance aircraft on the 12th at 15.00hrs. Could it be the ship left, there, with the *Royal Oak*. The silhouettes of the three battle-cruisers *Renown*, *Repulse* and *Hood* are very much alike and at night, confusing them would not be surprising. And neither Prien nor his superiors thought it was of primary importance to identify the ships precisely, a thing always difficult in the course of a night attack. Has there been a mistake? Has the Admiralty reduced a disaster to its smallest proportions by means of a subterfuge as simple as it was elegant: to tell the truth about *Repulse* without any other commentaries? But did they tell all the truth? *This is the question.*

This quid pro quo gave rise to doubts and doubt fostered suspicion on the behaviour of Prien, though the British 'fair play', through Winston Churchill's or Captain Roskill's writings, never missed the opportunity to pay tribute to the 'courageous commander of *U-47*', thus partially acknowledging his achievement. Nobody mentioned the presence of the second ship of the line, just as nobody ever spoke of the damage to *Nelson*. This only came later on, after the Germans had divulged the secret. If the *Iron Duke* was the one which was torpedoed, it is logical, then, that she would take refuge in the course of the same night, in her usual moorings of Longhope in shallow waters some ten miles away.

Three days later, on the 17th October, four Ju-88 light bombers of the 1/K.G.30 group attacked Scapa Flow under the command of Flight Lieutenant Doench. The *Iron Duke* was, technically, sunk by the explosion of a bomb of 500 kilos: a near-miss; officially the loss of the battleship was attributed to this air attack. The British had a splendid occasion to frustrate Prien and, consequently, the department of Dr Goebbels, of a tremendous potential of propaganda. For, in fact, the old battleship, partially disarmed, had been Jellicoe's flag-ship at the battle of Jutland. Already in October 1918 *UB-116* had tried to force the entrance to Scapa Flow with a crew of volunteer officers, with the aim of sinking the flagship.[1] But *UB-116* had been blown up on the minefield of the Hoxa Sound. In this case, Prien would unwaringly have avenged the honour of the German high-seas Fleet on the very spot where the Fleet was scuttled.

[1] The first attempt to enter an enemy's base by force had been carried out on the 20th December 1914 by the French submarine *Curie* in the Adriatic. Entering, submerged, the Austrian base of Pola, the *Curie* was detected. To prevent her from falling into enemy hands, her commanding officer, Lt Cdr O'Byrne gave the order to scuttle.

The *Hood*, battlecruiser of 42,100 tons, the biggest and fastest of the British ships of the line could make 31 knots. When seen again on the 21st October, eight days after Prien's raid, she was laboriously making 25 knots. For how long had she been doing this, and why?

In the second part of the book an analysis of the operation follows (Appendix XII) the official and unofficial German and British records gathered together with other entries after the account of the raid. All the known facts concerning this mystery are mentioned and truth is hidden among the information given there.

I should like to thank all those who have helped me in the course of my research, especially Captain R. F. Nichols, RN, Commander of the *Royal Oak*, Mr Herbert R. Johnston, Stoker, and Mr Norman T. Davies, Corporal of Marines, survivors of the wreck. My especial thanks are due to Grand Admiral Dönitz, who had meticulously planned this operation, for his willingness to see me, patiently answer my questions, and show me the pages of his war diary concerning Scapa Flow.

And last, I must express my gratitude to the survivors of *U-47*. Prien is dead—(he almost certainly died in the attack on a convoy, in the Atlantic in 1941); as did his two watch officers, Endrass and von Varendorff. The survivors of *U-47* have told me, among other things, the incidents not mentioned in Prien's war diary. The testimony of the only two German eye-witnesses of the attack, Ernst Dziallas and Gerhard Hänsel, have been most valuable. The retired Korvetten Kapitän Hans Wessels, then engineer officer, has told me about the damage to the engine and to the starboard propeller shaft; he moreover gave me some technical information and was kind enough to acquaint me with the names and addresses of the survivors of the crew of the submarine. The retired Korvetten Kapitän Wilhelm Spahr, navigator of *U-47* at Scapa Flow, described for me the depth charge attack, the damage to the gyro-compass and the incidents of navigation.

It is the accuracy of all this information which made possible the writing of this account.

I thank all the sailors and airmen who helped me so generously.

PARIS   September 1969   *Alexandre Korganoff*

1. Good heavens they're putting on the lights

U-47 was lying at the bottom of the North Sea. The pallid glare of the light, turned down low in the submarine at rest, was inciting to sleep but Leading Seaman Peter Thewes could not drop off. Sixty metres above, it was probably light by now, a grey light, on a grey sea above which grey clouds were running, chased by a south-east squall which had severely shaken them the night before. At this depth the movement on the surface was not felt. Apart from the men on watch in the control room, all the men had been ordered to rest in order to save oxygen. Lying on his back, Thewes was trying his best to keep his eyes closed.

The submarine with her crew of forty had left Kiel four days before, on the 8th October 1939. Part of the supplies and fuel had been left behind. The normal torpedoes, powered by compressed air, had been landed and, in their place, electric torpedoes of the latest model G7e had been taken on board. These arrangements had, of course, puzzled the crew. The taking on of the new torpedoes had prompted the leading seaman to think that *U-47* had been given an extraordinary assignment. Nobody in the crew's mess knew anything about the object of the cruise and, of course, this mystery had been the sole topic of conversation.

Thewes opened his eyes and came to the conclusion that to go on guessing would lead nowhere. He put the blame for his lack of sleep on indigestion for he did not want to admit that the continual pinching he felt in the pit of his stomach was caused by fear of the unknown. Still, he was not, normally, frightened easily. On the contrary, a sailor well thought of, he had always managed to come out of the most unexpected situation to his advantage. True the war had only been on for five weeks. Still, *U-47* had already managed to score three successes: the *Bosnia*, the *Rio Claro* and the *Gartavon*, three freighters sunk on the 5th, 6th and 7th September.[1] Those were operations carried out

[1]	Gross tonnage	Position when sunk
Bosnia	2,407	42° 29N 09°45W.
Rio Claro	4,086	46° 30N 12°00W.
Gartavon	1,777	47° 04N 11°32W.

in the sunlight. One knew where one was and what one was doing. This time an unaccountable something seemed to make the atmosphere strange, but he could not say why. From the beginning of the cruise, as soon as a ship was signalled, instead of attacking her, the commander carefully avoided her and, from such a commander, this behaviour was, to say the least, peculiar.

Thewes made an effort to think of nothing, but he did not succeed. He tried good old tricks to find sleep, as, for example, spelling difficult words backwards. This exercise only kept him more awake than ever. His back brushed against the pressure hull and he shivered. It was like ice. Thewes imagined what the cold and hostile world on the other side of the hull was like, this world lying in wait to engulf them. He watched a drop of condensation shimmering on one of the pipes running above his head. The submarine oscillated in an unexpected way under the tow of the current and the keel crunched on the sand. The drop fell on the blanket.

A noise nearby made him start. The leading seaman pricked up his ears, then shut his eyes again for a while and swore between his teeth after he had recognised the familiar snoring from the next berth, a kind of short raucous and deep chortle, like the humming of a bomber, followed by a long, high pitched wailing resembling the whistling sound of an aircraft in a nose dive. A warrior's rest, thought Thewes. He smiled at the idea and looked at his wrist watch. It was noon. He had been there since 08.00hrs on his narrow damp berth, overcome by the presentiment of impending action. What other reason could justify this waiting at the bottom of the sea? The 'chief' alone knew. His thoughts crystallised on Captain Günther Prien and Oberleutnant Endrass the First Lieutenant: these two, Thewes was prepared to follow anywhere. He crossed his hands behind his head and began to count methodically the drops of condensation within his field of vision. There were so many of them that the leading seaman was not long in falling asleep.

The crew had just finished their dinner. Muffled sounds indicated that the men had returned to their occupations in the various corners of the submarine. Obersteuermann (Chief Quartermaster) Wilhelm Spahr entered the control room just under the conning tower and glanced at the binnacle clock: 18.45hrs. Spahr was a well proportioned man, with broad shoulders, and was of slightly above average height. He was thirty-five and nobody on board had ever seen him otherwise than calm. The chief quartermaster assumed the double charge of navigator and

Günther Prien on board the *U-47*.

chief of the watch. He sat down at a small table fixed in the hull itself, on the port side near the forward partition, behind which was the captain's tiny office. He lit the lamp, lowered the lampshade mounted on a flexible leg and spreading a map, he began to study the submarine's estimated position, shown by a small circle he had drawn in pencil, south-south-east of the Orkneys. This reckoning could only be most approximate, because for three days the sky, continually overcast, had prevented all observation by the stars.

Getting under way had been carried out on a magnificent sunny Sunday, but the weather worsened during the night and, on the following day, *U-47* ploughed laboriously in a swell heaved by a depression from Ireland. The wind was still freshening and the men on the bridge put on their oilskins and sou'westers. At the end of Duncansby Head, situated at the north-east foreland of Scotland, the barometer suddenly showed a serious drop. The wind was getting stronger and blowing a gale. Heavy lead-coloured clouds were pouring incessant squalls on a wild sea. Visibility worsened. Under the combined action of winds and currents the submarine had drifted and Spahr hoped that the course, such as he had estimated it, was not too different from the correct one. He took a pair of dividers and fixed one of the extremities on his estimated point to determine the distance which separated them from the land. Absorbed by this problem he did not see Oberleutnant Günther Prien, commander of *U-47*, lower his head and step over the threshold of the watertight bulkhead leading into the forward part of the control room. He stopped for a while, buttoned up his old jersey on top of his polo neck pullover, then came near Spahr. Bending over his shoulder, he examined the map quickly.

"Well, Spahr, is that where we are?"

Startled, the chief quartermaster raised his head.

"Yes, sir, at least I hope so. With the currents, cross-currents and swirls from the Pentland Firth, the reckoning is difficult."

"I know the currents can reach 10 knots. In any case, we'll soon know. We'll draw nearer to the coast in order to take the bearings. I must have an accurate position."

Spahr was getting ready to say "aye aye, sir" but Prien had already turned away. The navigator put down the dividers and switched off the light.

It is all very well to take the bearings but try to do it in a pitch black night with no moonlight, on a wild sea, with, no doubt, on top of it all, a sky overcast and low. Still, things would not be at their worst if it did not rain because, if it did, one would not be able to see much in any case.

His thoughts were stopped short by a series of brief orders calling the crew back to diving stations. Behind Spahr, on the other side of the control room, on starboard, the engineer officer, Oberleutnant Hans Wessels, a giant, easily taller by a head than the rest of the crew, set about easing the submarine off the seabed.

"Hydroplanes to rise! Pump the trimming tanks."

Engine Room Artificer (ERA) Böhm quickly turned the control wheels of the valves. The pumps began panting. Slowly *U-47* got off its sandy cradle.

"She's rising—1 metre . . . 2 metres . . . " said Wessels.

The two electric motors each 375hp started with their characteristic note which settled into a continuous high-pitched sound.

The submarine rose at an angle of 10°, about 1m a second. The engineer officer standing near the board of the signal lamps went on calling out the depths. The humming of the electric motors of the hydroplanes resounded clearly amidst all the other noises which filled the control room. Prien and his two officers, Endrass and von Varendorff, with Petty Officer Meyer, had already put on their oilskins. Spahr did the same.

"Periscope depth! Both motors half speed," ordered Prien.

The waves could already be felt. Legs wide apart, Meyer began meticulously cleaning his binoculars, which hung round his neck. At a depth of 20m Wessels stabilised the submarine, then took her down again for a few seconds, as some of the men had had to change position. Given the length of the submarine, 66.5m, the shifting of their weight had influenced the trim of the ship according to the principle of the lever. The engineer officer was taking into account each litre of water in the ballast tanks. His curt orders followed in quick succession and Böhm operated the numerous controls of the valves without pausing.

The submarine rolled and pitched with more and more erratic movements as it approached the surface.

Prien climbed the ladder leading to the conning tower.

"Up periscope!"

His eyes followed the long steel tube slowly rising from its shaft. When the sights reached the level of his eyes, he grasped the handles and looked all around. Night had fallen. Nothing anywhere. He straightened himself and folded back the handles along the tube.

"Down periscope! Course south-east!"

To surface on a heavy sea it had to be head on with a good buoyancy of the forward ballast tanks.

"Course south-east," said the helmsman.

"Surface!" ordered Prien, putting on his oilskins.

The air, compressed at 205 kilos, rushed whistling into the ballast tanks from which the water was forced out gurgling. Wessels looked at the depth gauge—13m . . . 12m . . . 11m. He switched off the light leaving only the red lamps on. The characteristic sound of the cataracts falling from the superstructures indicated that the submarine had surfaced.

"The hatch is above water," he said.

The voice pipe and the hatch of the conning tower leading to the bridge had been opened; the barometer showed a pressure differential of less than 5mm. Standing on the ladder, Endrass was already unclipping the hatch which he pushed down with a dull sound on the deck of the bridge. A gush of cold air rushed inside. Prien jumped on the ladder and in less than three seconds joined his first lieutenant on the bridge which was still streaming with water. Listening intently, the two men tried to pierce the gloom. They knew that the first moments are decisive, for the enemy is sometimes very near. The night was black as ink. It was not raining but the stars remained invisible.

"Both diesels?" asked Prien.

"Both diesels on!" replied a voice from the depths of the ship.

"Both engines slow ahead!"

"Stop the electric motors!"

The starboard engine was the first to start with a dull rumble, followed, almost immediately, by the port engine. For an instant their roar rose above the tumult of sea and wind.

A slight jolt indicated that they were into gear. *U-47*, casting a cloud of spray, sprang forward on a foaming sea.

Von Varendorff and Meyer, having taken up their posts on the bridge, reported to the commander—

"Nothing to starboard!"

"Nothing aft!"

"Course north-west," ordered Prien into the speaking tube.

He straightened himself and scanned the sea.

"Close the conning tower hatch," he shouted without turning his head.

With a quick gesture, von Varendorff gripped the rail of the bridge with his left hand and, with his right, seized the hatch which he swung into place.

"Hatch shut, sir," reported the third hand.

The sea was coming from behind. The waves were lifting the stern and propelling the submarine forward, sometimes giving her a bow down angle—unpleasant, almost dangerous; dangerous because, if another wave were to submerge the prow while the ship glided down a trough, she would be unable to straighten herself quickly enough and would nose dive. The speed and her slim lines favoured this dive. In no time she could find herself 50m below the surface and tons of water could pour inside by the two air inlets of the diesels.

The deck was covered with foam. The water frequently rose halfway up the 88mm gun. Prien leaned on the speaking tube and addressed himself to Wessels who had remained on watch in the control room.

"Blow the ballast tanks completely with the exhaust gases and watch the hydroplanes in case of a dip."

Ceaselessly the ship in flight climbed the moving slopes which overtook her, rolling all the while. When the sea gave way, her stern plunged in the trough and, with a roaring crash, hurled up a splash of foaming water. Looming out unexpectedly from the darkness, liquid mountains continuously threatened to break on the conning tower. Her ballast tanks emptied of all water, the submarine behaved less heavily.

On the bridge the four men sheltered, after a fashion, from the blustering wind which was heavy with spray. In that atmosphere, saturated with water, salt everywhere—in the eyes, in the neck, its bitter taste was on the lips and in the throat. They had omitted to put on their breast-ropes, and a fierce lurching laying the submarine on port side brutally sent them sprawling on top of each other against the metallic casing of the bridge. Von Varendorff was the first to recover his balance. Raising his head, he saw the rest of a wave higher than the others or rather he made out the wan reflections of its foaming ridges rushing on the stern.

"Look out! A wave! Hang on . . ." He had no time to finish his sentence. *U-47* dipped in the void which the wave hollowed in front of itself. A dull booming. The conning tower struck by a direct hit of tons of water vibrated under the blow.

Slowly the submarine was emerging, covered in a coat of foam. On the flooded bridge the four men were spitting water, snorting and swearing. They were soaked to the skin. Streamlets of icy water were running down their backs and along their legs.

"Filthy weather," grumbled von Varendorff, wiping his eyebrows with the back of his left hand.

His eyes burning from the salt, the lieutenant took up his watch again. He was wondering when on earth the captain would make up his mind to announce the aim of the cruise.

He averted his head for a while and glanced sideways at the silent shadowy figure of the captain. He was itching to ask but he knew it was useless. Several times he had tried to draw Endrass and Wessels into conversation. Rightly or wrongly he supposed they were in the know of the secret, but these attempts had not come to anything. Little by little the lieutenant had come to the conclusion that their objective was a night attack on a big unit of the British Fleet at the exit of the famous base of Scapa Flow. This assumption was logical. Their course, the day spent at the bottom of the sea, the attitude of the captain, everything confirmed him in his idea. Scanning the darkness he was weighing the chances they would have of getting through the screen of destroyers and cruisers which would certainly keep a vigilant watch over the battleships and the aircraft carriers. He reassured himself by thinking of Korvetten Kapitän Schuart who had succeeded in piercing that screen with U-29 and in sinking the aircraft carrier *Courageous* in the Atlantic, three weeks before, on the 19th September, to be precise. After all, he said to himself, they were quite able to repeat the feat of the U-29 and may be, even, to do better. The lieutenant stopped wondering and concentrated on his watch. A shadow darker than the night attracted his attention then melted away in the darkness and disappeared—a cloud probably. The coast remained invisible. Supposing their reckoning was correct, the distance was too great to hope to get a glimpse of the islands in the moonless night.

The normal watch at sea was at 20.00hrs. Endrass, Bootsmann Sammann, Bootsmaat Dziallas and Matrosen Obergefreiter Hänsel came on watch successively instead of von Varendorff, Spahr, Meyer, and Matr. Ob. Gefr. Dittmer and Marquard, without there being more than four men together on the bridge. Some ten minutes later Prien too, left the bridge.

The wind was blowing from the south-east, force 6 to 7. The tide was high, nearly slack. The tidal stream, a knot or a little less, was flowing from the north with a leaning to north-north-east. These conditions of wind and currents of a fairly opposite direction caused the sea to be somewhat choppy and hard on the ship.

It could not be long before the land became visible. Spahr climbed on the bridge and wedged himself up as well as he could between the side of the bridge and the mass of the periscopes. He was glad to note that the wind was losing some of its strength. He took his binoculars, conscientiously wiped their lens clear and swept the sector where he thought he would find the horizon from abeam on portside and to the bow. Nothing to be seen. It was not easy. The sea and sky merged in to each other in the dark. Not a trace of anything like a coastline.

Spahr had outstandingly keen eyesight. He never wore the red spectacles which the men on watch were supposed to put on to get used to the darkness before going up on the bridge. Anxiety was creeping into his mind. Had he made a mistake in his reckoning? Or was it a squall hiding the shore, in which case visibility could fall to less than a mile and the situation of the submarine became dangerous. You had to be cautious about the strong, changing, insufficiently known currents, frequently carrying you on to the rocks.

He was on the point of asking the control room for the depth on the echo sounder when a mass slightly darker than the night emerged from the waves. Then his reckoning was not incorrect and he was relieved. The land he observed to port was looming up vaguely, about 45° from the bow, and its dim lines melted into the cloudy sky and the sea. The Orkneys were there quite near, plunged in the most intense darkness. No trace of life, nobody about on the shore. He wondered if there were men on the watch to keep a look-out to the open sea. There were few chances to be spotted in this darkness, but you never knew.

A squirt of spray blurred his vision through the binoculars. He let them hang from his neck and took out of his pocket the damp chamois leather he had used a few minutes before.

While drying the lens, he attentively studied the outlines of the cliffs on the portside, trying to get a general picture of the coast. To his right, Dziallas scanned the darkness ahead.

"I thought I could see a headland but I cannot find it again. It was there, straight ahead," he said in an unsteady voice.

Spahr turned to the direction mentioned, stared at the distance but could discover no sign of the land. He took his binoculars again without any more success.

"I cannot see anything," he said, lowering his binoculars.

"I must have dreamt it," apologised Dziallas.

"Maybe you did not."

Endrass had a feeling they were coursing towards a reef without his being able to see it. It was a question of instinct. He guessed the approaching danger. He had no right to take any risk.

"Starboard 20°," he ordered. In the conning tower the helmsman repeated the order and the submarine altered course to starboard. Spahr

Chief Quartermaster Wilhelm Spahr./Wilhelm Spahr

Petty Officer Ernst Dziallas, one of the two German eye witnesses still living, who was on watch on the bridge during the operation. / Author

endeavoured to scan the islands in the hope of discovering an outstanding point which would allow him to check his bearings. He had spent a lot of time studying the hydrographic pilot and had kept the topography of the place fresh in his mind, but in the darkness one hill looked like another. He tried to pinpoint Ward Hill which dominates the island of South Ronaldsay and is situated on the centre near the east coast.

Suddenly a shaft of light spurted from the night. Spahr quickly turned his head and was struck dumb by surprise. Before he had time to recover, a second beam of light pierced the darkness, then a third. . . .

"Good heavens, they are putting on the lights," Dziallas could not help shouting.

On the portside, covering nearly 180° the intermittent beams of the lighthouses and beacons marked out the coast and its dangers as in peace time.

U-47 was near land, going northward, parallel to the coast. Endrass took the decision to head for the open sea.

"Steer starboard."

The lights slid aft.

"Steady as she goes. . . ."

He looked at the luminous dial of his wrist watch: almost 22.04hrs, then he leaned again on the voice pipe and called the captain to let him know about this unforeseen event. Now they had to hurry to take the opportunity offered them to get their bearings without possible errors, for the British could switch off the lights as quickly as they had switched them on. The sky remained covered but visibility was better.

"Keep your eyes open! It is not for our benefit that they are lighting up the coast," he cried to the watch.

Before he had time to finish his sentence, Endrass realised that his advice was unnecessary. The attitude of the three men proved their vigilance. With their binoculars stuck to their eyes, they peered in silence at their respective sectors. The sea was still apparently empty.

Prien went up on the bridge. While he was fixing his sou'wester and his oilskins which he had not buttoned up in his haste, Endrass reported to him.

"Course east-south-east. The British lit the coast lights at 22.00hrs sir, I changed course just before, for we were afraid of being too near the land. Apart from that, nothing to report."

"It is something! Did you get the depth?"

"I was going to do it when they switched on the lights sir."

"Good," agreed Prien, while staring at the lights.

Spahr stepped a short distance away and leaned on the rail of the bridge, trying in his turn to identify the lighthouses. He watched, closely the nearest beam, the one which shone aft on portside. He counted the intervals between darkness and light.

"It is Copinsay lighthouse," said Prien at the very moment when Spahr opened his mouth to announce it.

"Yes, there's no doubt sir. The one slightly on its right, a good ten miles farther away is therefore, Auskerry, whose light reaches sixteen miles. Consequently the lighthouse straight behind can only be Rose Ness."

"Perfect," continued Spahr, still speaking, "we now know where we are: abeam of Burray at five or six miles from that island."

His hands firmly clutching the rail of the bridge, Prien reflected on the situation. The enemy allowed him to take precise bearings without difficulty. This was the good aspect of the incident. What could be the reason, surely important, which had caused the British to put on the coast lights? Very likely the move of one or more heavy units of the Home Fleet, battleships or aircraft carriers. But were these ships going into Scapa Flow or, on the contrary, were they leaving the base? Despite an exceptionally keen watch, they had still noticed nothing. This fact did not mean a thing, for the night was black as ink and the British were probably sailing with ships darkened far enough on starboard in the direction of Hoxa Sound, used as the principal entrance of Scapa Flow.

It was necessary at all costs to avoid being found by light craft which must be escorting the enemy formation, for the latter could pass as well by the west as by the east of the Pentland Firth. On her present course, the *U-47* would find herself abeam of this channel, far enough in the open sea, in a sector which was still unhealthy. He decided to change course to the east for two or three hours then to double back to remain in the vicinity of the outstanding points they had been lucky enough to situate so well. He leaned forward and looked at his wrist watch.

"Port helm, steer 085°," he ordered without hesitation.

The wind no longer blew in squalls but the cold was increasing. In spite of his gloves, Prien was feeling the icy touch of the metal making his fingers numb. He took his hands away from the rail of the bridge and rubbed them energetically, one against the other, to quicken his circulation.

Suddenly all the lights went out.

Prien heard Spahr announce 22.30hrs. He turned towards the chief quartermaster.

"Change course at 01.30hrs. Go about so as to come back in the sector. We'll dive to lie on the sea bed towards 04.30hrs."

Besides the uncertainty caused by this nocturnal naval move of the enemy, Prien had something much more serious to worry about. Early in the evening, Wessels had informed him of the existence of a leak of sea water in the external diesel-oil fuel tank supplying the starboard engine. The engineer officer thought that this inflow of water was to be attributed to the valves, defective, in his opinion, because of their mode of construction. These valves close against the pressure and were not, therefore, held in position by the latter. Wessels thought, at first sight, that he would be able to remedy this damage in the course of the night while the submarine was resting on the sea bed. If this plan did not work, the mission would be irrevocably spoilt. If ever the sea water were to seep into the injectors, the engine would become useless and it would be impossible to continue on the port diesel alone. To go

25

where they were going, the difficulty was mainly caused by the navigation. Then *U-47* would need all its power and all its manoeuvrability. The risks were such that the commander in chief of the Submarine Fleet had left to Prien the alternative of studying his chances of success before accepting or refusing the responsibility of the operation.

2. What do you think of it, Prien?

For Oberleutnant Prien, everything has begun in Kiel less than two weeks before, to be precise on the Sunday, 1st October.

On the depot ship of the submarines, *Hamburg*, the officers were chatting in the ward room after lunch when the door opened and an orderly let Commander von Friedeburg past.

"Your attention please, gentlemen, Commander Sobe and Lieutenants Wellner and Prien are asked to present themselves to the commodore of submarines."

Von Friedeburg saluted, turned and left.

The officers looked at one another without saying anything. Prien gave a questioning glance at Sobe, his flotilla leader, but the latter did not react; he was staring at the door which had just been closed. Korvetten Kapitän Sohler, captain of *U-47* broke the silence:

"What have you been up to, Wellner? Prien! Come, we want to know as well," he said, making a visible effort to take an ironical tone.

"I do not see what we might have been guilty of," Prien replied drily.

The three officers went on deck and stepped into a launch, the engine of which was already started. During the crossing of the harbour Prien wondered what could be the reasons for this summons, unusual for a Sunday. The launch slowed down, then the mechanic engaged forward gear, letting the boat advance on its own, alongside the hull of the *Weichsel*.

The helmsman, standing on the stern, gripped the ladder of the *Weichsel* with his hook. Nearby, on Tirpitz quay, Commodore Dönitz, commander in chief of submarines, was reviewing the crew of a U-boat.

Sobe, Wellner and Prien were waiting patiently in the wardroom of the *Weichsel*. They were waiting lost in their thoughts without exchanging a word. First Sobe, then Wellner, were introduced to the commodore.

Once alone, Prien left the armchair and, his hands in his pockets, came near to a porthole. Absentmindedly, he let his eyes wander round the harbour. The sound of clicking heels made him turn round.

"Will Oberleutnant Prien please go and see the commodore of submarines?" said the duty orderly.

Following him up a few steps, he entered a large room. In the centre, standing behind a table covered with maps, his arms crossed, Dönitz gave him a look of welcome. His personality radiated an extraordinary magnetism. Sobe and Wellner were at his side. Tall, slim in his blue naval uniform, the commodore had a face with a striking broad forehead. His features, fine and energetic, were lit up by clear blue, almost grey eyes. Prien came near the table and saluted stiffly. With the ghost of a smile, Dönitz shook his hand and without more ado asked him to listen closely to what Wellner, who had carried out operations in the Orkneys, was going to say.

The Orkneys! Prien's heart beat quicker, but he did not let his emotion show. He gave a quick glance at the table to convince himself that he was not dreaming. It was real: 'Scapa Flow' stood out clearly in big letters on one of the maps. Wellner, who had leaned on the table to begin his report, raised his head for an instant. Face to face, the two officers looked at one another for a second, straight in the eyes then Wellner began his explanations in an even voice:

"Before describing in detail the observations which I have been able to carry out with *U-16* on the defences, the setting of buoys, the lighthouses and currents, I am going to try to give you a general view of the difficulties of penetrating Scapa Flow."

Wellner paused an instant, appearing to reflect on where to begin and Prien realised that Dönitz and Sobe did not stop looking at him. The lieutenant began to speak again.

"The enemy has naturally blocked the different entrances of the bay with nets, mines, booms and blockships. The principal channels, Hoy Sound, Switha Sound, and Hoxa Sound, are especially well protected. The shipping appears to flow by Hoxa Sound, guarded by at least one patrol boat and closed by a submarine net which is opened for entrances and departures of warships as well as fishing boats. During the opening of this net it is possible to slide in submerged behind one of the entering ships. On the east coast Kirk and Skerry Sounds which follow Holm Sound are obstructed by wrecks dating from the first world war. Moreover, the tidal currents are very strong there. The other channels, Water Sound and East Weddel Sound, are impracticable because of shelves and shallows. I have noted temporary lighting of lighthouses and buoys on the occasion of the exits and entrances of ships of the fleet, at night. According to my experience of these regions one of the best defences of Scapa Flow against submarine attack is the sea itself. I have had great difficulties with *U-16* in the Pentland Firth, at the approaches to Hoxa Sound. We have been forced to surface, luckily at night, being unable to overcome the speed of the currents when submerged. In certain places these exceed 10 knots in the spring tide. At its strongest, the sea breaks wildly across the whole of the channel. It is evident that our submarine, doing at best, no more than 7 knots submerged, and that only for a short time, would be at the mercy of whirlpools, currents and cross-currents before operating in this region, and especially in the Pentland Firth, so it is essential to study the tidal currents and the times when they turn very carefully.

Wellner was now going into detail in his observation. From time to time he slid his forefinger on the chart to show precisely the defences obstructing a channel. While listening to him, all sorts of ideas went through Prien's mind, seething with excitement at the prospect of an attack on the famous base of the Home Fleet.

When he had recovered, the checks of the submarines at Scapa Flow during the 1914–1918 war came back to his memory in a flash. Von Hennig, Hansen and Emsmann, who had got under way with a crew of volunteer officers to torpedo the flagship of the Grand Fleet, the battleship *Iron Duke* flying Admiral Jellicoe's flag.

Wellner finally stopped giving explanations. The silence which followed unleashed a reaction in Prien's subconscious, for he felt ashamed at letting his thoughts wander which had prevented him from concentrating on what Wellner was saying.

Dönitz, in his turn, began to speak. Employing, as usual, a minimum of words, he emphasised the danger of an attack against Scapa Flow. He took up a pair of dividers and showed Hoxa Sound on the chart.

"Emsmann perished here. *U-16* was detected in the minefield constituting the external defence of Hoxa Sound. This minefield was controlled electrically from the land. The British closed the circuit. I do not think you can enter by Hoxa Sound and still less by Switha Sound or Hoy Sound because of the obstructions there."

The point of the dividers slid over the map and stopped on Kirk Sound.

"There across Kirk Sound there are only two sunken steamers. Another, sunk on the north side has pivoted under the force of the current parallel to the coast of Mainland and has been carried out a little more towards the east. Between this blockship and Lamb Holm islet is the first gap, 17m wide, up to the low tide mark and where

29

Grand Admiral Karl Dönitz, organiser of the raid on Scapa Flow. / K. Dönitz

the depth reaches 7m. A second, narrower gap opens between this blockship and the north coast of Kirk Sound. The shores are not inhabited. In my opinion a determined commander can pass at night on the surface in the slack of the tide. Certainly navigation will not be easy; on the contrary, it will be the most delicate part of the mission." Dönitz placed the dividers on the chart and, frowning slightly, gave Prien a questioning stare:

"What do you think of it, Prien?"

Taken by surprise, the latter lowered his eyes on the map. Before he had had time to recover, Dönitz went on:

"I do not want an answer just now. You will take with you all the documents in our possession about this plan. It will allow you to study the various aspects of the problem and to evaluate the chances of success. I will wait for your answer on Tuesday."

Prien had listened, and stiffened as if at attention.

He gathered the notes lying on the table and slid them in a large envelope Sobe was offering him. Then he rolled up the maps.

The envelope in his left hand and the rolled chart under his arm, he waited for the commodore to dismiss him, but Dönitz spoke to him once more:

"I hope you understand me well, Prien. You are completely free to accept or refuse this mission. If you come to the conclusion that it is impossible, you will report to me. In any case, be sure you will not be blamed at all, for I am certain that your decision will rest on your sincere and honest conviction."

Dönitz held out his hand:

"Of course the utmost secrecy is indispensable to the success of the operation."

The meeting was concluded. Prien saluted and left the room.

Still under the influence of what had just taken place, he went back to the *Hamburg*, unaware of the world outside. He carefully locked the documents in a safe and decided to go back home for dinner.

He walked like a robot, answering the salutes of the passing sailors and soldiers on the way. He reflected on his responsibilities. Was the mission possible? If so, what were its chances of success? Once more, he took mental bearings on the meeting he had just attended: he himself had remained practically silent, so did Sobe; Wellner had shown himself to be rather pessimistic while developing the result of his observations, the commodore thought the mission was possible and this man knew what he was talking about. The opportunity, so long dreamed of, to become famous by a brilliant feat was at last within his

33

grasp. Should it be allowed to be lost? He felt a mad impulse to accept blindly but reason won the day. He had two days in front of him to study objectively all the information available, before deciding solemnly and sincerely about the possibilities of success or failure.

Prien dined with his wife and their young daughter. At meals he was in the habit of describing in a jovial manner the incidents of the day or the actions of his men. He also had a gift all his own for telling anecdotes in a jesting way. But you were not to be fooled by this good natured expression. At thirty-one, Prien was a stern man, hard with people as well as with himself.

On that night, in spite of his efforts, he could not follow the conversation. His wife quickly guessed that something of importance was on his mind. She did not ask any questions, for experience had taught her that when her husband kept silent about his preoccupations it was better not to speak about them. She only cleared the table earlier than usual, alleging as a pretext that she wanted to take their daughter for a walk before bed time.

Prien left the table, took his cap, and kissed his wife, who was getting ready in the hall.

"I have something to do, it won't take long," he said, as an excuse on the threshhold.

He went back to the *Hamburg*, took the envelope and the maps, then went back home. His wife was out.

He went to his room, spread the charts on his desk and began to work. He carefully studied all the documents one by one dealing with the information as with the data of a mathematical problem. Deep in his task, he did not hear his wife coming back with their child and did not realise their presence until they came to say goodnight at the narrowly opened door.

To work more easily, Prien eventually spread the charts on the carpet. Late in the night he had to grant that the British had done whatever they could possibly do to create impassable obstacles. The only weak point was Kirk Sound with its two gaps, the passages of fantastic tidal currents.

He made up his mind. He would go.

To slide in between the blockships would not be easy, but the commodore was right, the enterprise was feasible.

Prien gathered the documents, put them back carefully in the envelope and again rolled up the maps. He went into the hall, put on his coat and his cap, went back to his room, took the envelope and the roll of charts, switched off the light, went out of the house and softly closed the door.

Outside, the stars shone in the sky of a beautiful autumn night, already somewhat cold.

He felt relieved and walked briskly in the empty streets towards the *Hamburg*.

After locking the safe where he had put the papers, he went out of his way, to the wardroom, deserted at this time. He took a bottle of beer and a glass and sat on the bench. Seeing a half empty packet of cigarettes forgotten on the table, he lit one. What unforeseen events, begun in this very place, had been his lot in one day! This was to change the course of his career. For the first time he felt proud to have been picked out by the 'Great Lion' from all his comrades. Tomorrow and no later, he would tell him of his resolve to accept the mission. His submarine was perfectly seaworthy and the crew well seasoned. He wondered how they would take the news of such a daring operation. He could not hide from himself that the risks were enormous, but the more he thought of it, the surer he became of its success. He was pleased to think he was seconded by men of exceptional quality like Endrass—his irreplaceable number one, Wessels and Spahr.

Prien crushed his cigarette in the ash-tray, emptied his glass and got up to go back home.

On the way he walked without haste, his hands in his coat pockets, thinking with melancholy about the years gone by.

Prien had never had an easy life. The inflation, rife in Germany in 1923, had ruined his family. In Leipzig, from the time he was a teenager, he had to fight the harsh realities of life. His mother was at pain to provide food for her three children, Günther, Hans Joachim and Lieselotte. Günther, the eldest, used to go and sell in a shop, bundles of lace bought in the country by an aunt, all the while trying not to be seen by his fellow schoolboys. His mother painted pictures and to increase her small income, let the best room of the flat to a student called Buzelius.

As long as he could remember, Günther had dreamed of foreign travel. In his little room looking on to the courtyard, there was a single portrait above his camp bed, that of his favourite hero, Vasco da Gama, who at the age of twenty-seven set out for the unknown with three small sailing ships, went round the African continent, resolutely set a course on the ocean which opened before him and discovered the sea route to fabulous India. That was the life!

Then arrived the day when Günther told his mother of his wish to

Günther Prien, commander of the
U-47. Signal, 1941

enrol in the school for naval petty officers of Finkenwärder in Hamburg. Frau Prien put no obstacle in the way of her son's vocation.

At Captain Oelkers' school, training was speeded up. Three months after admission, the Head shook hands with the pupils and wished them a good start in life. Günther began his apprenticeship as a deck-boy on board the three-masted square rigged ship *Hamburg* cleaning the lavatories. The life of a sailor was not as he had imagined it. However, on the *Hamburg* he became a man among real men and the latter taught him to be a sailor, after their fashion, which was rough and often brutal.

He was more than ever determined to become an officer. After having embarked as seaman on the freighter *Pfalsburg*, to complete his course in navigation, he prepared for the examinations of the School of the Merchant Navy. At the end, his certificates as a deep sea officer and radio operator allowed him to find a place as fourth officer on the steamer *San Francisco*.

He now wore a fine uniform with a thin golden stripe on the sleeve and had a comfortable cabin.

At the end of January 1932, Prien successfully passed the examinations concluding his studies. With his captain's ticket he had reached his goal, the summit of the hierarchy. He was finally to be the Master of 'his' ship 'after God'.

In succession he called at the offices of the main ship owners, la Hapag, Slomann, Riedeman, then at other smaller ones. Surprise, discouragement, dismay. Nobody attached any importance to his certificates; unemployment was rife and the reply was always the same:

"You're unlucky." "Times are difficult. Leave your name and address in case there's something available, but we promise you nothing."

Not wishing to lose the least chance of getting a ship, he remained at Hamburg living on his savings. To hold out longer, he undertook the translation of the book *China Clipper* but lacking money for food and fuel he had to give it up at page fifty. Harry Stoewer, the former bosun of the *Hamburg* helped him as best he could. He too had realised his dream by becoming owner of a small bar 'At the Star of David' in the Davidstrasse. There, Prien had food and drink on credit. The two men loved to speak of their time on the three masted square rigged ship. Over a toddy, they recalled the storm which had thrown the sailing ship on the south coast of Ireland between Hook Point and Cape Head, the shipwreck, the fire in the hold in the open Atlantic, or the desertion at Pensacola of the cook Balkenhol. About this, Prien revealed to Stoewer how the crew nearly died without knowing it after deck boy Prien, detailed to cook, had coloured the white cabbage with a sauce of red lead, fearing corporal punishment from the sailors because Sunday's dinner included obligatorily red cabbage. Yes, Stoewer remembered having been violently sick, like everybody on board, despite the good weather, after which the 'old man' had administered without any comment opium and castor oil to all the crew.

"I never suspected it," said Stoewer, his huge torso shaking with laughter.

"The 'old man' knew. He had come to search the galley. Having seen the pot of red lead, he had guessed. I thought he was going to strangle me in anger. But to cut a long story short, he told me that, in my own interest, it was better for me to keep quiet."

Despite the friendly help of Stoewer, Prien could not stay any longer in Hamburg, waiting for a ship, daily harder to find. Against his will he took the train for Leipzig. It is not easy to go back home after being absent eight years, without a penny in one's pocket.

Prien was not the type to live at his mother's expense. Every day he went through the advertising columns. It did not take long. The columns were filled with requests for work. Then the day flew by, exhaustingly, walking through miles of streets looking for work.

The period after leaving the school of Finkenwärder before he enlisted on the three-master, had marked him deeply. Without money to return home and especially wishing to get a berth, he had lived for some time at the school of Captain Oelkers, obliged to put up with all sorts of bullying. There he had learnt that 'after two days, a guest and a dead fish stink'. At the age of sixteen you do not forget. But now, he was going under morally and physically. He had to take himself in hand, do something.

One day he joined the newly born National Socialist Party. He did so as a reaction against the disorganised world in which he lived because this party had a programme of realistic economic revival, but also to have more chances to be admitted to a work camp. He was twenty-four years old.

At Vogtland, Lamprecht, the head of the camp, quickly marked him out among the rough men in his charge and made him his assistant. But the sailor was not made for this sedentary life. So, as soon as he heard that the Navy was giving equivalent ranks to officers of the Merchant Service, he jumped at the chance. He left the camp and in

January 1933 enlisted at Stralsund. He chose submarines. He was in the Navy and without worry for the morrow. His life changed completely: period of instruction, technical training at the submarine navigation school, commanded by Commander Slevogt, training on *U-3*.

Lieutenant Prien received the appointment of third hand of *U-26*, commanded by Lieutenant Commander Hartmann.

The submarine was at Bremen at the Deschimag shipyards. He left from Kiel by train taking advantage of the change of lines at Hamburg, and took the chance to pay a quick visit to the old district of St Pauli, to see Harry Stoewer. He had not forgotten the bad days and wished to pay off his debt.

At the 'Star of David' he had a shock. The former bosun of the three master had hanged himself two years before. Ruined by his good nature, the old sailor had preferred to end his life.

Deeply saddened, Prien left, his head down, without being able to think of anything but his friend. Stoewer had been beaten by life because he was too trusting. When, in his turn, he found himself in need, everybody turned their backs on him. Such was life.

U-26 went on a cruise in Spanish waters. Spain was shaken by the revolution and the ship had a mission to protect German national interests. The crew had a good example for Hartmann was an 'ace'.

Six months later, Prien married. He obtained his first command in December 1938. After presenting himself to the flotilla leader, Lieutenant Commander Sobe, on the submarine depot ship *Hamburg*, the new captain had hastened to get acquainted with his ship moored at the wharves of the Krupp Germania shipyard.

The *U-47* made a good impression on him. The long steel fish was thin and fine as a thoroughbred. Workmen were giving the final brush strokes to the superstructure. Prien made his tour of inspection as a connoisseur with legitimate pride.

The following day, at 10.00hrs under a pale wintry sun, on the bridge of *U-47*, the officer in charge of the ship, Wessels, engineer officer, presented the crew to the captain. Prien, somewhat moved, reviewed the thirty-eight men drawn up in two ranks and made a short speech, using very simple words which came quite naturally to his lips. Then to improve acquaintanceship he exchanged a few words with each sailor.

The daily trials started in the spring of 1939 and in the first days of August *U-47* was ready to undertake her cruise in the Atlantic. Then came the war.

U-47 in dry dock.

This war, in which nobody on board had seriously believed, had lasted scarcely a month and already he was going to accept a mission which most of his comrades would have considered as a suicidal operation. Up to now, Scapa Flow had remained inviolate. But he was entranced by the sporting side of the adventure and felt himself able to carry out this naval exploit. He was in the same state of mind as the knight preparing for single combat.

He thought of his daughter and of his wife. What would she have said if she knew? In the name of his little family, was he right to take such risks? He passed his right hand over his forehead as if to chase away these ideas which worried him and saw that he had arrived at his door. He took a key from his pocket and went in without making a noise. A quarter of an hour later, he was fast asleep.

The next morning, Monday 2nd October 1939, he knocked at the door of commander von Friedeburg, chief of staff of Commodore Dönitz. He went in and saluted.

"I wish to have an interview with the commodore of submarines as soon as possible, sir. It is urgent," he said to the officer seated at his desk.

Von Friedeburg stretched out his arm, took up the telephone and dialled an internal number.

"Hello, is that the commodore? This is von Friedeburg. It is about Oberleutnant Prien. He wants an interview ... yes ... this very day. ... Very good, sir."

He hung up and looked at Prien.

"Well, the commodore expects you at 14.00hrs."

Before going on the *Weichsel*, Prien went to look for the papers locked in the safe on the *Hamburg*.

At 14.00hrs exactly he was received by Commodore Dönitz. The latter was standing behind his working desk.

"Yes or no?" he asked immediately frowning slightly.

"Yes, commodore," replied Prien without hesitation. He stood at attention, clutching under his left arm the roll of maps and the envelope.

A smile showed on Dönitz's lips. He placed his hands flat on the table, leaned forward and continued.

"Have you thought of von Henning, Hansen and Emsmann? Have you taken fully into account the difficulty and dangers of this mission?"

"Yes, commodore, I am fully aware of the risks but I think I have good chances of success."

"Perfect, Prien. In that case, if you succeed in entering the bay of

Scapa Flow, attack only the big ships. Take no risks with the small ships. According to the papers that I have given you, you have noted the presence of heavy ships to the north of Flotta and in the channel between Switha and Risa."

"Yes, commodore."

"Is your ship prepared to get under way?"

"Yes, commodore."

"Unload the excess food and fuel, as well as your torpedoes. I will see that electrical ones are given you. They leave no wake. Do it without delay so as to hold yourself ready to cast off in the shortest time."

Dönitz straightened himself and added, "we will fix the sailing date later. Keep the papers till then, they could be useful to you as additional information in case you might have forgotten a detail."

"Very good, sir," said Prien saluting. He turned about and left the room with the roll of maps and the envelope which he still held tight under his left arm.

Wednesday 4th and Thursday 5th October 1939. Some of the food and fuel had been landed to the great astonishment of the crew.

Friday 6th October. Unloading of the compressed air torpedoes and loading of the electrical torpedoes G7e.

Helped by Endrass, Prien directed the operations without paying attention to the continuous coming and going of sailors, soldiers and civilians on the quay where the *U-47* was moored:

"Well, Prien old boy, you are getting ready, aren't you?" questioned a voice amplified by a megaphone.

Prien turned around and saw Sohler, on the bridge of the *U-46*, coming back from his daily trials.

"Yes, as you can see!" he shouted, curving his hands round his mouth, trumpet fashion.

The *U-46* advanced slowly on a parallel but opposite course. A good 50m separated the submarines. The noisy conversation of the two commanders had attracted the attention of the crowd. Some curious passers by had turned round while walking on, others stopped to look at the manoeuvre of the *U-46*.

Prien saw Sohler take the megaphone again. "Say, the big boss wouldn't have had the idea of sending you to Scapa Flow, by any chance?"

Sohler's amplified voice reverberated by some sheds nearby, was reflected over the harbour.

Wilhelmshaven, 8th October 1939. The preparation of *U-47* for Scapa Flow. On the bridge from right to left: Günther Prien, Amelung von Varendorff—third hand and on the extreme left Wilhelm Spahr chief quartermaster./Wilhelm Sparh.

Prien's blood grew icy cold in his veins but he reacted immediately. He drew a gulp of air and shouted as loud as he could:

"No! unhappily! You'll have to speak about it to him some day. He probably did not think of it."

Then he burst out laughing loudly.

Drops of sweat were forming like pearls on his forehead and temples, still he refrained from showing his anguish. His eyes fell on von Varendorff who was passing by. Ostensibly he gave him a series of orders in the hope of checking Sohler's exuberant joviality. He avoided looking in the direction of the *U-46* and effectively he heard the thundering voice of her commander:

"Well, wherever you go, good hunting old boy!"

"Phew!" Prien heaved a sigh of relief. He made no reply to Sohler and only waved his hand. He was trying to remain calm, but Endrass noticed his trouble.

"Could we really go to Scapa Flow, captain?" he asked in a low voice, a smile on his lips.

43

"What a question! My word, Scapa Flow is an obsession with all of you," replied Prien ambiguously.

"Scapa Flow, not yet. It is better to wait before going there! Your cheese stinks but give me a bit of your 'Harzer Roller' to taste, all the same."

Prien and Endrass turned round and saw two dockers seated on the quay, a few feet away, their legs dangling above the water, having a snack while exchanging impressions in a loud voice.

"Where is Spahr?" asked Prien, to change the conversation, although he knew very well what the latter was doing.

"In the shipyards because of the echo sounder, captain."

"I would like to see you both, this evening after dinner. Come to my cabin on the *Hamburg* towards 19.00hrs."

On the forecasing of the submarine a torpedo had got jammed in its loading casing and the sailors were beginning to get irritated.

"There! Use the pulley a bit. Lift up the 'fish' a little, no use spoiling it," said Prien addressing himself to Torpedo Petty Officer Bleeck who was supervising the manoeuvre.

Endrass went away to give them a hand, wondering why the captain had reacted in this way to Sohler's chatter. He was puzzled. Was it this incident which had caused Prien's wish to meet him and Spahr in his cabin, without witnesses?

For his part, Prien hoped that the mission was not going to be abandoned after the ill-timed intervention of Sohler. Why such a coincidence? What had made him bawl the name of Scapa Flow across the harbour? Life was funny indeed. He tried to convince himself that the situation was not as black as it seemed to him. Who then, could believe that the *U-47* actually was getting ready to cast off for Scapa Flow? Yes, on reflection, all that wasn't dramatic. One would see the reaction of the commodore if word of this ridiculous incident reached his ears. Meanwhile one must carry on as if nothing had happened.

Night had fallen on the town obscured by the black-out. Prien climbed the gangway of the *Hamburg* with a quick step and went towards his cabin.

A quarter of an hour later Endrass and Spahr left the wardroom and took the same direction without exchanging a word. Endrass had put Spahr in the know of the incident of the afternoon and both had reached the conclusion that something serious must be causing the behaviour of the captain. The two men stopped in a passage and Endrass knocked at the door of a cabin.

Lieutenant Engelbert Endrass, second in command of *U-47*.

"Come in . . ."

Prien was sitting opposite his bunk which was covered with charts and photographs. He turned round in his chair and rose. The first lieutenant and the chief quartermaster saluted him. He closed the door and put his back against it, his hands in his trousers pockets.

"Sit down and make yourselves comfortable."

He looked at them as if to test them then he said abruptly "We are going to Scapa Flow!"

He expected some kind of reaction but Endrass and Spahr continued to stare at him without moving a muscle.

"Here are the charts and papers relative to the defences obstructing the channels," he went on, taking his left hand from his pocket to indicate the bunk.

The two men followed his gesture with their eyes.

"Sohler doesn't know anything, does he? His remark was made by chance?" enquired Spahr.

"Yes, of course. This operation demands absolute secrecy to achieve the effect of surprise, but now we are sharing it with thousands of people because of this babbler."

"Maybe it's not as bad as all that," ventured Endrass, with his Bavarian accent.

Prien kept silent, and he went on:

"Supposing there were some enemy agents in the crowd. They won't ever take Sohler's joke seriously. On the contrary we are cleared of all suspicion which might have arisen because of the partial unloading of food and fuel combined with the changing of the standard torpedoes for electric torpedoes of the latest model. Our crew is the first to be puzzled. You have heard, like me, the men asking questions and making the most extravagant suppositions."

"That is roughly what I told myself, but I could willingly have done without these outpourings, for if the British suspect our intentions, we are well and truly sunk."

Spahr rose and bent over the charts.

"Have you already selected the channel that we must force, sir?"

"Yes, we are going to try to slip through Kirk Sound—this passage is the only possible access."

Prien, with a movement of his shoulders, stopped leaning on the door and planted himself before the two men.

"I would like you to examine these papers and tell me whether, in your opinion, this mission is feasible or not. I am going to shut you in here and I will come back at 21.30hrs."

He took his cap from the coatstand.

"See you soon, work well!" he said before closing the door.

At half past nine precisely, Prien followed the corridor leading to his cabin. He gave two hard knocks on the door, turned the knob, and went in. Endrass and Spahr were smoking quietly. He slipped into a chair, looking at them.

"I'm listening to you."

"It is feasible at slack water," Spahr replied briefly.

"Yes, I think that we will succeed in getting through," added Endrass, crushing his cigarette in the ash-tray.

This phrase, so simple, resounded in such a convincing fashion that immediately Prien had no doubt that with men like these two he could not fail. He did not try to hide a smile of satisfaction. Becoming serious again, he outlined the programme.

"We cast off the morning after tomorrow, the date of the operation is fixed for the night of Friday 13th to Saturday 14th because that will be the new moon. You would do well to study carefully the hydrographic pilot of the currents, their strength and the times when they change direction. It is of prime importance."

Judging that he had said enough, he rose, opened a locker, and took out a bottle of white Rhine wine and a cockscrew.

"Open it," he said, throwing them to Endrass, who caught them in the air, while he turned round to look for glasses.

"To our success!" he remarked, pouring out the wine.

Having chatted for a few monents, Endrass and Spahr took their leave.

"Of course not a word to anybody and don't dream about it tonight," advised Prien, his hand on the door knob.

The two men went away into the deserted corridor.

"You must not be superstitious, to cast off on a Sunday and stake your all on Friday the 13th," whispered Endrass in a bantering tone.

"Let's hope that this will bring us luck. We will really need it."

3. In the Headlights of the Car

Prien had lain down fully clothed in his cabin to think. Now that the submarine had come within a few miles of its objective, a stupid technical failure threatened to ruin everything. The operation was to begin the following night. Wessels and his mechanics had only a few hours in front of them to repair the damage. He could see the commodore's face again and the idea of going back to base was unbearable to him.

He threw his legs out of his berth and stood up. He glanced at the mirror which showed him the picture of a full face with energetic features. The eyes framed in well-traced eyebrows, shone with a cold grey-blue gleam reflecting a good deal of will power. His eyelids, slightly down at the end, lengthened by lines going up to his temples and the small folds round the sides of his thin lips gave him an expression both ironical and full of authority. Absentmindedly he passed his left hand on his cheeks darkened by a five days stubble, then took his cap and put it on. Pushing aside the green curtain hiding his cabin, he stepped out and turned to the right, in front of the small cabin of the listening post and radio. In the latter Telegraphist Steinhagen, earphones on, looked at him for an instant, then turned back to his dials.

The storm seemed to wear off for the submarine was no longer shaken by such jerky and abrupt movements. Keeping his legs wide apart, Prien went across the control room, watching over the four men in charge of hydroplanes, the pumps controlling the movement of water and the turbines for draining or air flushing. He then went through the petty officers' post, round the folding table fixed in the centre, then addressed a wisecrack to Leading Seaman Walz, the cook, who was busy in his tiny galley, and went through the door of the diesels compartment. In spite of the ventilation it was very hot there. He looked with anxiety at the starboard engine that was out of action. The regular roar of the port engine (M.A.N.) turning at full speed was deafening. From the other end of the compartment, Wessels saw Prien

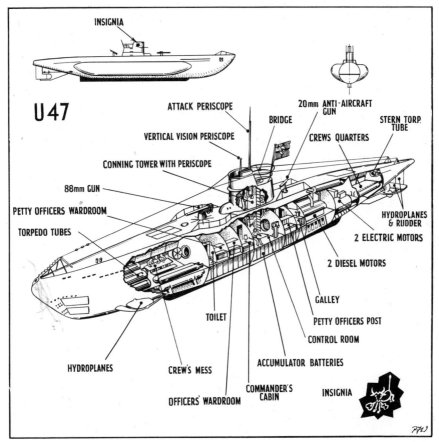

INSIGNIA

U 47

ATTACK PERISCOPE

20mm ANTI-AIRCRAFT GUN

BRIDGE

STERN TORP. TUBE

CREWS QUARTERS

VERTICAL VISION PERISCOPE

CONNING TOWER WITH PERISCOPE

88mm GUN

PETTY OFFICERS WARDROOM

HYDROPLANES & RUDDER

TORPEDO TUBES

2 ELECTRIC MOTORS

2 DIESEL MOTORS

GALLEY

TOILET

PETTY OFFICERS POST

CONTROL ROOM

ACCUMULATOR BATTERIES

HYDROPLANES

CREW'S MESS

COMMANDER'S CABIN

INSIGNIA

OFFICERS' WARDROOM

Cross-section of the U-47

immediately. The captain watched him saying something to the CERA, Strunk, then Wessels, wiping his face streaming with sweat, with a white cloth taken from his dungarees pocket, turned towards Prein.

"I think it will be all right," he shouted.

"Do you reckon you'll be long?"

"I can't say but I should say not."

"At what time do you think we'll bottom."

"At half past four."

"Good! Then we'll set to work immediately after."

Prien went back to his office completely reassured. He knew that the engineer officer was not in the habit of speaking lightly.

The damage to the engine had brought his thoughts back unconsciously to the difficulties he was going to meet on the way to Scapa Flow. Sitting on his bunk, he tried to imagine the appearance of the blockships obstructing the channel.

He mentally re-enacted the manoeuvres to slip between them following absentmindedly the weird angles imparted by the rolling of the submarine to his jersey hanging on a hook. He had studied the documents so well that he could have redrawn the map of Kirk Sound in the smallest details. Without a doubt he could not do without the 1,400hp of each of the two diesels.

A nasal voice came through the speaking tube.

"The captain is wanted on the bridge."

He looked at his watch: 04.00hrs. Yes it was time to go up on the bridge. He slipped on his boots, put on his oilskins and went towards the ladder of the control room.

Endrass gave him a report on the change of course effected at 01.30hrs: there was nothing more to mention.

The sky was still overcast and the sea covered with foam. Icy spray whipped his face and he pulled his sou'wester tighter.

"Are the engineers going to start the diesel again?" asked the first officer.

"They are going to begin the repair as soon as we are on the bottom. Wessels is positive: he won't take long to put everything right."

Visibility had become excellent. Prien took his binoculars. His keen eye soon made out the dark mass of the island emerging from the waves. He let the binoculars drop on his chest and saw a star.

"Course 130."

Then turning towards Endrass:

"We'll dive in 10 minutes. Gather all the men in the forward post at 04.45hrs."

"Very good, sir," replied the first officer, thinking, 'that's it, he's going to tell them that we're on the way to Scapa Flow. I wonder how he'll do it.'

The clouds broke up, showing open patches of sky. Prien took his binoculars again and trained them aft in the direction of the land. The islands were now scarcely visible. He leaned over the speaking tube and requested:

"Depth by echo sounder?"

"90 metres."

"Diving stations," he ordered, pressing the diving klaxon.

Frozen, their eyes and eyelids reddened by wind and salt, the men on watch had waited for this order impatiently. They dropped down the hatch in a record time. Prien himself secured the hatch and went down into the conning tower.

"Down 90 metres! On the bottom!" he shouted to be heard above the whistling of the air going out and the roar of the water rushing in already into the ballast tanks. At the same time he closed the voice pipe between the conning tower and the bridge.

Since the klaxon had sounded a whole series of manoeuvres had been carried out in the diesel compartments, in the electric motors compartment and in the control room: the engineers had stopped the port diesel; they disconnected it from the electric motor and closed the tube air induction valve and the valve of the silencer, all things they had already done on the starboard engine when it stopped. As soon as the diesel had been stopped the electricians started the electric motor; the tubes 'fresh air' and 'stale air' had been closed. The men in charge of the main ballast vents had opened them all, except those of the central ballasts.

In the control room Wessels watched the pilot lamp panel showing the securing of the hatches and ducts, as well as the opening of the main vents. When Prien, from the conning tower, ordered to submerge to 90m, he opened the vents of the midship ballast tanks.

The rolling and the pitching diminished, then stopped. The submarine was going down at a very slight bow down. The engineer officer was calling out the depth.

The humming of the electric motors stopped—a light impact—the U-47 had just settled on the sand.

The men were beginning to arrive in the forward compartment. On the doorstep, Endrass counted them to be sure they would all be present. Because of the small size of the compartment, they were obliged to find room where they could. Those who had placed themselves on the upper berths had to bend when sitting.

In the compartment, nobody moved or spoke. The slight grating of the hull on the sand, the only noise to be heard, took on an unusual importance.

They heard somebody walking in the gangway and Prien entered. Long ago, he had prepared a short speech, but what he said was brief and very different:

"This evening we are going into Scapa Flow," he said, every syllable quite clear.

The news was received in complete silence. A drop of condensation fell noisily on the metal floor.

51

"I'm not hiding from you the fact that the operation won't be easy, still it is quite feasible, otherwise I would not have accepted it."

Their features tense, the men looked at him attentively. Prien scanned the wan faces under the crude light of the electric bulbs and saw there, intense astonishment but also the relief of knowing at last the aim of the mission. He had the ghost of a smile, pursed his lips, as he often used to do, and went on:

"The engineer officer has to carry out a job on the fuel-oil pipe of the starboard engine. All those of you who are not on duty, either on watch or in the engine room must remain in your berths and sleep. The watch will awaken the cook at 15.00hrs. We will eat at 17.00hrs. Then during the whole operation there will be no hot meal; only sandwiches which everyone will eat at his post. Moreover, everybody will get a bar of chocolate. We must save electricity and any lamp not specially needed must be switched off. Nobody must move unless it is necessary so as not to use up the oxygen because we'll stay on the bottom till the evening. Don't make any noise. In spite of the depth, the listening apparatus can detect us with precision. During the mission itself, silence will be complete: I want total silence. No order or message will be repeated."

He stopped speaking and lowered his head slightly, letting them believe his speech was finished, but he straightened up almost immediately and added:

"It's in our own interests to be in perfect form when we awake and so we must sleep. Goodnight."

Imperturbable, the men remained rooted to the spot. He turned round and left, followed by looks he could feel on his nape and in his back.

Drops of condensation could again be heard falling somewhere on the floor.

Prien went into his office, drew up the green curtain behind him and took off his cap. He allowed himself to drop on the berth and remained thus a long time, lost in his thoughts.

He sat up, ran his hands through his hair. His attention was attracted by the war diary. Stretching his arm, he took it to enter the events of the day. He pushed himself to the small table drawn down next to the berth and began to write.

"12.10.39. Wind SE, 7-6.
Sky overcast.
Remained submerged, at the bottom, off the Orkneys.
Surfaced during the evening and got near the coast to take accurate

bearings. From 22 to 22.30hrs the British have been kind enough to switch on all the coast lights so that I could obtain a very precise position."

He put down his fountain pen. Now he had to mention the damage and note the presence of sea water in the fuel-oil tanks of the starboard engine, but he was no longer in a mood to go on. He decided to sleep for a while, thinking there would always be time enough to complete the war diary.

He took off his jacket, lay down, and switched off the lamp. Through the gaps in the curtain, hastily drawn, a ray of light caused a chiaroscuro, then somebody lowered the light in the gangway leaving only a night lamp. He closed his eyes with the intention of sleeping. From the diesel compartment, the muffled noise of the mechanics working reached him at intervals. Behind the partition, within the control room, four feet away from the green curtain, the men on watch were whispering in a monotonous rhythm. Now and then the current gurgled on the hull and in the superstructure.

Prien opened his eyes and tried to estimate roughly how long he had remained half asleep. He listened intently but no sound came from the engine room. He only heard the men on watch murmuring nearby. Unable to wait any longer, he got up, put on his shoes, then lifted up the curtain and on tiptoe went towards the diesel compartment. The clearing of a throat or the rustling of men rolling over on their berths testified to the fact that he was not the only one to be awake. When he went silently through the petty officers' compartment a few heads rose to see who was passing there.

The diesel compartment was in semi-darkness. A single small lamp was throwing a light on Wessels' face, bent over the engine room log. Absorbed in what he was writing, he did not hear Prien and only straightened when the latter patted his shoulder and began speaking in a low voice.

"Has it worked out as you hoped?"

"Yes, I think the damage is repaired, sir. We'll know for sure tonight when we get going," replied the engineer officer with a slight smile.

Prien scowled and said, "no jokes, Wessels, it has to work and work well. You know, I'm going to ask the maximum from it. It must not break down in Scapa Flow or in Kirk Sound, when we have a current of 10 knots on the nose. If you are not sure and certain of the result, better tell me while there is still time. Understood?"

Lieutenant Hans Wessels, engineer officer of U-47./Hans Wessels.

"Don't worry, sir, we'll be all right. There is no reason for a mechanical breakdown. Sure enough, the repair is not permanent but I assure you that the two engines will give all their power as before," the engineer officer promised quietly.

"Perfect, Wessels, that's exactly what I wanted," replied Prien in a conciliatory tone.

He moved away a few yards, but retraced his steps and added: "These notes can wait. You must be tired and it's better for you to go and rest. Tonight will be rough."

"I've almost finished, sir. In five minutes I'll be sound asleep."

This reply from Wessels reassured him completely and surprised him at the same time. The engineer officer did not look much upset at the idea of entering Scapa Flow, handicapped by an engine repaired with the means available on board. He admired him for remaining so phlegmatic and for being able to fall asleep within five minutes.

Retracing his steps towards his cabin, Prien saw the light shining in the wardroom. He looked in. Spahr, his head in his hands, his elbows on the table, was sitting in front of the map of Scapa Flow.

"I'm studying the details of Kirk Sound for the last time, sir," he explained in a low voice.

So as not to wake up Endrass, whose bunk closed by a curtain was behind the table, Prien said nothing and went back into his cabin.

He lay down and closed his eyes thinking of the crew and of the effect produced by his announcement. He heard Wessels passing in the wardroom to get back to his berth. Muffled murmurs from Spahr and the engineer officer reached him from the other side of the curtain. These murmurs grew faint, became a hum, and Prien fell asleep.

Endrass drew the curtain of his berth while the man on watch was passing by, going into the 'house of lords', as they called the forward torpedo compartment, to wake up Walz, the cook.

Prien slept lightly because he heard him too and understood that it would soon be time to get up. As soon as Walz passed behind the curtain, he opened his eyes and, through the gap, noticed that his boots were wrapped in rags, which allowed him to walk silently on the metal floor.

At 16.00hrs, von Varendorff went into the wardroom. On the other side, behind the green curtain, nothing moved in the darkness. He told himself that the captain had nerves of steel to rest so quietly a few hours from an operation from which they would only escape by a miracle.

The third hand was twenty-four years old and seemed just turned twenty. He was slim and because of his height had acquired the habit of holding himself in a slight stoop. He remained on the spot, for a moment, thinking of Prien, with a mixture of admiration and envy.

He yawned, then passing his hand through his flaxen hair, decided to go into the galley and warm up some coffee. Endrass put his head out of the curtain and took the coffee which von Varendorff offered him amiably. The latter came back with a coffee pot on a tray, a tin of condensed milk, two cups and two slices of brown bread with smoked ham. They drank and ate their sandwiches without saying a word. At the last sip von Varendorff broke the silence:

"I have a funny feeling at the idea of taking part in the attack on Scapa Flow. Doesn't it mean something to you to think that soon we'll be part of history?"

"Yes, of course, our fame will be world wide and we'll be talked about in every country. Or at least, we'll be decorated and granted a good leave. If we mess up the job, well, we will simply go to lengthen the list of our unfortunate predecessors. In any case, we can be sure that they will speak about *U-47.*"

"You mustn't say that. We'll come through, I'm sure of it. I don't see myself staying in Scapa Flow."

"That will depend largely on Spahr. By far the hardest will be to cross the boom with very little water to manoeuvre in a current of 10 knots.

"At least it's sport and it's just that which excites me. Spahr knows his business well. For that I have confidence in him. As for the captain, with his composure, he is capable of getting the submarine through wherever there is enough water to float."

"He is hard with the men. You can't like him but he enforces respect and in danger you are glad that he is there."

"Yes, I agree, I think we'll pull through and come what may, the game is worth the candle, isn't it?"

"We'd better stop talking, in case the skipper is no longer asleep. He'll give us a dressing down for wasting oxygen," said von Varendorff, looking towards the green curtain.

In his cabin, Prien reopened his eyes and kept them open. He heard stifled murmurs and, without making out the words, he could easily imagine what the topic was. He felt rested and fit. He hoped the men, too, had managed to sleep.

Familiar noises indicated that the submarine was awakening. The pungent smell from the fuel-oil, the oil and the sweat, were mixed with the sweetish smell of eau de cologne from the men sprucing up, and cooking smells. He inhaled and guessed that Walz was preparing veal chops and cabbage. It was nearly 17.00hrs. In the wardroom the table had been laid for the meal and they were waiting for the commander to join them. From where he stood, Endrass saw the green curtain drawn brusquely. Prien appeared and went to his seat. The clanking of knives and forks on the mess tins came from the 'house of lords' and from the petty officers' compartment. As everybody kept silent, the atmosphere hung heavy. Prien then spoke, thus lifting the order to keep silent. It was necessary for their morale and, in any case, the air would soon be renewed when next they surfaced. Von Varendorff could no longer hide his agitation. His eyes, bright with excitement, he began speaking profusely, without noticing the effort of all those present to welcome his cracks. They had not yet finished their coffee when ERA Böhm and Chief Petty Officer Electrician Römer went through the wardroom. They were going to set explosive charges which were meant to scuttle the sub if she was disabled and fell into the hands of the enemy. The first man set the explosive in the control room, the second in the electric motors compartment. Meanwhile, Torpedo Petty Officer Bleeck did the same in the 'house of lords'. Prien had given this order to Wessels and the engineer officer had chosen the three men for their coolness. If the crew had to leave the ship, these men were to remain on board and set off the charges before leaving the submarine in their turn.

In the 'house of lords' where they had cleared the table after the meal, Torpedo Petty Officer Bleeck, helped by Leading Seamen Thewes, Loh and Herrmann, were busy taking from under the floor two spare torpedoes, to place them in position for quick loading of tubes one and two. The four men undertook to move the port torpedo. Bleeck and Thewes guided the steel fish with their hands, Loh and Herrmann dragged at the pulley, hoisting the latter little by little towards its loading rail, fixed above their heads, until it reached the level of tube two. Thewes straightened up and wiped his unshaven cheek, which was streaming with sweat, with the back of his hand. The confined, stale air made a hard job of the smallest effort and he was panting. Small drops of condensation sparkled on the sides of the hull, on the doors of the tubes, on the ducts, wherever he looked around him.

Then it was the turn of the starboard torpedo. In the control room, the hand showing the seconds on the panel clock turned unflaggingly. It was nearly time to surface. One by one, the men went to their posts before being called to diving stations. Leading Seaman Hölzer found ERA Böhm in the control room at the venting and blowing control panel and went towards the echo sounder. Spahr came then, and sat in front of the small table on which he spread the map of the Scapa Flow approaches. Wessels arrived shortly afterwards. In the conning tower, Leading Seaman Schmidt at the helm, saw all those who were to be on watch on the bridge, come in succession, with their oilskins already on: Chief Petty Officer Sammann, Petty Officer Dziallas, Leading Seaman Hänsel, von Varendorff, and Endrass.

The first lieutenant, his legs wide apart, had crossed his arms on his chest, Sammann was intent on cleaning his nails and Hänsel was rubbing his chin with the look of concentration of a schoolboy during an oral test. They heard somebody climbing the ladder of the control room and the head of Leading Seaman Smyczek appeared through the hatch. Without saying a word, the latter settled in front of the torpedo data computer (TDC).

"I wonder what the weather's like up there," said von Varendorff to himself, just for the sake of saying something.

"The storm is certainly over. This morning the wind was progressively weakening and so was the sea, it was very plain," answered Endrass.

Heavy silence fell back on the group. Faces were grave, for nervousness before the action held them all.

Prien had put on his oilskins on top of a blue polo neck pullover. He straightened up his stained white cap and leaned with the palms of his hands on the frame of the small cabin for the listening apparatus. Funkmaat (petty officer telegraphist) Blank, his features tense, was listening for signals from everywhere. He turned round and reported:

"No propeller noise, sir."

"All right, Blank."

He passed into the control room, gripped a bar of the ladder and climbed into the conning tower. Discreetly von Varendorff glanced at his watch: 18.57hrs.

All eyes turned to the captain. He seemed to be weighing up his decision, then, little by little, his usual sulky look appeared on his face.

"Stand by to surface!"

These four words had an immediate result. The general tension slackened at once. In the conning tower the lamps were switched off.

"Periscope depth!"

The pumps were started. With precise gestures, Wessels corrected the trim as the submarine rose off the bottom.

The electric motors started with a mewing noise.

"She's rising . . . 1 metre . . . 2 metres," announced Wessels.

At periscope depth the movement of the surface was felt less than formerly The submarine was not shaken as on the previous day It meant that the sea was calm . . .

"Up periscope!"

Prien pushed back the peak of his cap and looked all around. Something had probably aroused his suspicion for he went on in his observation still turning the periscope.

"Böhm, did you clean the prism?" he asked aloud, without leaving the sights.

"Yes, sir. I cleaned and checked it carefully" answered the ERA from the control room.

"Funny. It looks as if it was covered with a white veil". He straightened up and folded back the handles.

"Surface! . . . Down periscope," he ordered.

He turned to Endrass. "It is dark, isn't it? I wasn't crazy. It could not be the reflection of the Rose Ness lighthouse on the clouds and it's a new moon."

The periscope tube slowly slid down into its well.

The first lieutenant opened his mouth to say something but changed his mind. The hissing of compressed air in the pipes and on the sheet plates was covered by the noisy gurgling of water rushing out of the valves, then Wessels' voice rose above all the noise:

"The hatch of the conning tower is above water!"

Endrass slowly opened the shut-off valve of the voice pipe, conning tower–bridge, so as to balance the external and internal pressures. The air of the submarine under high compression rushed whistling in the duct. Prien took his binoculars from their hook and hung them from his neck. Going up the ladder, he unclipped the hatch, opened it, and jumped smartly on the bridge. An icy breeze hit his face. A strange diffused glow seemed to enclose the submarine. He looked towards the sky when the watch was taking possession of the bridge.

"Starboard . . . nothing."

"Port . . . nothing."

"Nothing aft."

"What about the two diesels?" asked Prien with a twinge at his heart remembering the repair.

"Ready to start, sir," said a nasal voice in the voice pipe.

"Both diesels slow ahead!"

The starboard motor groaned in two keys. Quicker and quicker it started roaring, misfired once, twice. Prien gnashed his teeth. But the pumps were now well primed. The motor started again at a quarter turn and worked normally.

The port diesel started with a roar while Prien was bending over the speaking tube:

"Congratulations, Wessels. That was a good job."

Von Varendorff was looking at the sky in wonder. The glow took, in succession, all the colours of the rainbow, disappeared only to come back a few moments later with the same intensity.

"Well, this is a wonderful aurora borealis," said Endrass.

"Ventilate the ship," ordered Prien.

The blades of the two ventilators began to turn with a drone. The submarine progressed to the regular rhythm of her diesels. From the bridge you could see distinctly the white trail of the wake.

Behind the horizon, towards the north, the Northern Lights lit the clouds from above. Prien raised his eyes. If the breeze from the north-north-east cleared the sky as it seemed it might, the glow would be still brighter. Then the dark outline of *U-47* would stand out clearly against the silver background of the sea. What should they do? Everything had been foreseen except the Northern Lights. Should they put back the operation to the following day? This natural phenomenon very rarely happens two nights in succession. He closed his eyes for two or three seconds. A rush of ideas crossed his mind. Could he keep up the morale of the men for the next twenty-four hours which could become unbearable? Abruptly he took his decision—the die was cast. They would go that night. After all, the glow would help them both to find the enemy and more especially to see their target.

"Both engines full ahead!"

The bow wave cleaving the sea at 17 knots grew bigger. The two blowers, the ducts of which ended against the conning tower, gave out a kind of pig-grunt, difficult to stand for long. Because of the tides the timetable was calculated to the nearest ten minutes.

Down below, the men breathed with delight the fresh night air which cleared away the heavy foul atmosphere. In the control room Hölzer carefully watched over the dial of the echo sounder. He heard the diesels change their speed and a little later he saw the floor gradually come up at a slight angle. Spahr took a pencil and marked, on the map, the estimated positions as the second petty officer announced in the voice pipe the figures of the soundings on the bridge.

The islands seemed to be drowned in a kind of halo. The cliffs stood out clearly enough on the milky sky but the shore still merged with the sea because of the light and of the moving shades and glare of the aurora borealis. Impervious to the swell through which she cut like a dagger, the submarine rolled no more. Fantastic clouds, lit up as by the fires of hell, constantly shaped themselves into new monstrous silhouettes. Their shadows fled, twisting over the waves. These flames grew in intensity then died down until they disappeared, only to shine later more strongly than before. Was that, down there, the reflection of a cloud or a wave? Was it an illusion or a ship appearing and disappearing in the waves and troughs.

The groaning of the blowers was lessened by the wind whistling in Dziallas's ears. He lowered his binoculars, wiped the lens with a chamois leather, and trained them again on the horizon. He made a painful effort to see through this intangible veil which blurred the outlines.

"A ship in the line of the lighthouse!" shouted Dziallas without taking his binoculars from his eyes.

Though Prien scanned the waves, the sea seemed always deserted.

"You must have had a vision. There's nothing," said von Varendorff addressing Dziallas and lowering his binoculars.

"Ship straight ahead. It's merging into the coast line. Seems to be a trawler or a small cargo boat," Endrass confirmed.

They must not at any cost risk being seen, even if the other was only an innocent neutral. Without hesitation, Prien pressed the klaxon.

Hänsel jumped into the hatch way. Flattening his hands and feet on the ladder rail, he let himself slip in a single dash, to the bottom where he jumped sideways to avoid the boots of Sammann who was approaching. Dziallas, von Varendorff and Endrass followed. Nine seconds after the klaxon, Prien was hanging from the hatch cover to close it quicker with his weight.

"Open the main vents," ordered Wessels.

"Five, four, three, two, midship main vents!" thumped out the men almost with one voice, their hands on the control -levers of the valves.

Wessels did not let his eye leave the signal lamps of the ballast tanks. They lit up simultaneously. That showed that the vents were open.

The diesels had been stopped and the propellers were being driven by electric motors, the induction and exhaust pipes closed. Noisily the water gushed into the ballasts. The floor dipped 5°, 10° and seemed liable to go on swinging. The angle became dangerous because the depth was less than the submarine length. "One," shouted Wessels swiftly. The engineer officer had left the aft ballast closed to the last moment in order to speed up the dive by increasing the angle of the ship.

The floor straightened up. The plates were shuddering under rapid vibrations. The electric motors turned at full speed. "Ballasts open—10 metres . . . 15 metres . . . 20 metres," counted out Wessels.

"Bring her to periscope depth! Both motors half-speed," ordered Prien.

Leading Seaman Gerhard Hänsel the second of the two German eye witnesses still living, who was also on watch on the bridge during the operation. / Gerhard Hänsel

"Blow 'Q'!"

The last words of the engineer officer were drowned in the whistling of the compressed air. The five tons of water, roaring, rushed out of the tanks, usually kept full to counter-balance the tendency of the submarine to surface.

"'Q' blown, 'Q' Kingston shut!"

From the corner of his eyes Wessels looked at the two pairs of hands which turned the valve wheels. The air pressure in the tanks became too great and Böhm lowered it immediately. On the contrary the pressure of the atmosphere inside the ship rose causing a buzzing in their ears. You could carefully check the circuits, valves and taps of compressed air, but they were never completely water or air tight. It was a common occurrence and existed in all submarines.

"14 metres," warned Wessels without moving his eyes from the pressure gauge. Prien was in the control room, next to the engineer officer, his back against the ladder leading into the conning tower.

"Up periscope," he ordered calmly.

In spite of the glow pervading above the surface, he could not find the ship through the translucent veil.

"Confound it! What on earth is happening?" he swore aloud.

He straightened himself up and folded the tube handles.

"Down periscope!"

He climbed into the conning tower and connected the motor of the attack periscope. Endrass and von Varendorff had just joined him when Blank's voice spurted out from the voice pipe.

"Noise of propellers at 320."

"Motors slow ahead. Stop the sounder and the auxiliaries," ordered Prien, pressing his face against the rubber of the sights.

Now the characteristic noise of the propeller blades churning the water was heard clearly inside the submarine.

Pcht . . . Pcht . . . Pcht . . . Pcht. . . .

All eyes were raised, as if looks could pierce the steel places and see the hull of the ship. Prien continued to manoeuvre the periscope.

"They are not turbines. It must be a merchant ship and it's not going very fast," said Endrass.

"Yes, but what I can't understand is that I cannot manage to see it through this soup and still it's clear," said Prien adjusting the periscope. The ship was probably very near, judging by the sound. Then little by little, the Pcht . . . Pcht . . . Pcht . . . grew fainter.

Prien turned away from the periscope and addressed his officers. "I give up. See for yourselves if you have any better luck."

Endrass came first and looked for a good minute before giving up his place to von Varendorff.

"It's hopeless. Nothing. And yet it's not far," he said.

"We are off the coast of Scotland, don't forget. Maybe it's a ghost," replied von Varendorff leaving the tube in his turn. "In any case, a periscope attack is practically impossible in these conditions. It's good we realised it," commented the first lieutenant without paying attention to von Varendorff's wisecrack. "Yes it's rotten," concluded Prien, his face showing concern as he brought down the periscope into its well.

"Can we start the sounder again, sir?" asked Spahr's low voice, coming from the control room.

"Yes."

In the conning tower, silence fell on the group. You could only hear the muffled drone of the electric motors.

Then Spahr spoke again.

"To the captain—it is time to change course. Starboard 15."

"Starboard 15," repeated Prien.

23.25hrs. He waited a few moments then ordered:

"Surface! motors half ahead!"

"Blow main ballast! Surface," echoed Wessels.

The submarine emerged and the watch resumed their position on the streaming bridge. The first movement of von Varendorff was to scan the sea aft trying to see the ship which had just passed by them. He had no difficulty in finding in his binoculars the silhouette, dimly outlined, of a small steamship heading for the open sea. He announced his discovery immediately to Prien but the latter, busy studying the islands, did not answer him.

Now, only a few light clouds lingered in the luminous sky before disappearing south-south-west. The coast had become clearly visible. On the portside the sheer cliffs of Ronaldsay Island and, behind it, the distinctive mass of Ward Hill, the highest point on the island, stood out clearly on the white sparkling sky. Farther away, towards the north, Burray Island, separated by the narrow Water Sound, seemed to prolong the coast of South Ronaldsay. In front was the south-eastern extremity of Mainland Island, the most important of the Orkneys.

His binoculars glued to his eyes, Prien slowly scoured the length of the coast. The Rose Ness lighthouse appeared in the sights, then it was the turn of the stone beacon, 10m high and topped with a cross, which marked the entrance of Holm Sound into which they would soon penetrate. He lowered his binoculars and bent over the speaking tube:

"Course 320!"

"Course 320," replied Schmidt.

The bow swung to port and Hol Sound opened before the eyes of the men on watch.

An invisible hand put out the lights in the sky plunging it, and the land, into darkness.

The tidal current had taken the submarine and was pushing it into the narrows. As abruptly as they had vanished, the thousands of lights twinkled anew, throwing an orange coloured glow on everything.

"Ten metres . . . 9 metres . . . 7 metres . . ." announced Hölzer untiringly.

"Trim down until the casing is awash in case we run aground," ordered Prien through the voice pipe.

At the central post, Wessels had the vents of the midship ballast tanks opened until the boat went down 40cm.

"Trimmed down, sir. The draught is 5.10 metres."

To avoid the wild waters forming off the low headland of Burray Ness, Prien decided to hug the coast of Mainland.

"Starboard 20! . . . Steady as she goes."

Holm Sound, the entrance of which stretched a little over a mile, seemed to end in a cul-de-sac. The land surrounded it on all sides and no exit was yet to be seen. As they approached it, the current became stronger.

"Port 20° starboard, course 310 . . ."

"Course 310," replied Schmidt from the conning tower.

Over to starboard the lighthouse of Rose Ness appeared, strangely near. When the submarine passed under it, it towered over her as a mirador, livid and hostile. To port, the north-west bay, of considerable size, loomed up in the half-light. They sensed the presence of the beacon, the highest point on the island, at 73m in its west part, rather than actually seeing it.

As foreseen, the silent shores seemed deserted.

"No trace of look-outs," murmured Endrass as if to reassure himself.

Prien was the first to sight the sunken ship:

"Blockship across the channel, distance 2 miles, bearing green 60," he said with a certain amount of excitement.

Even clearer than the luminous sky, the sheet of the bay of Scapa Flow stretched out as far as the eye could see behind the black ghostly skeleton which was supposed to block the entrance.

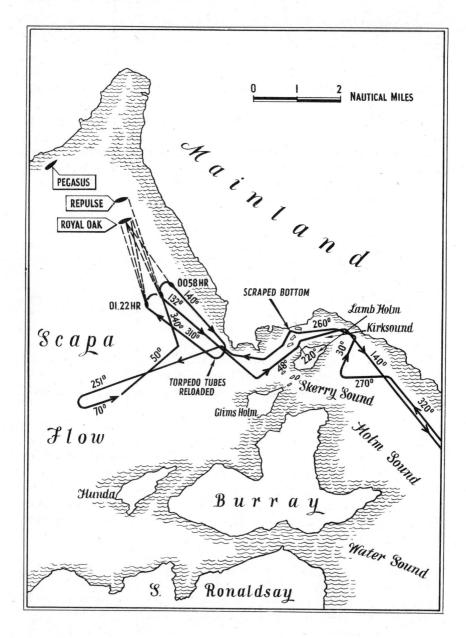

The route taken by *U-47* on the night of 13th/14th October 1939,
reconstructed by Petty Officer Ernst Dziallas, one of the two German eye
witnesses. This formally accredits the theory of the presence of a second
ship of the line to the north of the *Royal Oak*.

Scapa Flow! This magic name roused in Prien a storm of feelings and emotions that he would have been incapable of analysing. At last he could, at leisure, contemplate with his own eyes this forbidden bay.

"Course 270," he ordered firmly. He trained his binoculars on the sunken steamer and added, "We're in Kirk Sound."

The blockship quickly grew bigger. He looked for the three other blockships in a free and easy way. To his disappointment they did not prove to be easy to find. Impatiently, he examined the channel several times without success. This blockship was, for some unknown reason, alone.

"Damn it! Where are those wretched blockships?" he said, gritting his teeth.

Hölzer's voice went on ceaselessly, made nasal through the speaking tube:

"Four metres under the keel . . . 3 metres . . . 2 metres 50 —"

Suddenly Prien realised the situation and felt something like a blow in the stomach. In the control room Hölzer's voice had also caused a reaction. As if stung, Spahr jumped on the voice pipe:

"Hard a-starboard, sir! We aren't in Kirk Sound, we're on our way to Skerry Sound!" he shouted in a hurry.

Above, shut in the conning tower, Schmidt receiving the captain's order turned the wheel as quickly as he could and repeated, "Hard a-starboard—steady as she goes."

On the bridge the watch, petrified, held their breath. Prien was in a cold sweat, recognising his mistake: he had seen only one blockship where he should have seen three instead of the two islets Glims Holm and Lamb Holm. The sunken ship blocked not Kirk Sound, but in fact Skerry Sound. Given the speed at which the submarine was cruising, they would certainly have run aground.

U-47 was going about to starboard, almost at a right angle. Prien swallowed and looked for a last time at the skeleton ship quite nearby. She seemed to mock him, then slid towards the left, together with the two islets.

In the control room, a lump still in his throat, Spahr was recovering from his fright. He turned his head towards Hölzer. Drops of sweat stood like pearls on the forehead of the leading seaman in spite of the cool draught. His features contracted and his eyes still fixed on the sounder, Hölzer enumerated in a voice which had become subdued:

"2 metres . . . 1 metre . . . 0·50 metre . . . nil under the . . ."

Crunch . . . crunch . . . The grating of the keel crushing the sand reverberated with an overwhelming intensity inside the submarine

67

acting as a sound box. Still the ship did not seem to slow her course.

"Full ahead!" roared Prien.

For a moment he thought fleetingly of the repair to the supply system of the starboard motor, but already the throbbing of the two diesels went up several tones. U-47 bounded forward still quicker.

"0·50 metre under the keel," panted Hölzer. His mouth was dry. He felt a mad wish to stop his ears as if the fact of not hearing again the sinister grinding had the power to save them from disaster. Beside him, Böhm looked fixedly in front of him, biting the inside of his upper lip. Wessels, slightly bent, kept ready to empty the tanks. Leaning on the map, Spahr heard him mutter. Absorbed in his work, he paid no attention, listening to Hölzer's counting—

"One metre . . . 1 metre 50 . . . 2 metres . . ."

No doubt about it, the depth was increasing. He swallowed and called the bridge.

"Sir! No more risk of running aground. Course must be changed 30° to starboard to avoid the shallows of Lamb Holm. Careful! We'll soon be in the Kirk Sound channel."

U-47 pushed straight towards the dark and high mass of Mainland Island. Lamb Holm islet was outlined forward to port.

"Green 030, motors half speed both engines," Prien replied immediately.

The diesels changed speed and the white moustaches crowning the stem slowly grew smaller.

Endrass tried to get his bearings, The blockships obstructing the channel were still hidden by Lamb Holm. Von Varendorff examined the landscape with curiosity. Sammann, his mouth slightly open, glanced frequently towards the sky. He had never before seen the Northern Lights. Noticing his behaviour, Prien turned round to admonish him but could say nothing when he saw the childish expression of wonder, mingled with astonishment of the chief petty officer.

Hänsel, himself, continually passed his tongue across his lips. Dziallas did not take the binoculars from his eyes. The men on watch in the port and forward sectors saw at the same time the superstructures of the wrecks emerge from behind Lamb Holm.

Kirk Sound opened widely on the left. Carried sideways by the current the submarine progressed crab-fashion.

Less than 250m from the sheer, wild looking cliffs of Mainland, Prien ordered in a tone which had become calm again:

"Hard a-port!"

"Hard a-port," repeated Schmidt from the conning tower.

"Course 300!"

Once more the ship turned fiercely. Like a shadow she slid through the middle of Kirk Sound between Mainland and Lamb Holm, with the tide under her stern.

A thousand will o' the wisps gave out a blue light which slowly turned to orange-yellow. The steep shores and the interior of the islands plunged in total darkness gave the impression of being uninhabited.

Von Varendorff suddenly found the throbbing of the diesels deafening. Accustomed to this sound, he had grown to ignore it but the contrast with the almost palpable silence which surrounded them was too striking.

His fingers gripped the binoculars hanging on his chest. It seemed to him inconceivable that people on the shore should not give the alarm. He looked sideways at Endrass. The face of the first lieutenant, unmoved, showed no feeling. He had strong nerves, that one. Discreetly he pushed his elbow in Hänsel's ribs.

"They will awake eventually with the din that we are making and then there'll be fun," he whispered in the ear of the leading seaman.

"Unless they are all deaf and that's what it seems like," replied Hänsel in a whisper, not to be overheard by the captain. Von Varendorff shrugged his head to show his doubt then took up his watch again.

"Stop the diesels! Half ahead group up!" ordered Prien as if he had overheard the whispering of the two men.

The roaring of the two engines 'M.A.N.' stopped suddenly. Silence fell like an axe and enveloped the submarine. It was not only an absence of sound but a physical presence. The hissing of the current was heard above the feeble humming of the electric motors. *U-47* was merging into the environment becoming a shadow among shadows. Tension relaxed on the bridge. Unconsciously each man had the feeling that the protection of the night and the silence offered an invisible shield against the eyes and ears of the enemy. A flimsy veil floated in a cleared sky. The captain and the first lieutenant trained their binoculars in the direction of the blockships.

"The last obstacle before Scapa Flow," exclaimed Prien almost joyfully.

"Stop the sounder," he added into the voice pipe.

"Exactly as on the photograph," said Endrass without taking his binoculars from his eyes.

Prien agreed, congratulating himself inwardly for having taken the

69

trouble to engrave on his mind all the details of the charts and the aerial photographs, for what he saw corresponded exactly to these details.

Below, in the control room, bent over the map, Spahr also followed, as best he could, the progress of the submarine.

The current had reversed about three-quarters of an hour before and since 23.12hrs it was bearing to the west, that is towards Scapa Flow. The commander was, without a doubt, going to choose, as foreseen, the north channel. The latter was less deep than the south passage, but this last one had a cross current under the south-east coast of Lamb Holm. They would go through this channel about 00.15hrs. Spahr began to check the height of the tide in Kirk Sound. He took up again the sheet of paper on which he had noted the times of High and Low tide at Burray Point, chosen as reference position:

13th October: Low Tide at 17.13hrs
　　　　　　　High Tide at 23.23hrs

14th October: Low Tide at 5.34hrs
　　　　　　　High Tide at 11.45hrs

Quickly, he calculated again and found the same figure as before: At midnight, the height of the tide in Kirk Sound should be 3.2m above chart datum diminishing to zero at 05.00hrs. He went back to the map to check the figures given by the echo-sounder, figures he knew by heart. With their draught of 5.10m the depth would be sufficient and no more.

Between the blockships there would only be a few centimetres under the keel. The submarine had reached the bend where Kirk Sound turned to the left.

"Course 260."

"Course 260," echoed Schmidt through the speaking tube. Prien estimated the distance which separated them from the blockships 6 or 7 cables away and they were getting bigger under his eyes.

"We'll pass north of the blockships," he tossed the information without comment.

He took his binoculars again and focused them on the blockship furthest away to the north. Her silhouette appeared still blacker than the background of the Mainland cliffs. The hull was outlined distinctly in the sights against the milky surface of Kirk Sound. It was all that was left of a two-masted sailing ship. The violent strength of the current had made her turn like a wicket gate towards the east in a direction parallel to the shore of Mainland.

Kirk Sound was now constricted between a Mainland promontory

The tidal race through Kirk Sound, where Prien passed, over which the Churchill Barrier was later built. / IWM

on the right and Lamb Holm on the left. The current was increasing speed appreciably in this bottleneck narrowed by the presence of the blockships.

The aurora borealis suddenly faded out, plunging the islands into an inscrutable darkness.

Prien let his binoculars drop on his chest without uttering a word. The hissing of the current was clearly audible. A blue light, cold as the icy air which lashed their faces, was pouring down from the sky.

The barrage was getting nearer at an incredible speed.

"Starboard 10 midships! Steady as she goes."

"Course 270!"

"Course 270," echoed Schmidt.

The current seized *U-47* and spun it to starboard towards the sailing ship as if it had been a mere straw. The submarine began yawing to right and left.

In the conning tower, Schmidt found it difficult to keep steady on course. The helm was powerless. Ceaselessly, Prien corrected the course. Down under him, Schmidt, his eyes glued on the compass, turned the wheel with dexterity, now in one direction, now in the other. The leading seaman was in a sweat.

On the bridge, the men remained motionless. Things were happening at a hectic pace but those few seconds lingered indefinitely. The

71

free space between the wreck of the sailing ship and that of the steamer seemed barely sufficient to allow *U-47* to slide through. The slightest mistake would be fatal.

The scene had an hallucinatory quality. The current breaking on the sailing ship lifted up an impressive bow wash and one constantly expected to see her ghostly crew loom out on the deck.

In front of the wrecks of the steamers sunk across Kirk Sound, the swell made an enormous rounded fold of water which was irresistibly sucked in by the depression forming between the shells of the sunken ships. The sea was flowing there with the wild strength and din of a torrent.

At last the wreck of the sailing ship came abreast the conning tower. It was then that their blood froze in their veins.

A huge anchor chain, jutting out of the northernmost hulk of the barrage, was cutting across the course of the submarine. The chain was taut in an angle of $45°$ with the boiling surface of the channel in which it dived right in the middle.

"Shit!" exclaimed von Varendorff.

"Port motor stop!"

"Starboard slow ahead!"

"Hard a-port!"

The composure of the voice giving these orders produced its effect. The evil spell of the danger which gripped them all was broken. The various movements of the men on the bridge did not escape Prien's notice. Action was restoring all his faculties. Each second counted and he no longer had time to be frightened. Solidly set on his feet, legs wide apart, hands on the flat top of the bridge rail, he was one with his ship, like a horseman and his mount.

The spectral wreck of the sailing ship with her deck at sea level shining under the twinkling lights of the aurora borealis attracted the submarine like a giant magnet. Collision was imminent. The starboard propeller was raising a whirl of foam. Slowly *U-47* obeyed Prien's will and fell off to port. The bow brushed the chain. The keel touched the obstacle which caused the prow to pivot to starboard towards the nearby shore.

The starboard motor and the wheel hard to port brought back the submarine towards the axis of the channel but, acting as the arm of a lever, the chain was unremittingly pushing the boat out of the deep water. Holding their breath, Prien, Endrass, von Varendorff and the three men on watch followed with their eyes the jerky progression of the chain on the plates of the portside. The heavy rusty links, covered

The Churchill Barrier over Kirk Sound, which was built by Italian prisoners of war.

with seaweed and barnacles had reached the level of the conning tower. The foam boiled furiously on the deck, flush with the water, of *U-47*. They felt with terror the ship bump slightly, stop, and roll on her keel. Prien opened his mouth to give the order to empty the ballast tanks when the submarine suddenly freed herself while the chain slipped grating towards the stern. The current seized her fiercely and drew her off to port.

Endrass moved away from Prien not to be in his way. Clinging to the icy side of the bridge, von Varendorff saw the dark mass of the wrecked steamer, lying on the left, charge towards them as if to crush them. He had no fear of dying for in his heart of hearts he was persuaded that his time would not be up during this mission. His fighting ardour, on the contrary, made him fear that the adventure might end there, against this rusty hull. He opened his mouth, grinning, when he heard the commander hurling out a succession of brief orders. The wreck slowed down her course and came to a standstill a few metres away. The third hand realised that *U-47* had beaten the current and was casting off to starboard.

Schmidt, at the wheel, his face shiny with the effort, held the ship, somehow or other, reeling like a drunkard. With swift and skilled manoeuvres, he managed to bypass the wreck without hitting her.

The danger was not yet over. From second to second, the submarine was in danger of running aground on the nearby shore of Mainland which rose in front of the bow.

"Hard a-port."

At once Schmidt quickly turned the wheel.

"Course 220!" continued Prien in his usual voice.

The cliffs of Mainland slid from the bow to starboard then aft. Without difficulty *U-47* reached the middle of Kirk Sound. The latter was broadening and the current lost strength appreciably.

The main obstacle was overcome. There remained the mines which probably barred the entrance of Scapa Flow between Skaildaquoy point of Mainland and Glims Holm. The memory of the end of *UB-116* in the minefield of Hoxa Sound in 1918 went through Prien's mind. He decided to hug the coast of Mainland—he could only hope that the devices had been made harmless by the current which must tilt them heavily on their mooring ropes. Moreover the British mines had a solid reputation for inefficiency.

Endrass turned towards Prien and saw him calmly put his binoculars to his eyes and examine for an instant the village of Saint Mary, sleeping peacefully at the back of the small bay of Ayre.

"This light, which we cursed so much has been providential. I wonder how we would have come out of it in complete darkness," he said to him.

"I don't know but the brightness may be awfully annoying during the final phase of the operation for which we have come; and the Northern Lights are getting stronger and stronger" replied Prien, raising his eyes towards the sky.

"Don't you think that it will help us to find the targets and aim better, sir?" hazarded von Varendorff.

Prien smiled contentedly without replying. Decidedly the morale of his third hand was of the highest. He turned his head to the right, looked at the land, and judged that they were too near the shore:

"Port 20. Steady as she goes!"

"Spahr don't start up the sounder again." He noticed that Endrass was sweeping the sea ahead with his binoculars. He was also thinking of mines.

If there was a minefield, *U-47* was now entering it. The critical distance to cover stretched over 500 to 600m.

"No, we cannot blow up so near the goal," repeated Prien to himself, with conviction.

"Starboard 35!" he ordered in a slightly hoarse voice.

The submarine took again a course parallel to the land. Prien trusted in his lucky star, but nevertheless he had never yet felt so ill at ease and each turn of the propeller brought him some relief.

On the right the small houses of St Mary, stretching in a line on the other side of the coast road filed off at a distance of barely 500 or 600m. No light came through the shuttered windows and the deserted streets remained plunged in complete darkness.

Von Varendorff uttered a muffled exclamation:

"A cyclist!"

On the bridge all eyes were following the movements of the man pedalling peacefully. Was he going to turn his head? He went off to the right and disappeared in an alley, between two houses, without suspecting the presence, so close, of a German U-boat.

The men had no time to heave a sigh of relief. A slight throbbing made them prick up their ears. The noise went on increasing until it was clearly audible above the lapping of the sea and the drone of the electric motors. It came from the shore Suddenly two points of light pierced the darkness.

"Good heavens, a car! We had to have that," groaned von Varendorff.

"Damnation! When this chap comes out on the coast road he might see us. Our black silhouette must stand out on the clear background of the bay as though in a shadow theatre," fumed Endrass, training his binoculars on the car.

The road along the cliff described a slight zig-zag, going down towards the village. Suddenly two powerful beams of white light swept the road perpendicular to the beach and the sea beyond. As the car drew nearer, the light became stronger. Was it going to take the submarine in its headlamps before the right angle bend on the shore at the entrance to St Mary? It was a question of seconds.

"They ought to put this chap in prison. Doesn't he know the blackout of headlamps is compulsory?" raged von Varendorff.

The humour of the third hand made nobody smile for the conning tower was lit up as in daylight. The crude light of the headlamps was unbearable. The car stopped.

"That's it, he's seen us," exclaimed von Varendorff with anguish in his voice.

Blinking in the crude light, they heard the driver race his engine. At last the conning tower was back in darkness. Their eyes fixed on the intruder they watched his manoeuvres to turn round. The motorist must have been very agitated for he had to try several times, going forward and backward with jerky movements, before succeeding in retracing his way.

The car drove off at high speed. For a few seconds more its rear lights were visible then they disappeared, hidden by the bend of the little road.

"The fellow must have been rather surprised to see us sailing calmly on the surface," said Endrass.

"This time we're for it, the alarm will be given any minute now," groaned von Varendorff.

"Who will he be able to alert at this hour, I wonder? If he goes to Scapa, he will lose a lot of time waking up a villager or the policeman on duty at the police station, to phone Kirkwall or the naval base of Lyness. And then the fellow will be so excited that there is little chance of them taking him seriously straight away," continued Endrass, "I don't . . ."

"Stop chattering," Prien ordered them.

Skaildaquoy Point appeared very near, on the starboard beam. The danger of a minefield if there was one, was over without anybody having been aware of it.

"Start the diesels! Half speed! Stop the electric motors—Course 280!" ordered Prien firmly.

The groaning of the engines M.A.N. echoed in the calm of the night. Von Varendorff grinned and took up his binoculars.

The sparkling sheet of the small inland sea of Scapa Flow, lit up directly from above, opened ahead in all its breadth.

Inside the submarine, Prien's voice resounded in the loudspeakers of the ship's telephone:

"Battle stations! We are at Scapa Flow."

4. Open the tubes fast!

On the bridge the men carefully scanned their respective sectors. They heard Prien order: "Starboard 20!"

The submarine went round Cape Howequoy dominated by its cliff more than 16m high.

The hills around the bay of Scapa Flow began to look like mountains and their tops stood out sharply against the luminous sky.

The sea looked empty. The islands, without a light to be seen, were plunged in silence. This calm and this vacuum, which nobody had expected, set the nerves of the watch on edge.

The wind had lost some of its strength and at present the regular, set blow of an icy north-east breeze bore the characteristic smells of land.

Endrass lowered his binoculars.

"You can't say it's overcrowded," he exclaimed, vexed, with his drawling accent.

"Luckily the wind is coming from the direction of Scapa and does not carry the sound of our motors before us," said von Varendorff to him.

Prien tried to pierce the semi-darkness. Visibility was excellent, but still nothing to be seen.

"Let's have a look towards the main anchorage," he said to his officers.

"Port 20!"

"Port 20 it is!" replied Schmidt.

U-47 started its turning circle to port and the silhouette of Mainland was left behind. To the left the isle of Burray stretched out and seemed to melt into Honda islet.

"Ship's head?" asked Prien.

"Ship's head 251," came Schmidt's nasal reply through the speaking tube.

"Steady as she goes."

In front of them, the islands of Flotta, Fara, Rysa and Cava mingled with the rocky mass of Hoy Island. Already they could see the western end of Hoxa Sound, part of it still hidden by Honda islet.

"Look out for the patrol boat of Hoxa Sound. We can be its target in a few moments. If we are seen, all is lost," said Prien, training his binoculars forward to port. The seconds ticked away with unbearable slowness. Von Varendorff turned round to look at the wake and reassured himself with the thought that after all it could have been more visible than it was. The north-west headland of South Ronaldsay could now be seen behind Burray and the whole extent of Hoxa Sound appeared between the islands of Flotta and South Ronaldsay. The silhouette of the patrol boat stood out distinctly against the clear background of the sea.

Endrass let fly a volley of oaths in a low voice, got back his breath, and added: "Confound it! If she sees us as clearly, we're done for." Nobody replied, each man holding his breath, waiting for the inevitable, but nothing seemed to happen.

"Why doesn't she move? Her watch must hear us," grumbled von Varendorff.

"It appears they don't or, more likely, they don't expect to see a German U-boat on this side of the channel entrusted to their care," replied Prien.

Leaving his officers to examine the patrol boat as they pleased, through his binoculars he studied Gutter Sound between the islands of Cava and Fara. He knew that behind Fara there was the anchorage of the destroyers and farther to the south the naval base of Lyness, at the entrance of Long Hope, a kind of fjord which went about three miles inland deep into the isle of Hoy. As far as the eye could see, the sea was deserted. Scan as he would the shadows on the coast likely to hide the silhouette of a ship, he couldn't find anything.

He had to bow to evidence: not only was the main anchorage empty but moreover there was no ship to the south of Cava. He could not help swearing between his teeth. Endrass heard him and thinking that he had at last spotted something, asked him what it was.

"Nothing! Absolutely nothing! Emptiness and solitude all around. Cursed nuisance, the fleet has sailed."

"Pity! It must be a case of sheer bad luck."

"Very bad indeed," Prien said, in an abrupt, snarling way.

"They may even have got under way tonight when the lights went on," continued the third officer.

"It's possible, though I don't think so. A whole squadron would not have had time to pass through in half an hour," said Prien. "It must rather have been a single unit and her escort. But then, if the Fleet had left Scapa Flow more than twenty-four hours ago, the 'old man' would not have failed to let us know. He could not be unaware of it."

"Still it's funny," said von Varendorff, with astonishment, upset by the turn of events.

"Who knows, he may have learnt it too late, or maybe, they could not contact us for some reason or other," intervened Endrass.

Taking his binoculars, Prien once again swept the dim line of

Painting by Jean Delpech, naval artist.

demarcation between land and sea, from left to right, then he looked once more the opposite way and focused his attention on the patrol boat. On board her nothing moved. The boat seemed to have no crew, which was obviously not the case. He lowered his binoculars and looked at the patrol boat with an apparently disgusted air. Endrass noticed Prien's manner.

"Considering what they have to protect, I'm not surprised that they are sleeping the sleep of the just," he grumbled, "they would only have to open one eye and I wouldn't give much for our chances."

"Dear God, Please don't let the noise of our motors waken them. The wind is carrying straight in their direction," groaned von Varendorff.

"There certainly must be someone to torpedo in Scapa Flow," he went on, in his dry humorous way.

"Useless to continue in this direction. We shall retrace our steps to explore the north-east part of the bay, the length of Mainland," decided Prien, speaking aloud.

"Port 20!"

U-47 had the south-west extremity of Hunda Island on her beam when she started to go about.

"Ship's head?" asked Prien, after they had turned a half-circle.

"Ship's head 70!" replied Schmidt

"Steady as she goes—Steer 070!"

Once more, the shadow of Mainland rose up before them. The submarine proceeded almost exactly towards Skaildaquoy point, marking at about four miles from there the entrance of Kirk Sound from which they had come. They had covered a mile and a half since changing course. Prien looked straight in front of him. Without turning his head, he broke the silence:

"Port 10! . . . a little more to port . . . Steer 050—"

He took his binoculars again and trained them in the direction of the high cliffs of Mainland, he made out the phosphorescent fringes of the waves on the beach.

In the diesel compartment, his back against the frame of the door, opening on to the petty officers' room, Wessels was looking at the pipe work he had installed on the starboard engine. He raised his eyes to the clock screwed to the opposite partition separating the compartment from the electric motors. The hands pointed to 00.45hrs. He was surprised that only 30 minutes had passed since their entrance into Scapa Flow. He glanced at his wrist watch. No there was no mistake. He looked again at the engines shining under the crude light of the bulbs. Despite the ventilation, the gases made the atmosphere bluish. What could be happening up there?

A few feet away, on his right, Petty Officer Stoker Scholz was asking himself the same question. His overalls were sticking to his skin—they smelt of grease and fuel-oil and like all the other mechanics he never took them off at sea. Putting his hand in his pocket, he took out a white rag and wiped away the drops of sweat which were gathering on his forehead. He stared at the engineer officer with a worried expression.

Wessels sensed his look, turned his head, and caught the questioning look.

"Werner, shove some grease on the shafts," he ordered, to keep him busy.

The officer's voice seemed to relieve the stoker. He put down the oil-can which he was holding in his hand and with familiar gestures went away to carry out the order which he had just received.

On the other side of the diesels, Chief ERA Strunk took off his cap and conscientiously rubbed the leather band inside with a rag of doubtful appearance. Then he passed his fingers through his damp hair, put his cap back on, and pushed it by its peak on to the top of his head. He went across the compartment and approached Wessels.

"My word, the skipper is passing the British Fleet in review. We have been patrolling their base for more than half an hour without letting off a single 'fish'."

"I don't understand any more. Everything's so quiet that you would think we were in Kiel bay," answered Wessels.

"Spahr must know," said Walz who had heard the conversation from the kitchen next door.

"You're right. You have nothing to do. Go and ask him about it," replied Strunk.

"All right. I'll go if it's an order," answered Walz, with a pretence of respect. The two mechanics turned round and saw him going briskly towards the control room. He reappeared a few moments later, his face betraying nothing.

"Well?" asked Strunk.

"Nothing," replied Walz, staring at his boots always wrapped in rags.

"What do you mean nothing?" retorted Wessels. "You're kidding us."

"No, Mr Engineer."

"Anyway, what did he tell you? We are really at Scapa Flow, aren't we?"

"Yes, Mr Engineer," nodded Walz, his eyes still lowered.

"Tell us then! What are they doing up there?" asked Strunk

"They're looking for the British Fleet."

"Don't joke, you wretch!" exclaimed Strunk, beside himself with irritation, over Wessels' shoulder.

"Stop insulting me or I won't answer you," replied Walz. The cook was visibly enjoying the situation and did not hide it. Walz was a gallant fellow. He had enough self control to defuse the atmosphere in a case like this. Wessels gave him a look of admiration which he tried to hide under a rough manner:

"Good. Good. Keep calm my lad. Be serious and answer us properly."

"I am serious. You know quite well that I never joke."

"Ah! . . ."

Strunk stifled with difficulty a groan of rage which made the cook look at him. Walz frowned, raising his left eyebrow and stared at the Chief ERA.

"And we are where? At Scapa Flow?" asked Strunk in a manner which he forced himself to keep neutral.

"On the main anchorage of the Fleet—as deserted as the opera when the House is closed."

"What? You mean there's not a single ship? That we are all alone at Scapa Flow?"

"As for that, I don't know. In any case, we have just gone about, after pressing on until we were abeam of Hoxa Sound, without seeing a living soul except for that bastard of a patrol boat, at the entrance of this channel."

"And were are we going?"

"Towards the north-east part of the bay . . . I asked Willi to warn us if they find a target," added Walz casually going back into the galley.

On the bridge, Prien trained his binoculars in the direction of the cul-de-sac formed by the bay of Scapa which serves as a south port to the little town of Kirkwall. Inland, a mile to the north of the bay, more than four miles from their position, Kirkwall cathedral rose up. This building, dominated by a central steeple, with a spire, in red sandstone, is very easy to make out in daylight but, because of the distance and the darkness, Prien saw nothing clearly. He knew that the bay of Scapa offered an anchorage only to ships of medium tonnage. A rock called Scapa Skerry covered by less than 2m of water obstructed the entrance of the bay in the middle. This rock is very steep on the east side, and is linked to the coastal shelf on the other side, which extensively flanks the west part of the bay. The light buoy marking this danger was naturally unlit. If there were big ships in the vicinity, they had to be looked for to the south-east of this buoy. From the open they would be difficult to make out in the shadow of the cliffs. To see them from a certain distance, they would have to approach as near as possible to the shore, so that the superstructures of the vessels at anchor would stand out against the clearer background of the sky.

The Northern Lights created excellent conditions of visibility, much too good for Prien's liking. At intervals, there were periods of complete darkness, when, during an indefinite lapse of time, which could last a few seconds, a few minutes, half an hour, or more, you really saw no farther than the end of your nose.

Endrass was looking carefully at the inland sea on the left when the light in the sky suddenly went out as if a hand had drawn a curtain. He let the binoculars fall on his chest and said in a disheartened tone:

"Nothing to be seen." Neither towards the buoy 'Butter Barrel' nor elsewhere. A lousy day. It would be annoying, though, to go back home with an empty bag."

"We still have a slight chance along the north-east coast of Mainland," replied Prien, more to boost his morale than through conviction.

"I can't see the north shore yet, but I would be surprised to find anything of interest there," went on Endrass.

"We won't have to wait long to know for sure."

"Blast, it is dark—inky black," interposed von Varendorff.

The cliffs of Mainland, in spite of their nearness, remained invisible. The darkness was so opaque that Prien could not even guess their position any more. Judging from the last sighting, he assessed the distance at a mile.

The sky gradually grew clearer, allowing a glimpse of the outline of the Mainland heights.

"I see something on the portside ahead!" exclaimed Dziallas, with excitement.

Instantly, the three officers trained their binoculars in the direction indicated by the man on watch. Though they scanned the sea and the shadows of the coast, they did not make out anything suspicious.

"Your eyes need testing. The shore is as deserted as on the day of creation," said von Varendorff at last, without taking the binoculars from his eyes.

Dziallas was still studying the point of the coast where he thought he had seen a shadow darker than the others. Tension became painful at the end but he did not succeed in finding the blot. Persuaded he had been the victim of an illusion, vexed, he apologised:

"Yes, I probably made a mistake. I can't see anything any more With this nasty light it is not easy."

Prien lowered his binoculars and looked in the direction of Mainland.

"Hard a-port!"

"Hard a-port it is!"

"Ship's head?"

"Steer 350."

"10 to port, steer 340!"

The submarine was proceeding parallel to Mainland half a mile from the shore. If, within a quarter of an hour, no ship had been spotted, the mission would have been a fiasco.

In the forward torpedo chamber, Torpedo Petty Officer Bleeck controlled the four launching tubes with robot-like gestures.

"Say, that's at least the tenth time you've checked these tubes," exclaimed Thewes, passing his left arm around the starboard reserve torpedo.

"Oh well, it's become a nervous habit since we have been sailing round and round in Scapa Flow," replied Bleeck, turning round and straightening his forage cap. Everything was in order. The four launching tubes had already been flooded with the water from the compensation tank and the pressure in the compressed air drums was normal. It only remained to despatch the torpedoes to their target. Bleeck and Thewes had placed two in position of rapid reloading. Fixed to their respective serrated rails, the torpedoes were ready to be pushed in upper tubes one and two.

"Can you understand what's going on up there?" asked Thewes.

"No! Would you believe it? We have been cruising quietly for half an hour in the most formidable of the British bases? It's all very fishy. . . ."

"I feel that we are going to fire soon," interrupted Thewes.

"Your hair is still prickling your neck, I suppose," sneered Bleeck.

"You can laugh as much as you want. It never fails and you won't be long in finding out," retorted Thewes unperturbed.

Bleeck could not stand still. To calm his nerves and put a good face on it, he set about checking the temperature of the two reserve torpedoes which he had placed to warm up. It was important that the electric torpedoes should not be cold when fired, otherwise they risked operating badly or even not at all and of sinking immediately after ejection from the tubes.

"Do you trust these new devices?" asked Thewes, just to say something, for he knew the reply very well.

"No. I prefer the good old 'fish' with compressed air. Despite their wake, they have at least proved themselves, and anyway I don't see the importance of the wake in a moonless night. What do you think?"

"I don't know. No, not at first sight, but the 'old man' knows very well what he is doing. If he has given them to us, it's because he thinks they are safe."

"You're probably right," replied Bleeck, affectionately patting the torpedo on which Thewes was leaning his elbow. Carefully he wiped away a drop of condensation with the cuff of his sleeve.

At the other end of the submarine, in the rear torpedo chamber, Leading Seamen Herrmann and Loh were making somewhat similar remarks.

Herrmann smoothed his thick black hair above his right ear and straightened his forage cap. Gloomy-eyed, he contemplated the only torpedo tube, then turned towards Loh.

"Well, Willi, we don't need to worry much, it's Bleeck who's going to fire first as usual."

"Yes, he'll be the first, granting that we shoot our 'fish' too, which is far from sure as things are going. It will only be if up there, they stumble on several targets grouped together or if Bleeck makes a mess of his part of the job."

"You're a joker, you are, if you think we have run all those risks for nothing. Of course we'll fire. You don't really believe that Scapa Flow is empty of all ships? For the lack of thrushes, we'll make do with blackbirds."

"As far as I'm concerned, all I'm asking is not to finish like a rat . . . It's quite on the cards. War has just begun. I assure you, Herbertchen, I'd be as well at home."

"Don't fret, I'm sure that we'll see this adventure through. The skipper knows his job well. He's a tough guy."

"To be sure he is a tough guy, but nobody ever came back from Scapa Flow to tell the tale: it's enough to make you think that the British know their job too!"

Herrmann looked at his wrist watch and frowned.

"It won't be long now before we have actually been all round the base and still nothing to be seen. Blast it! What on earth are they doing up there?'' he grumbled, raising his eyes. He only saw the curve of the hull.

On the bridge, Dziallas tensed all the muscles of his face. The flitting vision of a shadow slightly darker than the cliffs appeared again for a fraction of a second in the sights, then vanished into the surrounding grey. Was it still an illusion? The breeze singing in his ears made his hand shake and the sighting for which he was searching escaped his narrow field of vision. The petty officer thought the night was really cold and he was beginning to feel numb. He lowered his binoculars and shut his eyes for a few moments, then he glanced stealthily around him. Nobody seemed to have noticed anything.

He took up watch again and almost immediately was shocked into new awareness. The blot was there, once more, ink black, its outlines remained dim. To make sure, he moved his binoculars slightly, then came back to the same spot which he pinpointed right away. No mistake. There was something there. He nudged Endrass.

"This time, I'm sure I see a big ship ahead, 10° to starboard," he murmured, watching him from the corner of his eye.

Dziallas saw him search for a few seconds for the suspicious point then steady his binoculars.

"Good heavens! You're right! Ship ahead, starboard 10°," announced Endrass with excitement.

Prien was trying to pinpoint the radio aerials on top of the eastern cliffs in the south of Scapa Flow bay. Immediately he brought back his binoculars in the direction mentioned and quickly examined the object which was provoking such a stir among the men on watch.

"Yes, I see her. It is a big one. Distance 4,000 metres at least," he pronounced at last.

In the conning tower in front of the TDC, Smyczek stiffened at the news he heard through the speaking tube. On the bridge, the atmosphere was getting tense. Endrass came near the sighting telescope.

The silence was broken only by the purring of the diesels, the hissing of the bow-wash and the lapping of the water sliding along the hull. Prien and Endrass had again taken up their binoculars. The shadow was beginning to turn into a silhouette. "It is a big tub with one funnel, her bow towards the land."

"I'd say it is a battleship of the 'Royal Sovereign' or 'Queen Elizabeth' class" said Prien.

"Rather a 'Royal Sovereign'. I can see her tripod mast aft. The 'Queen' class have a more massive superstructure."

"She is moored at right angles to the shore. . . . No, she must make

86

What Prien, Petty Officer Dziallas and Leading Seaman Gerhard Hänsel claim to have seen while on watch on the bridge during the attack. Reconstruction by the author.

an angle of 45°, or just about, it is difficult to say. I do not see any light showing."

"We cannot be very visible on the background of the cliffs—and we are full ahead of her. They're not expecting an attack coming from the land side," added Endrass.

Prien nodded and replied:

"Nevertheless! We must be still more careful. Our success depends on the effect of surprise."

A heavy silence fell on the bridge again. They all realised that if, through bad luck, the British watch were to spot them, the light guns of the battleship would send them to the bottom in a few moments.

"Second ship of the line behind the first one!" shouted von Varendorff. The captain and the first lieutenant took to their binoculars.

"Good heavens! But it's true . . . a big one, two funnels . . . they are moored in alternate rows . . . the first one covers two thirds of the second, moored nearer to the land," said Endrass, his eyes glued to the sights.

A bow tapering into a slight 'cutwater' stem, a free deck, two main turrets and part of the forward superstructure were visible behind the first silhouette.

"It's a battlecruiser ... *Repulse* or *Renown* ... She is much longer than the big one," observed von Varendorff.

"It must be *Repulse* for *Renown* is away on operations," replied Prien.

"Splendid targets and well placed for firing," said Endrass to himself, without taking his binoculars from his eyes.

Hänsel on watch aft was listening intently to the officers' dialogue. He was furiously eager to face the enemy who, even though his back was turned, could send him to the next world. He lowered his binoculars and cursed the light. It made the submarine's wake so obvious like a livid finger pointing at her. Barely a minute had passed since the second officer's remark had been made and still Hänsel thought the silence seemed to last inordinately long. What could be happening? He took his binoculars again and looked over the whole of the sector he had to watch. The leading seaman knew that the ship would go about as soon as the torpedoes had been fired. He was waiting for the commander's orders with impatience mingled with anxiety.

What was he waiting for? Now they must be within range. At what distance would he make up his mind to attack? He looked again at the wake. This seething water was probably visible miles away, he thought.

"Open the tubes fast! Tubes one to four prepare for surface firing!" ordered Prien.

Endrass bent over the voice pipe. In the forward torpedo compartment Bleeck frantically turned the wheels of the four tubes and bellowed in the voice pipe:

"Tubes one to four to the ready!"

"Tubes one to four ready, sir," reported Endrass.

"Depth 7m. Tubes one and two line of sight: forecastle of the ship to the south, tubes three and four: on the bow of the ship to the north. Distance 3,000 metres, torpedo speed 30. Director angle green three."

"Aye, Aye, sir" answered Endrass. He glued his right eye to the attack periscope, then, through the speaking tube, began a quick exchange of words with Smyczek. He gave him the distance, the position of the target and various other particulars. The TDC bearing was connected to the gyro-compass and the attack periscope. In front of the instruments Smyczek was watching the two dull red control lights which showed him that the orders had been carried out. After a few seconds, the humming of the TDC stopped and the two lights went out. Smyczek announced the result and then connected the TDC on the torpedo circuits: from now on the firing data were automatically transmitted to them. Another light went up in front of the leading seaman. It was now possible to fire from any position as long as the angle was not over 90°.

Endrass guided the aiming cross of the attack periscope on the superstructure of the battleship and without lifting up his head put his right hand on the torpedo firing control.

"Green three ready to fire, sir."

"Fire."

"Tube one, fire! Tube two at the ready!"

"Tube two, fire."

Prien was keeping his eyes on the second officer. He saw him move the attack periscope slightly to the right.

"Hard over to starboard," he ordered.

The sighting cross was just over the bow of the ship to the north.

"Tube three at the ready! Tube three, fire."

"Tube four at the ready! Tube four, fire."

In the 'house of lords' Bleeck, his hands on the control of the upper tubes one and two and one foot on the control of lower tube three heard the orders to fire, in the ship telephone.

U-47 was shaken three times. The first two shocks, at $1\frac{1}{5}$ second intervals, then the third one $3\frac{1}{2}$ seconds later told him that three torpedoes had left the submarine and were running at 30 knots towards their targets. Bleeck threw himself, swearing, on the hand control of tube four. Nothing happened. Frantically he tried to fire the fourth torpedo. It was in vain. A metallic voice came out of the speaking tube. He recognised Endrass' voice—

"What's the matter with tube four?" he asked calmly.

"I don't know yet," answered Bleeck, straightening up.

"Is the torpedo jammed?"

"I don't think so; the control must be, though. I'll see to it right away," said the petty officer in a grudging voice, as if he were holding himself personally responsible for the unfortunate incident.

On the bridge, as soon as the first torpedo had left the submarine, von Varendorff had pushed the spring of the seconds hand of his wrist watch.

In the control room Wessels was busy draining the torpedo tubes into the compensation tanks, adding water in equal weight to that of the three torpedoes fired. The balance and the weight of the submarine had to be maintained in any case to allow fast diving which was impossible otherwise.

The nervous tension caused by the waiting was becoming intolerable. Von Varendorff announced the thirtieth second of the third minute. Had the torpedoes passed by their targets? Had the detonators failed? Three failures on a sitting target—that was almost impossible.

Suddenly a whitish column of water rose strangely slow, hiding the bow of the battlecruiser. The sound of an explosion followed by a muffled roar resounded against the cliffs.

The shock of the underwater explosion carried well by the water, was felt more intensely by the men in the submarine.

Prien kept his eyes on the target. The white patch of the column of water had disappeared. For a moment he thought it had all been an illusion. The big ship remained dark and silent; she was there, as if nothing had happened.

U-47 went about.

Hänsel opened his eyes wide. The two heavy ships seemed to defy them. He could not stop looking at these giants, whose outlines appeared like shadows in a Chinese show on the bay lit up by the unreal flames in the sky.

For a short while, he doubted the reality of it all. It wasn't like this that he had imagined the attack on the British fleet at Scapa Flow.

"Open tube five—tube five at the ready!" came Endrass' voice.

Herrmann and Loh jumped to their feet.

"What did I tell you?" said Herrmann with delight.

Ignoring the remark, Loh wiped off the drops of sweat forming on his brow with the cuff of his left sleeve. Herrmann, ready to fire, his right hand on the hand control, remained silent.

"Tube five, fire!"

A new shock made the submarine tremble when the fourth torpedo left. On the bridge von Varendorff again set the timing on his watch. Still no reaction from the enemy. The deepest calm continued to reign on Scapa Flow.

"Another go, sir?" asked Endrass with conviction.

"Yes, reload tubes one, two and five: We're going to attack again."

The first lieutenant bent over the voice pipe.

"Reload tubes one, two and five and quickly, for a second round," he stressed.

The two ships of the line kept a ghostly silence. It was becoming inexplicable. Prien put his binoculars to his eyes. The bow of the ship to the north was sinking in the sea clearly below the water line.

"Hello, bridge! Tube four ready. Fire control freed. We're beginning to reload tubes one and two," panted Bleeck through the voice pipe.

"Good work, Kurt, but don't dilly-dally with the two 'fish', we're not going to stay here forever," replied Endrass.

"Nor us neither, we'll do our best."

The first lieutenant turned towards Prien: "tube four is ready, sir, tubes one and two are being loaded."

"Perfect—We'll fire three torpedoes on the ship to the south."

"Three minutes," announced von Varendorff.

The waiting and the ever growing anxiety as to the British reaction created an unbearable tension. The silence, light and shadows combined to make the atmosphere unreal. The seconds ticked away interminably.

To relieve the tension, Endrass decided to speak:

"Unbelievable! It's a mad joke. We torpedo a battlecruiser and her crew remains asleep. The base remains asleep as if nothing was happening. Everybody's asleep. Maybe we're asleep too. I hope we are not all dreaming together."

Prien gave a little smile and retorted:

"What is also unbelievable is that we have three misfires and a jammed tube. On the other hand, the inertia of the British is understandable. A submarine attack must seem to them so inconceivable that the idea of it has probably not even entered their minds. The explosion has been attributed, without doubt, to a magnetic mine."

On a south-east course *U-47* approached obliquely the shore of Mainland, which was already very near. Forward to port, almost on her route, there loomed up the massive projection which formed the south west part of the island. This rocky prominence which they had passed by when entering, marked the interior limit of Scapa Flow.

In the forward torpedo compartment, as soon as the tubes were emptied of water, Bleeck and Thewes opened the breech of tube one, then they dragged the torpedo, fixed with two hooks to its rail, and let it slide almost completely in the tube. It was not easy for it weighed more than a ton and a half.

Only the rudders and the propellers were still outside. Bleeck had his own way of getting torpedoes into their tubes. He pulled his forage cap down on his forehead, grasped the rail solidly in his hand, lifted up his legs and rested the hollow of his right heel delicately on the cone of the propellers, shored himself up, and at one go, pushed the torpedo right down into the tube.

Thewes closed the breech again at once and secured it carefully. Bleeck stood up again. Drops of sweat were running down his cheeks, bristling with fair hair.

"That's one gone," he sighed.

From the bridge, you could see clearly 200m away, the foam of the waves breaking on the shore with a perfectly audible hissing.

"Tube five ready," reported Herrmann through the speaking tube.

"Tubes one and two reloaded—tubes one, two and four ready," announced Bleeck a few minutes later, breathing in the voice pipe.

"Hard over to starboard!"

Prien had turned round to look at the shore of Mainland. Endrass glanced at him sideways and opened his mouth to say something but he heard him order:

"Steady as she goes! What's the ship's head?"

"Ship's head 310," replied Schmidt.

"Ship's head 310!"

U-47 moved slightly away from the coast. The battleship was not yet visible or, at least, nobody on the bridge was trying to find her. They sensed her as hunters sense the presence of game. The big ship must now be ahead 23° to starboard.

Until now, Hänsel had concentrated his search on the south part of his sector of watch, that is to say Kirk Sound. No sign of life. The leading seaman turned his eyes to the left and began to examine attentively the shore of Mainland. Maybe a ship or even several ships were lying there at anchor, in the shadow of the cliff ready to run them down unexpectedly. He scrutinised the smallest corners of shadow methodically. Nothing. Suddenly he made out clearly a ship anchored in a bay. In the background he seemed to see something resembling oil installations but he did not take time to make sure.

"Tanker moored abeam on starboard," he announced hurriedly.

Quickly, Prien and his two officers trained their binoculars on the point indicated.

"It's a small tanker, probably Merchant Navy. Her crew must be asleep for they've not seen us, going in or going out," commented Endrass.

"Let's hope they're heavy sleepers and don't hear us," added von Varendorff mockingly.

Prien lowered his binoculars and looked at his watch. The luminous hands showed 01.12hrs. Fourteen minutes had elapsed since the first torpedo had been fired. If they were to attack at the same distance as before there were only six minutes to go before the firing. He wondered what on earth could have caused the failures.

Had the estimate of the sighting of the course, speed and drift, not been accurate? Or was it a fault in the new detonators? The answer to the question was important. Three torpedoes out of four had not exploded. That was a lot. He had the unpleasant feeling that the torpedoes had been faulty. If such was the case, if the naval dockyard was issuing faulty torpedoes, then it was really not worthwhile to risk his life and his crew's performing feats of valour.

Dziallas lowered his binoculars and conscientiously wiped the lens. He had clearly studied the battleship. Still he thought he had seen something right ahead. The vision had been transitory and he was not at all sure of what he had seen. He did not say a word for there were as many chances of it being a ship as a shadow caused by the aurora borealis or an indentation in the coastline. He took his binoculars, again, but did not see anything which could be taken for a ship.

He looked again for a short while at the dark mass of the warship, then started to scan methodically the space on her right. Nothing to be seen, not even the masts he had vaguely made out a moment ago and which could have been those of destroyers.

He brought back his binoculars to the left until the silhouette of the battleship again came within the sights. A flash of lightning zig-zagged the darkness. Dziallas thought he was under an illusion. But no, a small luminous ray had just appeared on board the battleship, on the opposite side. The beam was partially visible when it went past the rear of the funnel. It probably came from the signalling bridge.

"Sir! They have put on a searchlight, sweeping towards the land."

The three officers again trained their binoculars on the battleship.

"No doubt they have woken up," commented von Varendorff.

"Yes, happily their attention is fixed on the wrong side," mocked Prien. His binoculars still glued to his eyes, he went on:

"Prepare to fire the three torpedoes to the centre of the objective. Oh! they have switched off the searchlight. They are on their guard all the same," he added.

Endrass leant on the attack periscope and regulated it so that the line of sight was covering the funnel.

"We'll fire from a shorter distance than last time," continued Prien.

Dziallas heard the first officer estimating the distances, the course and the drift, and transmitting them to Smyczeck. As for him, he

93

began quietly sweeping the sea with his binoculars. He scanned the sector in which he thought he had seen something suspicious a moment before. Slowly, methodically, he examined, with all the visual concentration he could muster, the dim line dividing sea and land. The effort he was under became hard to bear. The surface of the sea was whitish but this glow was not uniform. Here and there, bright spots alternated with moving shadows which, elsewhere, melted away in the grey of the shore. The light was continually changing in intensity.

Dziallas was one of the best men on board as far as the watch was concerned. His reputation was solidly established and he was doing his best to maintain it for he was more than a little proud of it. It was when, for the third time, he was back to the starting point of his sector, that he stopped at the sight of a small straight line. This line was almost imperceptible. It scarcely could be made out against the background of the hills. At its base was a slight discolouration. The careful study of this patch made it take the shape of a ship. No possible mistake. His heart began pounding a bit faster. The ship must be 3,000 to 4,000m away, maybe more. Taking account of the distance, it could be a tanker. On purpose, Dziallas turned his eyes away from it, to see if he could find it again. Yes, it was still there. A flat deck and the bridge right aft.

"Ship, red three-oh!" he almost shouted.

Endrass was startled but went on watching the battleship, all the while casting glances at the repeater of the target transmitter. Prien took a few seconds to discover the new ship.

"I'd say it's a small tanker anchored very near the coast, unless it is the old aircraft carrier *Pegasus*. Yes, that's what it is. That one won't hamper our attack but, with this light, we'll have to reckon with her afterwards," he said, his binoculars still glued to his face.

Turning his head, he looked towards the battleship. The silhouette of the latter had grown considerably larger. Now, he could see her clearly, with the naked eye. He assessed the distance and ordered:

"Open the tube doors!"

Letting his binoculars fall back on his chest, he went on staring at the warship.

"Endrass, are you ready to fire?" he asked brusquely.

"Yes, sir! director angle green three ready to fire."

His hand on the torpedo firing control, the first lieutenant remained stiff in an attitude of expectancy.

Dziallas shivered in spite of his two pullovers and wanted to sneeze. With difficulty he managed to keep himself from doing so. The breeze was stronger now, he thought. For a while he kept his eyes on the bow wave and then went back watching.

Tension was mounting by the second. Endrass wondered when the commander would make up his mind to fire. The distance from the target, he assessed, was now down to less than 1,500m. The shadowy form of the battleship was swelling enormously in the night.

"Hard over to starboard!" "Fire!"

Prien's voice, dry and sharp, made him jump.

"Tube one, fire! Tube two at the ready."

"Tube two, fire! Tube four at the ready!"

"Tube four, fire!"

The last shock indicated that the three torpedoes had been fired. At that same moment, in the 'house of lords' Bleeck was wiping his brow with his sleeve cuff whispering a vague 'bon voyage'.

On the bridge, von Varendorff pushed the spring of his chronometer for the third time. Prien looked at his watch. The hands were showing 01.13hrs 5sec. The issue of the game would be decided in the two long minutes which were to follow.

5. What should we answer, sir?

Hänsel now had the two battleships in full view. The leading seaman tried to guess the path of the three torpedoes for they did not leave any wake. He caught himself imagining which part of the battleship they might hit. After a while, the tension became unbearable. He moved his binoculars towards the left, to the limit of his sector or watch, trying to make out *Pegasus*. By luck or because his eyesight was excellent, he was not long in finding her. His teeth drawn tight, Prien did not move his eyes from the battleship.

His heart beat a little quicker: the white splash of a column of foam stood out on the dark mass of the ship, it went up high enough to hide the superstructures on the bridge. His fingers clasping the flat top of the bridge rail were so clenched that they hurt. He held his breath for an instant then his muscles relaxed and he recovered his usual calm. Thank God, this time, the torpedoes had behaved normally. Already a second geyser was rising at the rear of the funnel. Then a third, hiding the upper rear turret.

A triple blast was reflected back by the cliffs. A thick black pall of smoke began to rise from the second point of impact. Prien was watching with a certain amount of fear for the enemy's reaction but still nothing happened.

Endrass, lifted up his forearm and bent on his wrist.

"01.15hrs 40sec," he announced.

"Three torpedoes right in the middle of the target. If she's not done for after that, she's a ghost ship . . . ."

Suddenly a blinding light rent the darkness. Von Varendorff stopped speaking before he had finished his sentence. A second later a gigantic tongue of fire lit the whole rear of the battleship with an unbearable intensity. Its light was so strong that it lit up the inside part of the bridge and made the eyes of the men blink while they stood there, fascinated by the sight.

Endrass opened his mouth to speak just when the shock-wave hit the submarine with a terrific strength. The noise went through his chest and stopped his breath. Then there was utter silence. He thought his ear-drum had burst. His head down between his shoulders, he followed the trajectory of the huge pieces of steel torn from the battleship and thrown about like straws. The column of fire went out as suddenly as it had sprung up. A huge mushroom of smoke, still darker and thicker than the one from the rear of the funnel, rose in the sky where the will o' the wisps of the aurora borealis were sparkling.

Painting by Jean Delpech, naval artist.

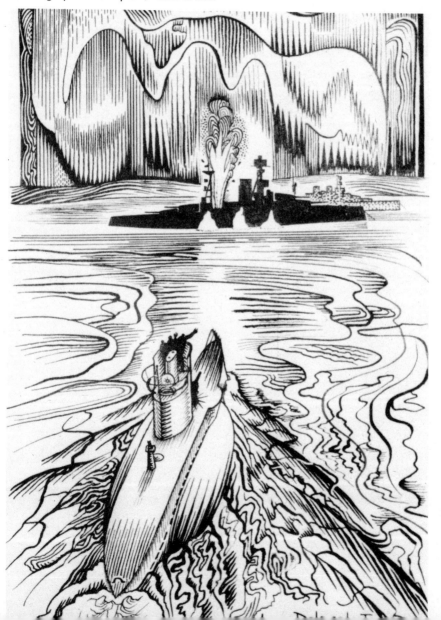

"I never heard anything like that," articulated Endrass in a hoarse voice.

"One of the magazines has probably been blown up. The smoke is from the burning of the cordite," answered Prien.

Endrass bent over the intercom and explained to the crew:

"The battleship which we have just torpedoed has blown up!"

"Look, she is listing!" shouted Dziallas.

Inside the submarine the series of explosions had been felt with an extraordinary violence.

The first idea which went through Spahr's mind was that a salvo from the main guns of the battleship had just crashed down nearby. In the 'house of lords' Bleeck, his face screwed up, had not even wiped the drops of sweat which were streaming down his cheeks. His chronometer in his right hand, he had remained motionless during the two minutes which had preceded the first detonation. A broad smile followed by a cry of joy welcomed the double explosion. Turning round towards Thewes he gave him a noisy slap on the shoulder. "The little dears have worked well, I knew it, they were warmed up just right." The fourth blast interrupted his monologue and made him almost lose his balance. The hull shivered as in the grasp of a giant hand but the submarine was not shaken, the explosion having obviously taken place near the surface.

Surprised by the violence of the noise, Bleeck and Thewes looked at each other anxiously. Thewes was the first to recover his calm.

"We must have made beautiful fireworks—it's time to get out of here before it becomes unhealthy."

He stopped speaking and listened, expecting to hear the firing from the enemy's defence. Instead of that, it was the voice of the first officer which came through the speaking tube with a nasal tone.

"The battleship which we have just torpedoed has blown up."

Bleeck and Thewes were listening, their eyes fixed on the mouth of the speaking tube, hoping to get information. But Endrass said no more.

Thewes scratched the back of his head.

"I've got the impression that soon all hell will be let loose. There isn't enough water to escape by diving. With the British chasing us the exit threatens to be much harder than the entrance."

"Never mind! Don't worry, leave that to the officers," replied Bleeck.

As if to prove him right, Endrass' voice came again over the intercom:

"Load tubes one and two!"

At the same time, in the rear torpedo compartment, Herrmann and Loh, waiting for the enemy's inevitable reaction, were also listening. Both were prey to the same fears. The British would not remain passive. They were going to send after them, if they had not already done so, all the available ships in the vicinity . . . and they were sure to be many.

The torpedo leading seamen were pricking their ears at the least little noise but did not hear any, save that of their own propellers churning the water with a regular rhythm. Endrass began to describe the operation in the manner of a radio reporter:

"The battleship has received a fatal blow. She is listing. A small craft, probably one of the servicing pinnaces, remains nearby, near the stern and sends frantic SOS. I would say that she is listing now at an angle of 45°. She is sinking slowly but inexorably. I cannot see her properly because of the distance and of the smoke covering her. . . ."

On board the *Royal Oak* everything was quiet. Within a few minutes that Friday the 13th would end to the relief of all superstitious men.

At midnight, the watch was changed. The two hundred men or thereabouts, on duty since 20.00hrs were happy to be allowed to go to their sleeping quarters, at last, secure in the base of Scapa Flow. All felt tired to death and it was easy to understand why.

The battleship had come back the previous day from an exhausting patrol. The weather had been so bad that most men in the crew had been sea-sick. The escorting destroyers being unable to keep in contact because of the violent storm, the *Royal Oak* had ploughed its way in a wild sea up to the vicinity of Fair Isle without any protection. Her deck had constantly been under foaming water. The waves had broken most of the rafts. The fury of the sea had been such that it had put the guns on portside out of action. The battleship reached Scapa Flow on the 12th October. An aircraft carrier, four ships of the line, ten cruisers and some destroyers were anchored there. The *Royal Oak* cast anchor in the north-east corner of the bay, near the battlecruiser *Repulse*.

A German reconnaissance aircraft was sighted towards 15.00hrs. The same thing had already happened the day before; this incursion could forecast a bombing raid by the Luftwaffe. The anti-aircraft watch on the battleship was, consequently, reinforced, for the number of land batteries and fighters was very small.

A little before 17.00hrs Commodore Dönitz had in hand Lieutenant Newe's radio message describing the number and type of the ships he had observed in Scapa Flow. The information was as heartening as it

HMS *Royal Oak* in September 1937. / IWM

could possibly be. The perfect visibility left no doubt about the identity of the ships. Effectively the latter was to be verified by the study of the aerial photographs.

At the end of a meeting held during the night at Wilhelmshaven, at which Lieutenant Newe was present, a message was sent to *U-47*. The submarine did not get it, for at that time she was asleep somewhere at the bottom of the North Sea, near the Orkneys. It did not matter. What was important was that the hunting ground was not short of targets.

Prien's mission promised to be fruitful.

But the fateful 13th October was not going to end without a dramatic turn of events. The news burst out like a bomb. The cipher department gave the information that the British Fleet had got under way the previous evening. From this, Commodore Dönitz drew the conclusion that the Royal Navy, alerted by the two consecutive air reconnaissances, and fearing air attacks, had, for the time being, evacuated Scapa Flow. It was all the more irritating because the first aircraft, from the Second Air Squadron, had carried out this flight without order to do so.

Dönitz considered ordering *U-47* to come back but, thinking it over, did not take such a decision. The die was cast and there remained but to hope that all heavy units had not left the base.

At Scapa Flow, contrary to what could have been expected, the 13th went by without any alert happening to disturb the daily routine.

On board *Royal Oak* some marines had loaded the food while sailors were busy repairing damage caused by the storm and piling up the pieces of the broken rafts in a heap on the deck. The crew had not yet had time to find their strength back and the men were absolutely exhausted.

On the 14th at 00.58hrs an explosion of medium strength echoed in the night. A mild shock shook the battleship. Nobody believed in immediate danger. The men whose quarters were forward under the main deck woke up with a start and, with a few exceptions only, went back to sleep peacefully.

Those who were sleeping amidships or aft had only heard a muffled explosion which was not alarming at all. The 29,000 ton battleship gave them a comforting feeling of security. The fact that this floating fortress could, in a few minutes, disintegrate in the base of Scapa Flow was hard to consider. Officers, hastily dressed, had gone up to the deck and wondered about the origin of the explosion. Was it a bomb or a mine dropped by a plane. Nobody heard the telling drone. Nothing showed that the ship had been hit. Maybe it was an internal explosion. As a matter of duty, a safety party was sent to the paint hold, forward, where the noise seemed to have been heard stronger.

The possibility of an attack by a U-boat was not considered likely by most men, all the more because minutes were ticking away without anything happening to disturb the surrounding calm. An enemy submarine would not have been content with firing one torpedo, which seemed to have exploded somewhat too early, and then disappear. Would not a submarine have attacked again ? And then, how on earth could she have entered Scapa Flow ?

Still, a few sailors, forward under the main deck, were sure that it really was a torpedo attack and that they were in danger of their lives; they were doing their best to wake the men, but the latter were too tired to react. They turned their backs, grumbling that they wanted to be left in peace.

On the signal bridge a Leading Signalman thought he saw something suspicious on the water and reported it to the lieutenant on watch. The latter ordered him to switch on a searchlight for a moment. An empty whisky case appeared in the beam of light, drifting with the current.

A quarter of an hour had elapsed since the alert and most of the men who had gone up on deck were going to go back to their sleeping quarters.

Suddenly three strong explosions almost at the same time, shook the

The wreck of HMS *Royal Oak* as depicted by a contemporary German painting. This representation is incorrect, as the ship in fact capsized to starboard. / Verlag Erich Klinghammer

battleship. Columns of water, one abreast the bridge superstructure and the others abaft the funnel and near the upper turret left no doubt in their minds: it was really a torpedo attack.

A series of explosions were heard deep in the battleship. The lights went out causing the utmost confusion. A black pall of smoke, thick and greasy, covered the centre of the ship. *Royal Oak* began to list.

A dazzling flash sprang along the main mast up to its top. A frightening blast knocked down a great number of sailors and marines. Panels, steel sheets and debris weighing tons flew in the air. Suddenly the whole aft of the ship was on fire. A blinding flame, as if vomited from hell, jumped at a dizzy height, and went out in a second.

The main deck offered a dreadful sight with the dead, the dying and the wounded howling with pain. The acrid and at the same time sweetish smell of burnt flesh, cordite and fuel-oil caught the throat.

The ship was listing more and more every second. Groping among the debris, the damage control party collided in the dark, with the first-aid parties. The internal system of communication was out of order. Groups of men still unwounded, found themselves isolated in various compartments of the battleship. Orders were to be transmitted by messengers, but as soon as they tried to go down the ship, they were immediately pushed back by a human tide forcing its way up in quest of fresh air.

"Everyone for himself!" The cry of 'abandon ship' spread with a surprising speed.

Down below, the watertight doors were placed in alternate rows. It meant that to cross over a place, you had to go out through a door situated on the opposite side from the one you had entered. These heavy doors, impossible to manoeuvre by hand, had closed down when the ship listed to a certain degree. Trapped like rats, men exhausted themselves labouring to open them. Pushing dragging with the energy of despair, they always ended by falling on top of each other. Unbalanced by the growing list, heavy objects crushed the hapless men who could not see them fall in the dark.

To starboard, under the main deck, at the point of impact of the torpedoes, the place was in a shambles. In the marines' mess and in the stokers', unfortunate men went on burning like torches. Horribly burnt by cordite, dying and wounded were lying together with burnt up corpses in an unbreathable atmosphere.

The men who had succeeded in reaching the fore and aft gangways, where the ladders were to be found, fought with all their strength to push the bunch of people who stopped the way to the main deck. There were a few scenes of panic, but also numerous acts of courage and self sacrifice.

Five minutes had barely elapsed since the last explosion and already the deck of the giant was up by 45°. Water was pouring in through the portholes, open for ventilation, and blacked out but not watertight.

The drama had been so quick that the MFV acting as a tender linking the battleship with Scapa Flow and moored on portside, found itself in an awkward position less than a minute after the second attack. When listing to starboard, the *Royal Oak* had begun to lift the MFV out of the sea. Luckily the skipper was awake. He instinctively seized the axe and with difficulty, severed the mooring ropes, stiffened and hard as steel bars. With a hissing of wood against metal, the small boat slid on the hull of the battleship and fell back into the sea with a huge splash of foam. Happily the damage was not serious and immediately the skipper of the MFV started to try and save the survivors. A crowd of men half dead with cold were swimming in icy water covered with fuel-oil. The two big boats secured on portside and the hawsers of which had been released in time, had turned over under the weight of the survivors. They were floating upside down, next to the debris of the rafts thrown from the ship's deck. A few sailors had managed to hoist themselves on the boats, others clung to them or were trying to climb on them at the risk of upsetting them completely.

On board the MFV, the survivors were picked up with infinite care, for the slightest contact with their burnt skin drew from them howls of pain.

The list of the deck of the *Royal Oak* was becoming so pronounced that you could not move on it except by dragging yourself on your knees. One of her enormous propellers was above water. Fearing the whirl of sea when she would sink, groups of men, more and more of them, dived into the water. Phlegmatically, some officers helped the wounded or gave their own life belts. A great number of them refused to abandon ship until the very last moment.

Inside the *Royal Oak* the vertical ladders were almost horizontal. Men walked on the bulkheads.

The big ship stopped listing. She remained still for a few moments, shivered all over, then fell back in her movement even faster than before With her searchlight, the MFV was ceaselessly sending SOS messages to the aircraft carrier *Pegasus* anchored some two miles away. The skipper swore like a trooper; a battleship of 29,000 tons had just blown up and nobody seemed to have noticed it. At last he made out the low, moving shadows of destroyers or anti-submarine craft. Lights began to wink long-short-long signals.

"At last they are waking up," grumbled the skipper at the wheel. Suddenly without any warning, the giant keeled over, taking with her to the bottom a great number of men. She lifted up a wave which made the MFV roll like a nutshell.

When the sea calmed down, the skipper saw, to his surprise, heads emerging from the sheet of fuel-oil on the surface of the water. These survivors of the last minute had escaped from the upturned hull by sliding through an escape port after tearing out the black-out and ventilation apparatus.

The tragedy had not lasted 10 minutes. Where *Royal Oak* had been, a long rolling swell shone under the cold sparkling lights of the aurora borealis.

"I cannot see her—She must have sunk," concluded Endrass, opening his eyes wide.

Painting by Jean Delpech, naval artist.

"Destroyers and anti-submarine craft forward on starboard," cried von Varendorff.

Prien turned on his heels, looked in the direction mentioned, then replied dryly:

"They zig-zag in a disorderly way and do not suspect anything."

"Good Lord, if one of them sees us, we're done for," he thought.

Searchlights were flashing messages from more and more points. A long livid beam pierced the darkness, swept over the sea, hesitating, then went out. One, two, three other searchlights were switched on, pointing their long white fingers towards the sky, trying to pinpoint aircraft.

Von Varendorff expressed the thoughts of every one of them when saying, half mockingly, half seriously: "It won't be long before things begin to warm up. It is time to scarper."

On a south-east course, the submarine was running, using the whole power of her diesels, along Mainland, towards the exit from Scapa Flow, still about a mile distant. The cliffs were rising less than 200m away. In spite of the noise of the sea and the roar of the diesels, you could hear distinctly the humming of the motors from the cars speeding on the small coast roads.

"This time, we are done for. They are awake," said von Varendorff.

His eyes gazed with astonishment. The searchlight beams issuing from various points, crossed each other over the submarine, forming a luminous vault of the most beautiful effect. "They think it is an air attack. All the better," he thought to himself.

Hänsel was attentively following the movements of the destroyers which happened to be in the sector it was his job to watch. The shadow shrunk on itself as to become quite small. Then it began to swell imperceptibly, and above all to get rapidly higher over the water. The leading seaman frowned and his blood froze in his veins when he made out the huge bow-wave.

"Sir! A destroyer is going to ram us!"

The words had already sprung out of his mouth when he realised that the captain was following the new arrival with his eyes.

"Group the motors," ordered Prien in a neutral voice.

He felt light vibrations going through the bridge plates. Wessels had pushed the motors to their maximum. The effect of the current dead ahead was already strongly felt and the pursuer was gaining ground at a disconcerting speed.

"No doubt now, she has found us and found us well. Barring a miracle, she is going to destroy us," said Prien to himself. He was waiting to see the flashes of the first firing gun at any time now.

"Prepare tube five! Depth 2m, speed 30," he growled.

Endrass repeated the order to Herrmann through the voice pipe, then nervously turned his attack periscope on the destroyer. The first lieutenant realised plainly that tube five represented their very last chance of salvation. They must not mess up this shot.

With this idea in his head, he began to estimate, and as he did so, to transmit to Smyczek the speed, the distance, the bearing, the angle[1] and the drift, particularly important in that case because of the increasing strength of the current.

From the conning tower, Smyczek announced the result given by the transmitter of the target position, then connected the apparatus to the torpedo circuit.

The flame coloured lights in the sky sparkled more brilliantly than ever, pouring a luminous yellow glow on the bay. Endrass had no trouble in bringing the aiming cross of the attack periscope over the bridge of the destroyer. He put his right hand on the firing control without letting his eyes stray from the target:

"Tube five ready to fire, sir."

Prien did not react, but looked first at the pursuer, then at the land

---

[1] Distance off: distance of the submarine to the course of the target, measured perpendicularly to the latter.

Bearing: angle between the axis of the submarine and the line on which the target is seen, measured clockwise.

Angle on the bow: angle between the course of the target and the line on which you see it measured from the bow of the target on the left or on the right.

to estimate their speed. Von Varendorff often raised his eyes to the sky to watch the beams of the searchlights still criss-crossing overhead and changing place as the submarine did. He felt ill at ease and spoke to Endrass with a shade of anxiety in his voice.

"Confound it, Why are these beams always above us? They follow us as closely as if they were actually seeing us. Have they spotted us? Is it to mark the vertical of our position?"

"No, I don't think so. They are searching for aircraft. They simply follow the throbbing of our engines. They have not yet realised that a submarine could have had the audacity to enter the inviolable base of Scapa Flow."

"This destroyer is surely chasing us," grumbled the third hand.

"Don't think so," replied Endrass laconically, putting his binoculars to his eyes and training them in the direction of the British ship.

In spite of all the power of her engines, the submarine progressed with heartbreaking slowness, shaken by the current which raised a big bow wave. At last they came up with the Skaildaquoy headland and were slowly nearing Glims islet. At a short distance on the left, the sunken shells of the wrecks in the Skerry Sound made dark patches on the clearer surface of the sea. Broadside to port, Kirk Sound opened. Kirk Sound, the way home, the road to the open sea, the route through which they had come. The wrecks blocking the channel were still merging into Mainland Island.

Through the voice pipe Spahr's voice came out steady with a nasal twang.

"Hello bridge, tide's ebbing, sir, and not deep enough to go through the north channel again."

"We'll take the south channel," replied Prien.

"That's why I'm giving the Skaildaquoy headland a wide berth to slip between the Lamb islet and the wreck farthest away to the south, the one broken in two."

"You can come within 300 metres of Glims before going about. It will be deep enough there. Stop." answered Spahr.

Prien trained his binoculars on portside, towards the broken wreck about a mile away, but could not make out its different parts against the dark background of the islands. The current running from the south of Kirk caught the sub broadside to port. The abrupt rolling and pitching of the boat made it hard for the men to keep their balance unless their feet were wide apart. Prien reckoned that Glims islet was some 400m away and gave the order: "Hard a-port."

U-47 went right about against the current changing course at nearly right angles.

"Steady as she goes."

"Ship's head?"

"Ship's head 48," answered Schmidt.

"Stop the motors!"

The bridge plates ceased vibrating. The boat, slowing down slightly, found it harder to fight against the current. The aurora borealis turned to orange then to blue, losing for a while some of its intensity.

On the bridge, the men, with lumps in their throats, followed with increasing anxiety, the speedy progress of the destroyer. In spite of the darkness, it was no longer a vague shadow but a silhouette with a clear outline.

Hänsel could not take his eyes away from the destroyer. Confused thoughts went helter-skelter through his mind, threatening, it seemed, to make his head burst. So it was the end. He would not see his parents any more before the end of the war, supposing he would come out alive from the impending destruction of the submarine. Nevertheless, the leading seaman noticed with relief that the rage of the current was such that the foam of the wake was lost in the fury of the eddies. Suddenly the destroyer switched on a powerful searchlight.

For a while the chalk like beam swept the surface of the sea and went out. Hänsel did not get enough time to recover his breath, before a new searchlight blinked on the bridge of the destroyer.

"Good Lord, he is signalling to us in morse," said Endrass with an effort and without letting go of the firing control.

"He asks us to identify ourselves," murmured von Varendorff.

"What should we answer, sir?" asked Hänsel anxiously.

"Nothing!" barked Prien.

A blast of icy spray whipped the conning tower. The destroyer was still getting implacably nearer, sending a new, short series of light signals.

"He's got us and won't . . ." breathed Endrass; without finishing his sentence, he almost shouted: "Good Heavens! He's going about!"

His eyes popping out of his head, Hänsel looked at the destroyer changing course. When she showed her broadside, Endrass' hand tightened on the firing control but Prien kept silent.

A few minutes later the six men, flabbergasted, saw the destroyer dwindle away in the darkness at full speed, leaving a whitish wake trail behind her.

Endrass was the first to recover. He blinked as if to make sure he wasn't dreaming and turned to Prien exclaimed with a stronger drawl than ever:

"Well, tonight we've seen everything, sir!"

The latter was motionless. He did not seem to have heard anything. Von Varendorff, in his turn, roused himself from the listlessness which paralysed him. He wiped his forehead wet with spray, with the palm of his hand and said in a voice made hoarse by emotion:

"Can you make it out? The signals prove that we were well and truly spotted. With her 120mm guns she could destroy us in no time and here she . . ."

"Obviously she did not identify us," cut in Endrass. "She certainly took us to be a patrol boat or a trawler."

"It is extraordinary. Nobody will believe us and I find it hard to believe myself."

"Endrass is right. She probably did not see us. She was after a submerged submarine. To see one cruising on the surface at Scapa Flow in the present circumstances must in their minds be akin to madness."

"If she really noticed us, which I doubt, in the dark, we could quite easily pass for a trawler and as such, unable to answer them in morse," replied Prien.

Ahead of them, Mainland, Lamb island and the blockships seemed to form an impassable wall. Those sunk in Skerry Sound, on the right, showed them the course to adopt. The nearest one passed by less than 100m away. Suddenly a series of muffled explosions were reflected back from the direction of Scapa Flow. Von Varendorff turned to Endrass and muttered: "that sounds like depth charges to me."

"Yes, that's exactly what I thought. They are after a submerged submarine," replied Prien, still scanning Kirk Sound.

The two officers were intent on finding their way through the darkness. Without any warning signs, the boom emerged from the night, a stone's throw from the bow. Ahead, to starboard was the massive shadow of Lamb islet. Ahead on the portside were the blockships. The sinister skeletons were raised like wounded soldiers ready to prevent their going through. Was it exhaustion? Nervous tension? Their aspect was still more threatening, more hostile than when they first entered.

"Both engines half ahead!" shouted Prien.

The tidal current, some 10 knots, was causing a strong undertow which made the manoeuvre still more complicated.

"Both motors slow ahead!" he rectified almost immediately. To avoid the risk of running aground on Lamb islet, they had to pass close to the broken wreck. Vehemently the whirling water pushed back the prow of the sub towards the heap of rusty scrap.

"Starboard 10!"

Shut in the conning tower, unable to see the obstacles, Schmidt, his legs wide apart, manoeuvred as best he could to keep on course. His torso slightly bent forward, the leading seaman at the wheel, face screwed up, brow shining with sweat, tried to anticipate the submarine's yawing. The eddies which shook the ship in all directions did not make his task easier.

The bow of *U-47* was getting nearer the dismantled skeleton, gaining ground metre by metre.

"By Jove! I never saw such a current," said Prien leaning over the first officer's shoulder.

The streaming wreck came to the level of the conning tower. From the bridge, the men could plainly see the weeds and barnacles encrusted on the twisted sheets of metal. By leaning out a bit they could have touched them with their hands. The roar of the current in the bottleneck rose above all other noises, even the sound of the diesels and the explosions of the depth charges still going on in the distance.

The propellers raised a torrent of foam but the ship no longer advanced. The stern began to oscillate dangerously, threatening to throw the submarine across the channel.

"Increase speed: 200 revs!" ordered Prien.

His throat quite dry, Chief Petty Officer Sammann was staring at the wreck. She was still there, abeam of the conning tower. Her crew of ghosts was holding them back with invisible grapnels. His mind was troubled by what he had just gone through, and odd bits of legends about ghost ships came back to him. The icy damp breath of dead sailors polluted the air he took in. A wild push of the backwash stronger than the others, flattened him against the sides of the bridge and brought him back to reality. He looked at Prien and saw him leaning on the flat top of the rail on portside, towards the wreck, then whipping round to order in a thunderous voice:

"Give us all they can give! By Jove we'll manage to go past that dirty old wreck! Steady as you go!"

The sharp piles and girders of the wreck sunk into the sand were threatening to rip open the thin plates of the ballast tanks. Prien felt a shiver run down his back, for damage to the ballast would cut out the possibility of diving. The submarine would then find herself at the mercy of any small patrol boat.

The chances of forcing the allied blockade, on the surface, going back to Wilhelmshaven, would be flimsy indeed, not to say non-existent. Slowly, but more and more swiftly, U-47 was gaining on the furious current.

"250 revs!"

The dismantled skeleton fell back, brushing past them. Prien did not take his eyes off it. As soon as the stern of the submarine had passed the sinister obstacle, he shouted:

"Full ahead!"

Rolling and pitching in the undertow and eddies, the submarine regained speed, lifting up a cloud of spray.

A double yell, sprung as a single shout from the throats of Endrass and von Varendorff, ended with a roar from Prien:

"The mole!"

"Port."

"Port," replied Schmidt, turning the wheel quickly: a double line of sweat streamed from his temples down his unkempt cheeks.

At less than 100m, a landing stage sticking out from Lamb islet lay across their course.

His hand clenched on the flat top of the bridge railing, Prien thundered:

"Steady as she goes . . ."

The ship obeyed the rudder aided by the current which was bearing on the bow. She barely avoided the landing stage and surged in the direction of the sailing ship sunk near the shore of Mainland.

"Hard a-starboard."

"200 revs."

The blockship behind which they had entered Scapa Flow slid away to port. U-47 was back again in Kirk Sound, sailing with the tide, parallel to Mainland and Lamb. They were through the boom.

"Phew! We are out of the wasps' nest," von Varendorff sighed noisily.

A series of explosions in the distance made him turn round. Above Scapa Flow, the aurora borealis continued to shine with all its lights. The boat arrived in the middle of the bend of Kirk Sound, formed by Mainland island.

"Course south-east," ordered Prien.

In front of the bow was Holm Sound leading to the open sea. To port the cliffs of Mainland and the country behind were still as dark and silent.

"Full ahead!"

The throbbing of the diesels rose in pitch. Two miles still separated them from Rose Ness. Now, with each turn of the propellers, the current lost some of its strength.

The gap of East Weddel Sound which appeared to starboard was quickly left behind. Not a word was spoken on the bridge. Tension had lessened, but still everybody was silent. The pictures of his wife and daughter went through Prien's mind and he felt happier than ever to have come out of it alive.

The cape of Rose Ness, quite near, sprung at last from the darkness. The swell from the open sea was already making the submarine pitch slightly. Towards the east, the sky, like a vault, ranged from night blue to ink-black.

Unconsciously, Prien took his binoculars and watched the darkened lighthouse, then let them fall on his chest and went over to the intercom.

"The boat is out of Scapa Flow! Our course is south-east to our base! Your conduct has been as I expected and I am proud to command a crew of brave men! The mission has been carried out with success. In the so-called impenetrable base of Scapa Flow we have sunk a battleship and seriously damaged another. We are now at sea, that is to say in our element and, from now on, safety depends only on ourselves. Leave Action Stations."

In the control room, Spahr looked at the binnacle clock: 02.15hrs— He felt tiredness mounting and rubbed his eyes. In an hour and 45 minutes he would have to go on watch again. He put out the light and rose to go to his sleeping quarters. Passing beside Böhm at the control of the ballast, he noticed the drawn features on the round face, usually smiling, of the ERA.

"Well, Gustav, we've come out of it safe and sound," he said, giving him a tap on the shoulder.

"Heavens! It is tiring to remain idle. These three hours have been the longest in my life," replied Böhm, forcing himself to smile.

"Never mind, we're all in the same boat. I'm going to have a short nap and you should do the same. Nothing like it to put you right again."

"You're right, Willi, Werner won't be long in coming to relieve me. Cheerio!"

A sudden roll of the ship, sharper than the others, surprised Spahr and almost made him lose his balance.

"This time it is clear we're well at sea and 1 prefer that," commented Böhm sententiously.

Spahr was taking a step towards the petty officers' quarters when von Varendorff let himself slide down the ladder from the conning tower and made a noisy contact with the metal floor.

"A drop of the hard stuff for the valiant crew, boss's orders," he shouted, with a broad smile on his lips.

Spahr stopped disconcerted.

"It is surely the first time that I've heard such an order given since I've been on board," snarled Böhm.

"For my part, I won't refuse it. My throat's dried up," replied Wessels from the other end of the central post.

Böhm turned round to add something but von Varendorff had already disappeared in the direction of the galley.

6: The Bull of Scapa Flow

Von Varendorff breathed with delight the cold night air. Never before had he thus enjoyed the vast spaces of the open sea. Everything had fallen back into place. The regular throbbing of the diesels, the noise of the waves against the hull and the movements of the submarine pitching and rolling gently on the light North Sea swell, all this was familiar to him. The watch had gone back to ordinary routine: four men each of whom was in charge of a 90° sector. Visibility was becoming good again. Above Scapa Flow, the aurora borealis still remained visible. From time to time he heard the muffled explosions of the depth charges which went on bursting in the distance. He found himself thinking of the events which had happened since 23.30hrs.

What surprised him most was that this adventure had lasted at most, scarcely 165 minutes. But these minutes would make *U-47* the most famous submarine of the German Navy. He pictured the reception at Wilhelmshaven and the tales he would tell his comrades.

A little before 04.00hrs Spahr, his eyes still heavy with sleep, went up on the bridge to take his watch. In spite of his polo neck jersey, jacket and thick muffler, he seemed to be cold.

"Good morning, sir—not too cold?" he asked.

"All right, thank you," replied von Varendorff, passing his right hand over his forehead.

Spahr knew that the young officer made this unconscious gesture only when he was exhausted or in need of sleep. He looked, for a moment, at the sea and sky then continued:

"Where are we? What's our course? Is it still south-east?"

"Yes, course south-east—speed 15 knots. I took sextant shots on three stars about 10 minutes ago. We are roughly in the middle of Moray Firth. The captain has asked to be wakened at 05.45hrs for the dive. Apart from that, nothing to report. No ship or aircraft sighted," reported von Varendorff.

The well established drill of the relief was over quickly. The crew of the new watch had taken their position. A sailor brought up a small steaming coffee pot and a cup which he handed to Spahr.

Von Varendorff went down the ladder of the control room with stiff and awkward movements. His limbs were heavy and numb. He realised, then, that he could scarcely stand on his feet and contrary to his custom, he did not go through the galley to eat a sandwich, but went straight to his berth. Damp heat inside the submarine took away the remainder of his strength. He let himself fall on the bench of the mess, let his eye wander with pleasure from the familiar objects, to the green curtain behind which Prien was resting and began to unlace his shoes. He threw himself, rather than lay down, on his bunk.

It would soon be sunrise. In the east the sky was growing paler, letting the line of the horizon appear. Prien had not yet given the order to dive, so as to keep course on the surface as long as possible. Visibility was good, except towards land because of intermittent squalls. Frequently Prien and Spahr trained their binoculars in this direction for, from there, a ship could loom up unexpectedly. Autosuggestion? It was a shadow among so many others. But this one moved behind the curtain of a storm.

"Ship to starboard aft!" shouted Petty Officer Meyer excitedly.

Without taking time to check the accuracy of the statement, Spahr pressed the klaxon and rushed down the ladder after the watch, while Prien turned round for a moment to try to identify the intruder.

Merchant ship or warship? He didn't argue and jumped in his turn, down the hatch. He drew down the door and, with his legs in space, hung on to the closing wheel. Standing on a bar, he secured it quickly shouting: "Periscope depth!" The propellers had already been clutched in to the electric motors.

"Open the main vents! Five, four, three, two, midships!" ordered Wessels standing before his panel, littered with signal lamps on which showed the word 'Dive'.

"Five, four, three, two!" answered Leading Stoker Hölzer and Able Stoker Sollig almost at the same time, repeating each one after the other the numbers of the ballast tanks they were in charge of. Signal lamps lit up on the panel and the gurgling of water resounded in the control room. The submarine dived at a negative angle.

"One," exclaimed Wessels.

"One," retorted Böhm, opening the valve of the aft ballast tank.

Though small, the incline was increasing. They had to be careful, for the depth was probably no greater than the length of the ship.

The main vents were open—"10 metres, 15 metres," announced

the engineer officer to the captain. Then raising his voice:
"Blow 'Q'!"

The compressed air whistled in the ducts noisily pushing the water out.

"Q blown. Q kingston shut!"

Hölzer and Sollig turned the wheels quickly.

"Hydroplanes, ten of rise."

Slowly the deck came back to the horizontal. Wessels then finished emptying the air from the ballasts.

"Shut the main vents."

From the conning tower, Prien ordered,

"Both motors half ahead—"

"19 metres, 18 metres," enumerated Wessels.

The depth gauge steadied at 14 metres.

"Up periscope!"

From the listening post: "noise of fast propellers bearing 315," reported Petty Officer Telegraphist Blank who had just begun his 8 hour watch.

"I see her. It is a patrol boat and she looks as if she has seen us," exclaimed Prien, his eyes glued to the sights.

"Down periscope! Course 135! Slow ahead. Dive to 50 metres."

At the most silent speed *U-47* took her new course so as to offer the smallest surface possible to the sound waves of the patrol boat.

Ping . . . ping . . . ping . . . ping—the first sharp notes of the detector struck the hull more or less clearly then faded away.

Blank, his earphones on, attentively followed the movements of the patrol boat. From time to time he heard her propellers slow down: the enemy was listening too, trying to spot her prey.

The contact lost for a few moments was quickly re-established. The 'pings' were becoming more regular.

"The propellers are speeding up in the constant reading of 300," reported Blank.

"Get ready for depth charges!" ordered Prien calmly. "Course 120."

The men were listening anxiously and gave one another furtive glances and a wry smile.

"Passing: short range," warned Blank.

The ping . . . ping . . . ping . . . ping . . . ping . . . was now continuous. The distance grew shorter all the time.

In his tiny office, Blank was watching his reading dials intensely. Large drops of sweat rolled from his forehead on to his eyebrows and streamed down his cheeks without his making the slightest move to wipe them away.

"Bearing constant," he stated, uselessly, for everybody was aware of it.

Prien, for his part, did not remain inactive. From the conning tower, he had ordered the stopping of the auxiliaries and was directing the manoeuvres of escape. Orders were given in a low voice as if the enemy could overhear them. All efforts seemed useless. The persistence and surety with which the patrol boat was hunting them were becoming demoralising.

Vrr, Vrr, Vrr, Vrr, Vrr, Vrr, Vrr, Vrr, Vrr, Vrr, Vrr, Vrr, Vrr, Vrr, Vrr, Vrr . . .

The angry churning of the propellers went through the thick hull and seemed to throb in their brains.

"This bird of ill-omen is holding us in its claws," murmured Endrass, his eyes raised as if he hoped to be able to see the blades.

"I did have the idea of letting her have a torpedo, but she draws too little water," said Prien. "She was on her guard, the wake would have been quite visible and we had no chance of hitting her."

"If she had surprised us near the surface, things would have gone very badly for us."

Wakened suddenly, von Varendorff rushed into the conning tower.

"She let off the first one," shouted Blank.

The electric motors purred so slowly that you could scarcely hear them.

A strange and worrying silence was spreading throughout the ship.

"Three more!" added Blank grimly.

He switched off his apparatus and set to count the seconds, tapping his knee with his right index finger.

Wham! The din was terrifying. The explosion struck a violent ram-like blow, on the hull.

WHAM! WHAM! WHAM! Three new explosions resounded like the trumpets of the last judgement. The submarine shuddered from end to end. Endrass was clinging to the hoisting cable of the periscope, but von Varendorff lost his balance and fell on his knees. The light went out and the emergency lighting was switched on. In the control room the steel plates of the deck rose and fell again, with clashing slams. Böhm, gripping a big wheel which had begun to vibrate, grimaced as if the metal was electrified. The hands of the depth gauges jumped on the dials and sometimes crashed on the buffer. Sounds of broken glass could be heard from all other compartments. The air was filled with dust and particles of paintwork. Debris of every kind littered the floor.

Prien and Endrass looked at one another with consternation. The enemy was working to perfection. The first depth charges had straddled the submarine but *U-47* held well. From stem to stern the word 'OK' transmitted by the voice pipe was reassuring the officers.

The sizzling of the water churned up by the depth charges had stopped. Silence, a sinister silence, had again fallen on the submarine. Blank's voice assumed a strange volume:

"The noise of the propellers is fading bearing 090. She is slowing down."

"She is trying to check the effect of her first attempt," remarked Endrass.

"Engines dead slow! 30° to port!" shouted Prien sharply.

"She is ahead on portside but she is sure to come back," said von Varendorff.

Prien objected to the remark: "The enemy's listening; it is not the time to manoeuvre."

With anxious face, he was trying to find a way of getting out of this tight corner. Making up his mind, he addressed his officers to explain his plan:

"We are going to try to confuse her. Once she has spotted us she'll come to attack. Then, instead of tacking, we'll face her and pass under, in the opposite direction, our motors full on. At that moment she'll probably be too hampered by her own speed to listen and maintain ultra-sonic contact."

"She's starting again!" announced Blank.

Ping . . . ping . . . ping . . . ping . . . . The sound waves struck the hull with the whizz of a ball, diminished, then disappeared.

"She's passing on 080 and going away."

Everyone nurtured the same hope that the British ship had lost contact. The respite was short.

"She's coming back!" warned Blank a few moments later.

Ping . . . ping . . . ping . . . ping. . . —this noisy hammering took again unbearable intensity.

Blank quickly explored the other sectors and frowned. He heard clearly propeller noises in a direction totally opposite and the angle was very open. He turned towards the voice pipe and reported hurriedly—

"Propeller beats between 275 and 305 there are four or five ships."

"Damnation! we are caught in a vice," swore Prien, between his teeth. "This fellow must have alerted a formation of anti-submarine chasers operating in these waters." He said aloud, "They must all be on their mettle."

"The first is passing at short range!"

"Bearing movement?"

"Steady!"

The attacker was charging at 20 knots and in a straight line.

"The pig! She's falling on us as if she saw us," said von Varendorff in a grating voice, clutching the ladder of the conning tower.

The submarine was still dragging herself at a very low speed and Wessels had some difficulty in keeping the same depth.

"That's it—she's right ahead! Now's the time!" thought Prien.

"Full ahead. Give us the lot!"

The buzzing of the electric motors was raised, then remained on a high pitch. Rapid vibrations went through plates and partitions. U-47 lunged towards her enemy. The noise of ultra sonic waves and propellers increased then began to dwindle. A few drops of sweat formed on Prien's temples.

"Don't hold on to anything fixed rigidly to the hull" recommended Wessels in the control room.

Wham! Wham! Wham! Wham! Wham! Wham! Wham! The depth charges burst out in an incessant din, making the submarine roll, but this time the explosions happened farther away.

In his small cabin, the petty officer telegraphist uttered a cry of pain and tore off his earphones. Because of the speed, he had not heard the fall of the depth charges in the sea and had not disconnected his apparatus. Stunned by the noise, he rubbed his ears and let fly a volley of oaths.

"It's awfully painful to hear the ocean being lifted up," he said to Telegraphist Steinhagen leaning at the door of the post. He put on his earphones again and took back his watch grimacing.

"Sounds of propellers fading on 280. They merge into those of the arrivals. Detectors perceptible, in an intermittent way," he said in a hoarse voice.

"Dead slow!" ordered Prien.

"The British ship has been surprised by the manoeuvre; you charged like a bull," said Endrass, mocking but still somewhat pale.

From the stern, which had been the most dangerous zone during the last attack with depth charges, Herrmann, bent over the voice pipe, was the first to announce 'OK'.

The emergency lighting allowed them to make out the installations they all knew, eyes closed, in their least little detail. But at 50m under the surface, uneasiness increases with darkness. The men had man-oeuvred, like robots, without thinking, using automatic gestures so many times rehearsed in the course of countless exercises imposed by the captain. The electricians of the emergency team had repaired the damage to the main lighting circuit between the two attacks, and now they were replacing the broken bulbs. Morale was boosted by the return of light.

The group of submarine chasers did not attack immediately. Hope was increasing as time went by, until Blank said in a shaky voice:

"Propellers from 40 to 180 going through zero!"

Prien and his officers understood that they had taken their wish for an actual reality. The pursuers, obviously guided by the patrol boat, were closing down on them in a circle. Blank soon confirmed their fears:

"Propellers signalled from everywhere!"

The constant rustling of the ultra-sonic detectors against the hull left no doubt.

One of the hunters rushed on the submarine and jettisoned a string of depth charges. They exploded far enough away without causing much damage except some broken bulbs. Prien took the opportunity. The submarine cast about and threw herself towards the gap thus opened. Her free progress did not last long. Two pairs of irate propellers blocked her path and sent her back into the infernal circle.

U-47 manoeuvred, changing course, going right about, without succeeding in getting rid of her pursuers. Regularly one of them was in the way.

"Stand by for more depth charges!"

Brutal explosions, lights going out, emergency teams, nerves were put to a hard test.

To conserve electricity, they began to work their machines by hand, the hydroplanes with the help of big wheels. The latter demanded a physical strain which was telling in the long run.

A string of depth charges burst aft, very near, at a slightly greater depth than that at which the submarine was cruising. The din was deafening.

The ascending eddies pushed the ship up towards the surface. The light went out again. The shuddering hull was being compressed and extended. The electrician connected the electric current on the second lighting circuit. In the control room, Wessels gave a succession of orders to re-establish the balance of the submarine and come back to the 50m depth. A pipe cracked in the diesels compartment. Immediately the Petty Officer Stokers Schmalenbach and Scholz jumped to isolate it. A valve wheel leaped from its axis, fell on the floor, and bounded again noisily. Already the electricians were beginning to change the broken bulbs in an atmosphere still made heavy by particles floating in the air. Suddenly, one of the electric motors stopped. Prien, startled, took hold of the phone:

"Motor room; report on the damage," he ordered in a strained voice.

"The starboard propeller shaft seems damaged. That has made us stop the motor. We are trying to find out the nature and extent of the damage," replied Chief Petty Officer Electrician Römer.

"Take her to the bottom!"

With an extraordinary coolness, Wessels had succeeded in controlling the depth and re-trimming the submarine. As soon as he heard Prien's order, the engineer officer undertook a new series of manoeuvres.

The hull grated on the sand and *U-47* rested on her keel at a depth of 70m. With the port motor stopped, a sinister silence, like the onset of death, enveloped the ship. Wessels hurried to examine the starboard propeller shaft.

Prien went down into the control room. He had the conning tower evacuated and secured the hatch. All the men who were not wearing felt soles or slippers, or whose boots were not wrapped in rags moved about on tip-toe. Bending over the gyro compass, now out of use, Spahr examined the pieces carefully. The apparatus did not seem damaged. It was a stroke of luck. With 10,000rpm it could have burst, injuring someone or causing damage to installations. It would be necessary to put the compass back in working order. However, to regulate it would take a good six hours. The correct functioning of the gyro compass had a particularly special importance because the submarine on her return course would have to go through channels and across minefields. Inaccuracy in navigation could result in catastrophy. Spahr was awakened from his thoughts by the stifled voice of Blank.

"Echoes of detectors everywhere. Churning of propellers increasing in 170."

Prr, Prr, Prr! The external purring became perceptible to the ear in all compartments and every one got ready to be roughly shaken. The noise intensified, remained static, then decreased without anything happening. The hunter went away without launching any depth charges.

The situation was dramatic. Prien felt the looks of all the men present in the control room trained on him. He had to put a good face on it for each of his gestures or expressions would be interpreted immediately. He took off his cap by the peak, between his thumb and index finger, and scratched his head, an expression of aloofness on his face. The most urgent thing for the moment was to know the seriousness of the damage to the starboard shaft. With silent steps he went towards the motor compartment. If the damage was external, shaft or bracket warped, their return would be sadly endangered.

Surrounded by CERA Strunk and Leading Mechanicians Sporer, Behme, Lüddecke, the engineer officer on his knees examined the shaft at the entrance of the stern-post tube. The four mechanics stepped aside to let the captain pass. Wessels turned round and, seeing the bottom of Prien's trousers, raised his head.

"It's not too bad. I think we'll come out of it, sir," he said with a slight smile.

Prien kept silent. He noticed the drawn features and the dark rings under Wessels' eyes.

"Fortunately, there's nothing wrong with the shaft itself. It's the bolts of the shaft coupling which have been sheared," added the engineer officer.

He stopped speaking for the British ultra-sonic waves were resounding against the hull, as if someone was throwing peas against a tin. Then they heard, also, the churning of propellers. Ping . . . Ping . . . Ping . . . Prr, Prr, Prr . . .

Wessels got up smartly. Motionless and silent, the six men awaited the depth charges, holding firmly to some support.

Wham . . . Wham . . . Wham . . . Wham . . . The hull rebounded on the sand, but the explosions took place at a distance which deadened the shock fairly well.

Once calm had settled again, Wessels continued his explanations.

"We have to pull out the broken bolts to replace them," he said, looking down on the propeller shaft.

"How long will it take?" asked Prien, somewhat uneasily.

The engineer officer reflected for a few moments and, speaking to himself in a subdued tone:

"Let's see! I must cut and thread fourteen bolts, then take out the old ones and replace them with the new ones. Good, if everything goes well, I hope to complete it before 19.00hrs."

The captain listened to him, his face showing anxiety.

"Do your best, Wessels," he replied.

"You know that we'll try to part company with our awkward guardian angels after nightfall by taking French leave."[1]

The mechanics chuckled at the pun.

Prien went on:

"We'll surface and race for dear life!"

"You can say that again," added Wessels, with dead-pan expression.

"Until then, we'll pretend to be dead."

Reassured, Prien joked to cheer up the mechanics.

"Give me back the horse-power and I'll do the rest to get us out of this tight corner," he concluded, pursing his lips, as he often did.

"You can count on me, sir, we'll do our utmost."

Prien turned to go back to the control room and stepped over the sill of the door, leading into the petty officers' compartment. Passing by, he whispered 'OK'? and some comforting words right and left, to the men who remained lying on their bunks in order to use less oxygen.

So as to save power, Walz was asked to prepare cold sandwiches. In spite of the circumstances, the meal was eaten with a good appetite. By and large, morale remained good. The men suffered above all from not being able to do anything and having to endure the noise of the echoes against the hull, the sound of the propellers, and the explosions of the depth charges.

From time to time, between two successive depth charge attacks, one of the pursuers passed nearby without launching anything as if simply to reveal her presence. This trick was an extra trial for the nerves.

The afternoon was almost over. The damp heat was becoming overwhelming. In the engine room, the mechanics, streaming with sweat, were working on the sticky plates.

Spahr went across the control room and sat down at the small table of the officers' mess. Within a few minutes he would replace von Varendorff.

Ping . . . Ping . . . Ping . . . Ping . . . Ping . . . Prr . . . Prr . . . Prr . . .

Once more, Spahr, who had stopped counting the depth charges, did not react.

Wham . . . Wham . . . . Wham . . . Wham . . . .

The explosions shook the submarine violently. Torn off the seat to which he was clinging, Spahr was lifted up several centimetres. A bulb broke.

---

[1] Translation note: in the text, "Filer à l'anglaise", hence the mention of a pun.

"Good heavens! Will they never finish their stock?" swore Endrass from his bunk.

In the control room, von Varendorff, his right hand still clutching the ladder of the conning tower, was taking stock of the glasses of the depth gauges and other precision instruments which had just been broken.

"Curse it! What are they waiting for? Why don't they finish us off with a combined attack?" whispered Leading Seaman Mantyk in the ear of Dittmer, who had come to relieve him.

"Maybe to make us surface and surrender," said the other, when Spahr was coming into the control room to take up his watch from 16.00–20.00hrs.

The cold meal was eaten quickly. Prien was lying on his bunk when he heard the hydrophone operator signal propeller noises going away to the north-west. What he was hoping for had happened at last. He jumped from his bunk, quickly lifted up the green curtain, and stepped out. Leading Telegraphist Hebestreit turned his head and took off his earphones.

"There's only one left, sir. She is cruising slowly. I don't hear the others," he said in a low voice.

"Good! Watch all the sectors carefully, for we are going to surface soon," recommended Prien, going away.

Without stopping in the control room, he went towards the engine room. On entering he saw Leading Mechanicians Sporer and Lüddecke on their knees, tightening the bolts on the tail clutch. Standing, Wessels was supervising their work.

"We'll be at it for ten minutes more, sir," he said, glancing at the binnacle clock which showed 18.55hrs.

"Good show! You've done a good job—that's the least one can say. It's the second time that you've saved our bacon," declared Prien, smiling. He paused, then continued addressing Wessels.

"We'll get under way as soon as you're ready. There's only one hunter up there. We must take this opportunity to scamper before the others come back with their load of depth charges."

"We'll be ready within fifteen minutes, sir."

"I'll be in the control room."

"Very good, sir. By the way, the gyro compass is in working order. You've only got to supervise its adjustment."

As soon as the captain had turned his heels, Lüddecke, who was tightening a bolt, looked up and watched him going away.

"Did you hear the skipper patting us on the back?" he murmured to Sporer.

"Yes, and I hope that those upstairs will stop being so superior. I'm fed up seeing them consider the mechanics as useless," cut in Sporer.

"That's what I meant. It's thanks to us that the ship has been able to carry out her mission. And if she gets back safe and sound, it will again be thanks to us."

"Which does not change the fact that they will have all the honours, beautiful speeches, and long leaves."

"Let's get on. We mustn't lose time—it's not the right moment for discussion," intervened the engineer officer.

Prien asked Endrass, von Varendorff and Spahr to come to the control room to explain his plans to them

"If we get under way with the electric motors, we run the risk of being spotted, when starting them, by the hydrophones of the enemy who is always on his guard," he began.

"All the more as we'll probably have to make them go at a good speed to overcome the grip of the sand," agreed the third hand.

"We'll proceed in the following way" continued Prien.

"Blank will scan the whole horizon with the hydrophones very carefully, to ensure that there is not a single ship in the vicinity. Then, as soon as he signals that the hunter is getting farther away, we'll surface by slowly emptying the midship ballast tanks until we bring the deck to sea level. Only the conning tower will emerge. Then, we'll get away in the night, taking care to reduce our silhouette to the minimum."

Wessels entered the control room. Prien beckoned him to come nearer and briefly repeated the line of conduct he had mentioned. The engineer officer nodded his approval and went to his place near the panel.

"To your stations," said Prien in a muffled voice.

Near by, in his tiny office, Hebestreit, with earphones on, was following the movements of the pursuer and exploring the horizon carefully.

The men, their faces still strained, stood in front of their wheels and levers, waiting for orders. Prien, his arms crossed, Endrass, his back against the ladder of the conning tower, and von Varendorff, his hand on a bar, were all awaiting information from the hydrophone operator. Spahr, from his small chart table, looked, in turn, at these tired faces covered with a seven-day growth, and unconsciously passed the palm of his hand over his unkempt cheek.

In the impoverished atmosphere, breathing was becoming a

whistling process. The ship had been submerged for twelve hours and much oxygen had been used up because of the work on the starboard shaft and the repair of the various installations. The atmosphere was overpressured. When the submarine had rested on the bottom, the engineer officer had let some water in the compensation tanks to anchor the ship solidly on the sand and these tanks had been emptied of their air inside the submarine. The over-pressurisation had not been resolved, the ceaseless activity of the hunters having forbidden the starting of the compressors which would have been much too noisy.

A death-like silence reigned over all the compartments. The hull ground on the sand and an eddy rustled in the superstructure. The waiting was beginning to become unbearable.

"There it is, she has just gone right about and is going away on 040 at slow speed. The horizon is clear in every corner," announced Hebestreit at last.

"Surface!" ordered Prien, without moving.

Wessels turned towards Böhm:

"Blow the compensation tanks slowly to avoid the whistling of the air in the pipes."

The engineer officer knew that it was necessary to lighten the ship by several tons to counterbalance the effect of the suction from the bottom and he had calculated the quantity of water to release, to be able to reach the surface without emerging suddenly.

"Blow midship main ballast, but slowly."

The floor oscillated a little. The submarine rose slowly with a slight positive incline which was corrected almost immediately. Wessels' eyes did not leave the depth gauge. It was working in spite of the broken glass of the dial and the engineer officer heaved a sigh of relief.

. . . 60 metres . . . 55 metres . . . 50 metres.

The officers were straining their ears towards the hydrophone operator but Blank remained silent. It was a good sign. The seconds went by with a disheartening slowness. The success of the attempt was going to depend, in a large measure, on the first phase of the operation, that is, on their success in surfacing without being spotted.

. . . 40 metres . . . 35 metres . . . 30 metres. . . .

The submarine was steadily going up without incident.

Prien, followed by his two officers, climbed into the conning tower. The muffled voice of Hebestreit cut the litany of numbers which Wessels was calling out one by one.

"She's still going away. I scarcely hear her propellers at 010."

The ship was beginning to pitch and roll softly. The surface was near.

"Main motors ahead, slow," ordered Prien.

The motors started immediately and the submarine got back some balance.

"Course 190. Up periscope," he continued. He had not yet finished speaking when he realised that the compass was still out of order.

The long shiny steel tube rose from its well with a purring noise. He seized the controlling handles, unfolded them, and stuck his face to the rubber of the sights. To begin with, he saw only the darkness of the water, then vision improved. The sky was studded with stars and visibility was good. Still he could not spot the pursuer. Reassured, he was going to abandon his observations, when Hebestreit's voice made him jump.

"She went right about. The propeller noises are clearly perceptible and increasing in intensity."

Prien moved the periscope, but he could see nothing but the sky and the sea. He straightened up and clipped up the handles.

"Down periscope! Motors half-speed ahead."

Then he switched off the light in the conning tower.

The engineer officer spat out a series of orders to empty a small amount of water from the central ballast tanks by having their compressed air blows opened slowly and intimated a few moments later:

"The hatch is above water. Don't open it yet. I'm equalising the pressures."

Prien had put on his old leather jacket. Standing on the ladder, His binoculars hanging from his neck, he was waiting with his right hand on the hatch wheel. Under him, Endrass, von Varendorff and Spahr held themselves ready to jump out after him.

The air whistled in the voice pipe of the bridge. Wessels opened the valves only gradually, to protect the nose and ears of the crew. The noise of the air diminished.

"Pressure has fallen to 5mm. You can open now," warned the engineer officer.

Already Prien was unbolting the hatch. He pushed it down and jumped on the bridge. The fresh air was pleasant when hitting his face. A few small clouds lingered in a clear sky. Although the night was dark, it did not take long to locate the pursuer. The ship was going at low speed and could be seen three quarters ahead. He estimated the distance at less than two miles.

"Starboard twenty!" he ordered.

Obviously the enemy had not seen them.

"Steady as she goes!"

The courses of the two ships became almost in line. Prien watched the hunter through his binoculars. Still no reaction.

"We shall wait until she goes about before starting the diesels," he said to Endrass.

U-47 went away slowly and silently from her enemy, without leaving a wake. At present, her course was placing her towards the coast where visibility remained poor. This evening the respective positions of the antagonists were the opposite of what they had been at dawn. Low in the water, the submarine was almost invisible at some distance against the background of the land, blacker than the night. The hunter, on the other hand, could be made out clearly enough against the starry sky above the open sea.

Prien leaned on the voice pipe.

"Can you increase speed?"

"Yes, but not for long," said Wessels in a nasal voice.

"Will you hold on for another quarter of an hour?"

"Yes! But no more, otherwise, if there is an alert, we may not be able to manoeuvre submerged."

"It will not be long before he turns back," murmured Endrass.

Prien trained his binoculars in the direction of the hunter.

"Starboard 15," he ordered, to keep the outlines of the submarine as small as possible.

"That's it! He is beginning to change course," exclaimed Endrass.

In the sights of the binoculars, the shadow of the hunter grew thinner then stretched out all its length. It grew smaller again when the ship had ended her movement. Vision became uncertain because of the distance and the men had difficulty in maintaining contact. Ten minutes later, this flitting shadow was definitely swallowed up by the night.

"I hope that we have finally lost her," concluded Prien, lowering his binoculars.

"Tomorrow they will announce, no doubt, the destruction of a U-boat," replied Endrass mockingly.

"Diesels on!"

"Half ahead—with batteries to be charged!" ordered Prien.

One after the other, the two engines started at the quarter turn, throbbing familiarly. Two small jerks and the ship went forward into the night. A gust of wind carried the foam of the prow-wave and a cloud of spray flew over the conning tower.

Prien turned round and looked at the wake. The two propeller shafts were working normally. He took up his watch again and examined, for a moment, the Scottish coast visible from time to time. The cape of Kinnairds Head could be recognised by the white tower of her lighthouse 23m high. It was time to change course.

"Come back 25 to port."

At 20.00hrs, Endrass' watch, relieving that of Spahr, took on its normal form. Prien remained on the bridge.

A little before 21.00hrs, he gave his instructions to the first officer.

Shipping must be concentrated on the coastal route. We are going to follow it to have a better chance of getting a merchant ship on our way. Thus, we will avoid *U-20* which is operating on the open sea. I am going to listen to the news at 21.00hrs. If I hear anything concerning us, I will let you know over the intercom."

Prien went down into the control room, took off his binoculars and his leather jacket, and went towards the radio post. Petty Officer Blank was on duty.

"Tune into the BBC for the news."

Music stopped for the news broadcast.

"*This is the BBC Home Service. Here is the news bulletin—as it was reported late this morning, the Secretary of the Admiralty regrets to announce that* HMS Royal Oak *has been sunk, it is believed, by U-boat action. Fifteen survivors have been landed . . .*"

"Get a German station," cut in Prien.

Blank touched a switch and the familiar voice of a German speaker came out from the loudspeaker, in the middle of a sentence:

". . . on the radio, the British Admiralty regrets to announce the loss of the battleship *Royal Oak*. The British believe, as you could expect, that the battleship has been sunk by a submarine. They did not give any details about the time or place of the loss. In Poland, the advance of the . . ."

"Cut that out!" said Prien.

He called to the bridge, through the speaking tube:

"Hello, Endrass, we sank the *Royal Oak*!"

"Congratulations! A battleship of 30,000 tons officially to the credit of *U-47*: It's worth promotion and an Iron Cross first class."

Prien stifled a slight laugh and answered:

"I do not ask for personal recognition. The credit is due to the whole crew."

"What did they say about the damaged battleship?" asked Endrass to change to subject.

"Nothing—no mention of it. They simply gave a first list of 15 survivors of the *Royal Oak*, that's all."

He paused and then added:

"By the way, I won't go back to the bridge; I've got to rest for a while. Give the order to wake me at 05.30hrs for the dive."

"Aye, aye, sir."

"Good watch, Endrass, Cheerio."

Prien gave a slap on the shoulder to Petty Officer Telegraphist Blank and said:

"Well, we didn't manage it too badly, did we? We'll drink to that tomorrow."

He turned away and lifted up the green curtain of his cabin. He threw his cap down on the bunk and got rid of his leather jacket, which he hung on a hook. Then he sat down in front of the small table, took some paper and wrote the draft of a message to Commodore Dönitz:

Unternehmung planmässig durchgeführt. Royal Oak *versenkt.* Repulse *beschädigt. Erbitte Einlaufweg I 16.10 abends, da andere Unterlagen nicht mehr an Bord U-47.*[1]

From his small office, Blank saw the captain's hand draw the curtain. Prien stepped out and gave him a sheet of paper saying:

"Send this radio message to HQ immediately."

The curtain fell back on the captain. Blank read the text and started sending the message.

Endrass had ordered the speed to be increased. The tapered bow of the submarine, cruising at 15 knots, was throwing two foaming waves higher than the casing. Aft, the milky wake lost itself in the night. This trail could attract the attention of a patrol of the Coastal Command. Watching the threat from the air was made difficult because of the pig-like roar of the supercharger blower which was added to the high throbbing of the six cylinders of each diesel engine M.A.N. The men on watch scanned alternately the sea and the sky with increased attention. These waters were dangerous because the naval port of Rosyth was quite near. A large number of patrol boats were probably cruising at the entrance of the Forth precisely to prevent the U-boats from entering it. Through prudence, Endrass had decided to go a longer way round but in the open sea.

At midnight von Varendorff replaced the first lieutenant. It began to rain. The ship was only slightly pitching and rolling but the deck was covered with foam. An east-north-east breeze blew force 3 to 4. The

---

[1] "Operation carried out as planned. *Royal Oak* sunk—*Repulse* damaged. Please give information on route back home on 16.10hrs. I no longer have data about this."

night was cold. The monotony of the watch was not broken by any incident and at 04.00hrs Spahr appeared on the bridge to take up his watch. He found the third officer chilled by the icy spray.

Prien went up on the bridge at 05.45hrs. The chief quartermaster took a fix at 06.00hrs and made it to be 56° 20 N. and 0° 40 W. Immediately afterwards, Prien gave the order to dive. Spahr pushed the klaxon and the manoeuvre went on as usual.

The submarine touched the bottom at 72m.

In the control room, Endrass, his hands in his trousers pockets, looked at the binnacle clock and thought with annoyance of the two tedious hours he would still have to spend there. His back against the ladder of the conning tower, he was listening absentmindedly to all the small familar noises, the grinding of the hull on the sand or the slight creaking coming one knew not from where. Blank, on watch at the hydrophones, coughed discreetly. Pop! . . . a big drop of condensation crashed at his feet. Suddenly a dull explosion hit the plates of the hull and was reflected inside the sub. Blank swore in his tiny office. Endrass quickly raised his head.

"A depth charge," he whispered.

He went towards the hydrophone office and stood at the door. The look in his eyes asked the telegraphist what it was all about.

"I did not hear any propeller noise. In any case, the explosion must have taken place at a considerable distance, but with the amplifiers it's all the same, painful for the ear-drums," said Blank.

"Funny, only one explosion instead of the usual string of them," remarked Endrass.

Prien came out of his cabin and went near the post.

"It's not meant for us. Maybe they are after *U-20*. If we don't make too much noise, we don't run a great risk." Then, addressing the first lieutenant, he added: "circulate the order to wear slippers and not to speak loudly."

"Very good, sir!" answered Endrass going away.

Wheyom!

A new explosion, as weak as the previous one, made him turn round. He heard the petty officer telegraphist put the earphones on his small table and say:

"It's difficult to say for sure where the explosions come from because the bursts are unexpected and I do not hear any noise which could give me some pointer."

The explosions went on at irregular intervals. They did not worry anybody and lunch was quite lively. Prien did not have the heart to stop them speaking altogether. Whispering went on briskly in the officers' mess as well as in the petty officers' and in the 'house of lords'.

In the officers' mess, the topic was broadcast information.

"I expect the British will go on keeping silent about the damage to the second battleship," said Endrass.

"It would be refusing to admit the obvious. I saw it with my own eyes and it's a safe bet to say that our reconnaissance aircraft will take photographs, if it hasn't already been done," replied von Varendorff.

"I suppose the battleship must have got under way as soon as possible to avoid the reconnaissance. The torpedo exploded on the bow, probably causing only slight damage," said Prien.

"Yes, that's what I would have done, had I been British," approved Wessels.

"Are you so sure you hit his bow?" objected the third hand. "The British ships of the line have both their forecastle and their quarter deck open and free. Personally I would say we hit the stern."

"It doesn't make any difference. The torpedo need not necessarily have caused damage to a vital part. She might have kept under steam, controlled the leak by using her pumps, and got under way during the night," maintained Endrass.

Prien and Wessels looked amused at the two opponents—von Varendorff did not yield.

"But yes! It does make things different. With damage to her bow, isolated as it is by the watertight bulkheads, she could get under way and go to a naval dockyard, I grant you that. But, on the contrary, with stern damaged, all she could do is to take refuge in the Lyness base under the cover of the anti-aircraft guns there. I saw things all right. I clearly noticed her forecastle a good deal under the normal water line. A damaged bow would not be sunk as deep."

"If we hit her aft there is really a chance of two of her propeller shafts being damaged," said Wessels.

"Well, gentlemen, to go on supposing is wasting your time," protested Prien. "We all agree on the main point: a battleship was sunk and another damaged. This result certainly deserves a celebration."

He called the cook.

"Walz, a brandy for everybody to toast *U-47* and her courageous crew!"

"Very good, sir! The order will be carried out right away," answered Walz in a low voice, straightening up and bringing his heels

Drawings of Prien (left) and Wessels (right) produced as postcards to commemorate their feat at Scapa Flow. It is interesting to note that the drawing of Prien was in full colour.

silently together as at attention. He turned around, straight as the letter I and disappeared into the galley.

Walz began his issue of brandy aft. When he reached the 'house of lords' Leading Seaman Hänsel was once more describing the operation. He looked upon the sailors, packed tight at the small table.

"Would their lordships like a brandy?" he asked obsequiously.

Hänsel stopped short.

"Uncle Walz offers you a drink to toast the heroes."

"Skipper's order," sneered Steinhagen.

"OK, if you take it like that, you're obviously not in a hurry," answered the cook.

"Go on, pour your stuff and no more palaver."

Walz took a small glass out of his pocket and used it as a measure. He poured the contents of it in each tin mug then, keeping the last full glass for himself, stood near the door.

Lüddecke was sitting next to Hänsel; discreetly the latter, while going on with his report of the torpedo attack, stretched his right hand, took Lüddecke's glass and emptied it at one gulp, all the while going on with his description. The leading seaman noticed it and the result was a muffled hurly-burly which pleased Walz no end. He smiled smugly and lifted his glass in Lüddecke's direction:

"Your health, sweetheart!"

He smacked his lips to show his contentment, threw back his head and wiped his lips with his sleeve cuff, while looking at the able seaman who was red with anger.

"Farewell, your lordships," he said, more obsequious than ever. He

133

turned tound, straightened his forage cap, and went away in the passage, bottle and glass in his hand.

The day passed by slowly without any other incidents. Thirty-two explosions in all were counted, without possible error.

The getting under way had been fixed at 18.15hrs. The dinner was quickly eaten between 17.00hrs and 17.30hrs then the men went back silently to their stations.

At 18.15hrs, Hebestreit signalled a propeller noise. Prien, Endrass and von Varendorff, close together near the hydrophone operator, waited for details.

His earphones on, the telegraphist was dealing with all the switches, using both his hands.

"Slow propeller noises. It is probably a big merchant ship or a tanker," he said clearly, a huge wrinkle barring his brow.

"Ah! . . . The noises have stopped . . . funny, she must have stopped. I'm not getting anything any more."

He went on turning switches for some seconds more.

"There is no longer any propeller noise. She certainly has stopped," he concluded, turning towards the officers.

"It is funny, to say the least, a merchant ship stopping in the open sea and near a submarine. This does not seem clear to me, murmured von Varendorff.

"In any case, it is a big one," repeated Hebestreit.

"It's probably a merchant ship which has hove to for some reason. She does not suspect anything. If she was a naval unit who had spotted us, we would have heard her detector. On the other hand, a big ship of the line never cruises by herself," said Endrass.

"We'll see what it's all about when we get a bit nearer," concluded Prien.

He came back into the control room and ordered:

"Diving stations: we're getting under way!"

Using the electric motors with care, the submarine reached periscope depth. In the conning tower, Prien made a gesture with his two hands and the periscope rose from its well, humming. When the sights were level with his face, he seized the handles. The men saw him stop the rotation of the periscope and quietly study a certain point. Without saying a word, he looked around in all directions and came back towards the point he had just previously stared at.

Imperceptibly the atmosphere grew tense in the conning tower. Without looking away from the objective, he made up his mind to say:

"Merchant ship stopped at 300m ahead. He flies Norwegian colours. Give me the book of silhouettes."

Von Varendorff took the book and began to go through it rapidly.

"That's it, sir. I've got the Norwegians."

"Come and look, Endrass," said Prien, leaving the periscope. Taking the book from the third hand he went through the black silhouettes of the different ships. He turned the page and his forefinger pointed at a picture.

"Here she is. I think it's her. *Meteor*, a passenger ship."

Endrass lowered the periscope and leaned over the commander's shoulder.

"Yes, similar bridge and masts."

"Lower periscope. We're going to see what she's up to. Endrass, stand ready at the gun, in case of emergency. It might be a trap. Get everything ready for the gun. Hebestreit must watch for radio messages."

"Very good, sir," he answered, going down speedily to the control room. Prien switched off the light.

"20 to port—motors half ahead," he ordered.

A few minutes later, the head of the first lieutenant appeared through the hatch of the central post.

"Ready to load the gun, sir!"

"Surface."

"Steer for surfacing 010. Blow midships main ballast."

U-47 took a bow-up angle. The compressed air whistled in the pipes and the metal sheets of the ballast tanks. Prien climbed the ladder of the conning tower. Von Varendorff, Endrass, and the others went up a few bars after him.

"The hatch is above water!" shouted the engineer officer, lower down in the ship, opening the shut-off valves of the voice pipe to the bridge.

"Pressure balanced!"

Prien unclipped the hatch and jumped on the still streaming bridge. Endrass and the gunners quickly went down the external ladder of the conning tower and began manoeuvring the gun.

A fair breeze was blowing from the north-east. Visibility, under a cloudy sky, still remained good. The steamer was swinging on a swell from the east. The Norwegian colours were painted on her side, lit by searchlights.

"He's using his radio!" The hurried voice of Hebestreit came in a nasal tone through the voice pipe. Prien did not hesitate.

"Fire a warning shot ahead of her."

"Fire!"

The gun gave a dry bark. The shot landed about 100m from the bow.

"Reload," shouted Endrass.

"Ask him his identity and destination," ordered Prien to Hänsel who was holding his morse lamp. The answer came also in light signals: "Norwegian steamer *Meteor*, destination: Newcastle on Tyne, 238 passengers on board."

Carefully *U-47* came within hailing distance. Prien took hold of the megaphone:

"Send us your papers!"

Endrass had had the 88mm gun pointing at the Norwegian bridge. A boat was lowered from the steamer. Her crew had a lot of trouble putting it to sea because of the swell. At last the boat succeeded in getting away from the hull of the steamer: they rowed hard towards the submarine cruising at very low speed. Prien could make out an officer, a portfolio on his knees, and four sailors rowing.

"Stop motors," he ordered.

U-47 pitched and rolled heavily. The gunners found it difficult to keep their balance and the first lieutenant was wondering with anxiety how to hit the target if he received the order to fire.

When the boat was only a few metres away, Leading Seamen Dittmer and Marquard threw a rope, then helped the officer to get on board. Prien looked at him as he was coming to the conning tower. At that time, Hebestreit called the bridge through the voice pipe:

"Hello, sir, I made a mistake when I thought the Norwegian was using his radio. He remained absolutely silent."

"I prefer that," grumbled Prien, who was beginning to think that things were not moving fast enough. The officer quickly climbed the ladder of the conning tower and introduced himself to Prien in German. The first lieutenant was a young man, neatly dressed and with an intelligent face. He calmly took out the papers from his portfolio and handed them out to Prien. The latter examined them under the light of a pocket lamp. The papers were in order.

"You may proceed. I do not need to remind you that radio silence is the rule. Any broadcasting will be considered as hostile and force me to retaliate immediately and without pity," he said, giving him back his papers.

The first lieutenant put them in his portfolio without a word, saluted and went down on the deck.

"Bon voyage!" shouted Prien from the bridge.

The Norwegian officer turned round, made a sign of recognition with his hand, and smartly jumped in the boat, still held near the submarine by Dittmer and Marquard. The latter gave it a vigorous push, then waved their arms, howling noisily, "safe return".

"Ahead slow! Steer o!" ordered Prien.

U-47 went about 100m from the boat.

With the east swell, to go on southwards would have caused such a rolling that the gunners would not have been able to use their gun, had they had to.

"Steer 270! Half ahead!"

The submarine made a half circle and left with the sea astern. Endrass had the gun still trained on the steamer: she could have sent a radio message unexpectedly, and, in this case, they would have had to destroy her bridge at one go to cut short any broadcast.

The *Meteor* kept silent. At last, Prien reckoned the Norwegian could no longer see the submarine in the darkness.

"Secure gun, action stations!" He shouted to the first lieutenant. The gunners bolted the gun in its resting position and followed by Endrass, went quickly to the bridge.

"Course 140! Full ahead!"

The throbbing of the diesels increased suddenly. The bow plunged into a wave which swept the deck. *U-47* was proceeding towards the open sea. After some 10 miles, Prien ordered to go south again. The deep hollows of the swell were parallel to the sub and caused her to roll uncomfortably. The pendulum-like movement reached 30° or 35° and even more.

Going down to the control room, Spahr alternately torn from the ladder and sent smack on to it, was performing real contortions. On entering the petty officers' room, he heard the noise of broken glass and falling tins on the metal floor, coming from the galley. Walz let fly a volley of swear words while trying to pick up the tins escaping from his hands.

In the course of the evening, the north-east wind turned to full north and progressively lost its strength. At midnight when von Varendorff replaced Endrass, the submarine scarcely pitched and rolled. The weather was becoming milder.

"All we have seen were some small boats far enough away in the direction of the land," said Endrass. "In order not to stray too far from our course at 23.00hrs I set the course east-south-east. At least I hope so; the compass hasn't yet returned to its position."

"At dawn we must be on Dogger Bank."

"At least we shall avoid the vicinity of the British minefield. Are there special instructions?" asked von Varendorff.

"None, except to wake the captain at 05.30hrs."

"Good. I expect we'll dive between 06.00 and 07.00hrs to avoid the trawlers."

"He didn't say, though I don't think there'll be a crowd of them. We didn't spot any going," replied Endrass, throwing himself in the hatch of the conning tower. Visibility remained good, but the weather was still overcast. Still, towards 06.00hrs, the small west-north-west breeze tore away the clouds. The sky was getting slowly clearer. The day was breaking on a grey sea.

"Two trawlers starboard three-quarters!" signalled Dittmer.

Prien studied the intruders with his binoculars.

"They could well be Dutch," he said.

Spahr's eyes were attracted by black points appearing and disappearing with the movement of the waves. Mines!

"Three mines drifting a quarter to starboard," he shouted.

"Port 20!" ordered Prien in answer, lowering quickly his binoculars.

He soon spotted the mines. The man at the wheel reacted immediately and the bow swung to port.

"Good heavens, only a few minutes of inattention and we could be sent away to the next world, not even knowing how," thought Spahr staring at the sinister contraptions.

"It would be imprudent to blast them because of the fishermen nearby. I don't think they saw us," grumbled Prien.

"Pity! They can blindly kill innocents and if a passenger ship or a neutral hits one, you may be sure the U-boats will be blamed."

"Yes! It's a pity but we can't do anything else."

The three mines filed past some 10m away from the sub.

"Come back 20 to starboard!"

"Where on earth are they coming from? It's important to watch we don't fall in a minefield we know nothing about," continued Spahr.

"What's the depth on the gauge?" asked Prien.

"41 metres."

"We must avoid the south border of the Bank, limited at its contour line of 20m where the shallowest parts are to be found: 14 and 13m. Just now we must avoid the danger by going east," said Spahr.

"I'd like to be sure of that by getting an astro fix."

"Do you want me to take the height of the sun for a meridian passage?" asked Spahr, looking intently at the sky.

"No. That would force us to stop until midday. I would prefer to go on for two good hours. You'll be able to get two sun position lines, one towards 09.00hrs before the dive and the other . . . let's say at 15.00hrs, when we'll surface for that purpose. We'll spend the day at the bottom to allow the compass to stabilise and we'll surface to take the second sight and find our position at 15.00hrs."

"Very good, sir! I'll regulate the clock in the meantime," said Spahr, glancing at the reddening disc of the sun.

"While I'm at it, I'll get a check on our longitude."

At 15 knots, *U-47* cut, like a dagger, through the slight swell which could not make her pitch or roll.

"Top,"[1] said Spahr.

07.02hrs. He noted the time on a small pocket book and took his binoculars. He scanned the surface of the sea from the bow to the horizon. Suddenly he felt a shock. His fingers clenched the binoculars. One, two, five, ten rounded shapes bristling with horns appeared in the sights, placed in several rows.

Dittmer's howl made him jump:

"Minefield straight ahead at 600m."

"Stop port! Hard a-port, rear full astern starboard," thundered Prien. The bow swung immediately. The submarine took a list, and went right about.

"Steer o."

"Both engines slow ahead!"

The diesels lowered their rhythm and the ship slowed down.

"By jove! We had a narrow escape," said Prien, his voice quite hoarse.

"At night we would have been for it."

"This minefield wasn't here when we first passed. They must have laid it since then."

"Happily they must have done it in a hurry judging by the bad fixing of the buoy ropes. Otherwise we would not have been aware of it."

Prien thought for a while before murmuring: "All the same, I'm not going to go right about to avoid this blasted minefield. We'll go under it!" he added, with resolve.

Spahr turned round completely taken aback, scratched his neck, but remained silent.

"Hard over to port! Both motors half ahead."

[1] Translator's note: "Top" = voice signal ex: "One, two, three, top!"

The bow turned back towards the minefield.

"Course north."

The men on watch lowered their binoculars ready to jump through the hatch.

"Depth on the echo sounder," asked Prien.

"43 metres."

He pressed the klaxon firmly; 15 seconds later the hatch closed above his head and with both hands he turned the closing wheel.

"Down 38 metres. Both motors slow ahead," he cried.

Wessels barked out a series of orders. The throbbing of the diesels gave place to the hum of the electric motors and the water gurgled into the ballasts. The submarine dived in record time, with a very slight bow down angle. Prien went down into the engine room.

"Ten metres . . . 15 metres . . . 20 metres . . . 25 metres . . . 35 metres . . . 38 metres . . ." announced the engineer officer with his eyes fixed on the hand of the echo sounder.

"Course 180," ordered Prien.

The men, dumb with fear, imagined mines filled to the brim with 350 kilos of high explosive swinging at the end of their buoy rope, stretching their fragile horns in the dark cold water. Nobody spoke. The submarine progressed so slowly that even the usual rustling of the current in the superstructure could no longer be heard. From time to time, the starting of the hydroplanes motor was added to the muffled purring of the electric motors and the feeble murmur of the propellers.

Prien approached the echo sounder. The ultra-sonic echoes showed 3 to 4m of water under the keel. Suddenly a new sound made them prick up their ears. It came from outside. Everyone held his breath. . . . Crrr . . . cr . . . crcrcrcr . . . rrrrrr . . . crcrrrrr. . . . The noise came from portside. The mooring wire of the first mine rubbed against the hull at the level of the hydrophone office, a little forward of the conning tower. The grinding slid down to the diesels compartment. Time seemed to stand still. At last the rubbing stopped.

Spahr turned his eyes towards the binnacle clock: 08.05hrs. Prien, staring at the sounder dial, did not move. Von Varendorff took out a handkerchief from his pocket and wiped his eyebrows, damp with sweat, then looked at Endrass.

"Well, it's not on this mine that we'll be blown up," said the second officer in a low voice. Crr . . . crcrcrcrcrrrrrrr . . . rrrrrrr . . . crcr. . . . This time, the grating came from forward, on the starboard side. Prien prayed silently that the guards protecting the hydroplanes and the propellors played their part by preventing the wire from hooking

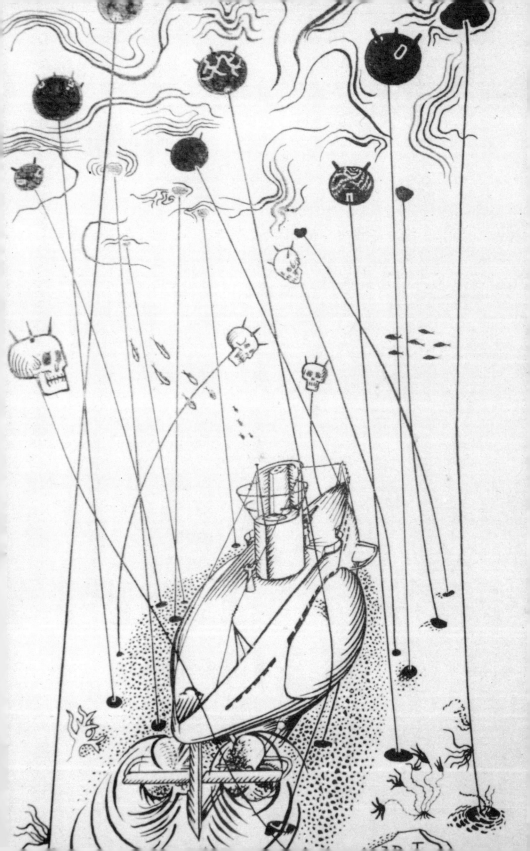

itself on to them. Wessels happened to look at Böhm, still seemingly petrified. The mooring wire pursued its course along the hull.

The grating was irregular, cut by long moments of silence as if the rope were clinging on the plates, then it slid more rapidly a few metres aft. A quarter of an hour went by without anything happening.

"We've probably got through the first row," said Endrass in a hoarse voice.

Soon the gratings began again—Prien ordered a few changes of course but the mooring wire went on scraping the hull. An unusual calm reigned in the control room. Faces remained strained, but tension had relaxed somewhat. The men were getting used to the presence of death on the other side of the steel plates.

"Careful! Only 2 metres of water under the keel," shouted Prien to Wessels. The latter had a few dozens of litres emptied from the midship trim tanks and the ship went up by 3m.

"That's all right! Do not go higher," said Prien without stopping to watch the sounder. Very slowly, the submarine progressed through the minefield brushing the bottom of the sea.

"It's a good thing the mines are not too tightly grouped," whispered von Varendorff. "Do they intend to overlap our own minefield by overflowing on the Dogger Bank?" he asked with some anxiety.

His question remained unanswered. The sinister gratings became less frequent, began again, and at last, ceased altogether.

"Both motors three-quarters ahead! Steer east!"

Silently, *U-47* slid under the sparkling waves of the North Sea. No sign of contact with the mines, The ship had reached the end of the obstacles. A few minutes after 10.00hrs Prien gave the order to surface after he had observed the horizon, to make sure no ship was about.

The sun shone on a green sea. The men on watch breathed with delight the fresh air of the open sea. Spahr climbed on the bridge quickly with the sextant in hand. His eye glued to the sighting telescope, he put the bottom rim of the sun on the horizon and 'swung' the instrument.

"Top."

The chief quartermaster took a series of five heights at intervals of ten seconds. Half an hour after they had surfaced, the submarine was diving again and softly touched the bottom of the sea.

In the control room, Spahr finished his calculations of the sun sight, switched off the lamp and got up to go to his bunk to rest a little before lunch. Prien, also, soon left the control room and went to his cabin. Then, Endrass took a small book from his pocket and began to draw bulls. He used up several sheets sketching, then compared the results. He cancelled them all except one of a savage bull charging and blowing through his nostrils with rage. Apparently satisfied, he closed the book and slipped it into his jersey pocket.

Lunch was succulent, Walz had obviously made use of his cooking talent and his popularity increased immensely. During the meal, nobody alluded to the testing hours of the morning, and Scapa Flow was once more the subject of all conversations. In the officers' mess, they spoke of the destroyer.

"I'll never understand it. With the electric motors grouped with the diesels, we were leaving a wake as visible as that of a battleship. She could not help seeing us, or at least our wake. I mean—what possessed her and made her go right about?" exclaimed Endrass.

"Yes, from what I understood, we were at her mercy," approved Wessels.

"We could not change the speed because of the current. With the drift the ship would never have reached Kirk Sound. On the other hand, time was more than scarce because of the low tide. Each minute counted. I assure you that the return has been much more difficult than the going in," said Prien.

"It's not what I intended to say, sir, but why did she go away so suddenly? Let's suppose that the submarine was much less visible on the background of the Mainland cliffs than the silhouette of the destroyer, cut out like shadow in a Chinese show, on the clear surface of Scapa Flow. Still it is time he signalled to us. So no problem! He saw us. But he was after a submarine and not a flying dragon."

"At the beginning, after the first hit on target, they may have believed it was an air attack but not after the battleship had been blown out," said Wessels smiling.

"Very honourable lieutenant, we could go on for ever about flying dragons and Chinese shadows," answered Prien, remaining very serious in appearance. "A wise man would say that we will only have the key to the solution of the mystery after the War, and even then, only if such is the will of Heaven. Don't we run the risk of losing face if we maintain that the fires of Heaven have blinded the enemy to the point of making him salute those who have made fireworks of his *Royal Oak*? To speak the picturesque language of Westerners, I would say that we will be labelled liars for I think that the British Admiralty will prefer to forget the incident, and 1 can understand it," he added. "However, I remain convinced that the destroyer did not recognise the submarine. It seems obvious to me—"

"I'll never dare to tell the story. Nobody will believe me," cut in von Varendorff, from the control room where he was on watch.

"Anyway, the main thing is that we are 'windward of our mooring,[1]'" said Wessels.

At 14.15hrs, Endrass went in the petty officers' compartment and addressed Spahr, lying on his bunk, his hands behind his head.

"Willy, can you let me have a chart?"

"What for?"

"I need it to cut down a design," answered Endrass with hesitation.

"What design?"

The first lieutenant thought for a while, then he made up his mind: it was simpler to tell what he had in mind.

"Well, to remind us of this assignment, I have drawn an emblem for our ship and I would like to paint it on the conning tower. I need a big sheet of paper to cut the pattern full size and put white paint on the contours."

"May we see this emblem?" asked Spahr, cautiously.

"When I have the chart, I'll draw it on the back of it."

Curious, Sammann, Böhm, Strunk and Römer were raising their heads from their bunks and asking Endrass a volley of questions but the latter remained adamant.

Spahr put his legs out of his bunk and went to fetch a chart. Endrass spread it on the floor and, with a few pencil strokes, reproduced the bull blowing through his nostrils.

"What do you think of it? Here is the Bull of Scapa Flow!"

They grouped around the first lieutenant who was sitting crosslegged near his drawing, and showed their approval with nods punctuated with exclamations.

"Not bad—not bad at all," approved Spahr, "but you must finish it without the skipper knowing. Then we'll get him to the deck for some reason or other to see his reaction."

"I suggest you wait till the beginning of the morning when we'll be under escort and in the shelter of the Westwall."[2]

"The skipper won't definitely be spending his time on the bridge any more," agreed Endrass, rolling up the map.

He looked at his wrist watch and added:

"It is nearly 14.45hrs and it is time to go. We'll cut the design later on. In the meantime, I prefer to leave it here."

---

[1] Translator's note: to be all right.
[2] Westwall: Name given to the German minefield between Dogger Bank and the island of Borkum.

The 'Bull of Scapa Flow' painted on the conning tower of *U-47* by Engelbert Endrass, second in command of the U-boat. / Friedrich Krupp AG

Der Stier von Scapa Flo

Spahr took the roll and placed it in his bunk against the side. Then he put on his jersey and followed the first lieutenant towards the control room.

The submarine broke the surface sending a dazzling foam on her sides. The men on watch jumped to their post. It was a beautiful autumn afternoon. High in the sky, huge clouds scattered the blue with their big whitish balls.

"It's almost warm! You can tell we are sailing south," exclaimed Spahr gleefully, his sextant in his hand.

He waited for the sun to show itself between two clouds and once again measured several heights to find the mean so as to minimise risks of error.

After spending half an hour on the surface, the ship dived and came back to rest on the sand. In the control room Spahr finished his calculations and marked on the chart the exact bearings at 15.00hrs: 54° 51′ N and 3° 21′ E. With the divider he measured their distance from the western edge of the hachured zone representing the German minefield.

"I want to reach the entrance of the passage before nightfall," said Prien, leaning on the shoulder of the navigator.

"By surfacing towards 19.00hrs we'll be there, sir, but we'll have to make 16 knots. Following the course 128° on the compass, we'll directly file in channel No 1."

Spahr corrected the estimated position at 07.00hrs: 54° 57′ N, 2° 58′ E, then he calculated the meeting point of the three floating mines and found 54° N, 2° 56′ E. Meanwhile, Endrass cut out his design in the petty officers' mess.

They were to leave the bottom at 18.45hrs. The submarine surfaced at 18.56hrs. The light breeze had changed to north-north-west. The sky remained slightly cloudy and the sea calm. Nobody in sight.

"We can't be very far from the entrance of the passage," remarked Spahr.

Daylight was turning into twilight and Prien gave the order to switch on the navigation lights. Spahr looked at his wrist watch and said, "we're coming to the entrance of the passage, sir."

"Ship straight ahead!" signalled Leading Seaman Mantyk.

The commander and the officer of the watch trained their binoculars on her.

"It must be one of ours, for she is obviously coming out of the passage," observed Prien.

"Yes and she also has her navigation lights on."

At about half a mile, the steamer turned to starboard and passed by on a parallel course at a distance of about 500m.

"Nothing suspicious," confirmed Spahr lowering his binoculars.

Prien relaxed and let his thoughts wander, which rarely happened to him. He had every reason to be satisfied. He had succeeded in carrying out with brilliance a particularly delicate mission and he took pleasure in imagining the reaction of the 'old man' at the announcement of the destruction of *Royal Oak*. Letting his eyes wander among the whitish spots of foam running the length of the submarine, he said to himself that each turn of the propeller brought him nearer to his wife and daughter. He immediately pushed away these ideas from his mind, for he had a horror of becoming sentimental. Unconsciously he turned towards the steamer and could not believe his eyes. The ship had gone right about! What did that mean? And yet, no—she continued on her way.

"Heavens! Her port-light has become green!"

"But it was red a moment ago!"

"Good Gracious! She's camouflaged!" exclaimed Spahr.

"Hang it! We're going to teach her a lesson," roared Prien.

"Careful, it's getting dark and if we give chase, we risk being unable to find the passage again."

Prien stifled a string of oaths and took up his binoculars to examine the suspect carefully.

"I cannot even fire at her. Nothing proves that she is not one of ours, but I have my doubts," he grated out.

The steamer at last melted away into the darkness and the submarine found herself alone on a glassy sea. Navigation continued without incident. They only had to be careful to remain in the passage.

When Endrass came to relieve Spahr, Prien decided to go down and rest to be in good shape the following day. That day promised to be tiring, with reports, visits, parades and other formalities which he could not avoid.

"Have me wakened at 03.30hrs. We will meet the patrol boat posted at the exit of the passage without doubt towards four," he said, before going down the ladder of the conning tower.

In his office, he took off his leather jacket and his cap, then sat down before the small table which served as a desk. He wrote out a telegram advising HQ of his arrival at Wilhelmshaven at 10.00hrs. He rose and lifting up the green curtain, handed the piece of paper to Blank.

"Send this message with a request for acknowledgement," he said.

A few minutes later, the petty officer telegraphist was transmitting the acknowledgement advice. Prien switched out the light and immediately dropped into a deep sleep.

On the bridge, the men on watch did not relax their attention, for other ships could go through the channel. But the monotony of the night watch was not troubled by any encounter.

At 03.45hrs, von Varendorff saw the captain climb the ladder of the conning tower.

"The watch did not signal any ship, sir," reported the third hand.

"We have scarcely left the minefield. I expect that the escort vessel is not very far now."

The ritual of the relief was quickly gone through. Besides the normal complement, Leading Seaman Hänsel had gone on the bridge with the signalling light. It was Spahr who spotted the trawler at 04.04hrs, three points on the starboard bow.

"Send her the recognition signal," ordered Prien to Hänsel.

No answer.

"Repeat the signal, twice: she did not see us."

Still no reaction.

"Damn, they seem to be sleeping. We'll try something else," exclaimed Prien, disappointed.

"We'll stand right in her way and when we are right ahead, we'll send her the signal full in the face. Impossible, then, not to see it."

"Steer 20 degrees to port."

The silhouette of the patrol boat was getting smaller as the submarine approached the grain of the patrol boat. Prien took up his binoculars. He made out clearly the bow wave.

"Send the signal three times," he shouted.

The sights of the binoculars were trained up on the bridge of the trawler, but the latter remained dark as if lifeless.

"It's a wonder! Ah, the dirty dogs!... With such fools one can expect anything. They would let a squadron through," exploded Prien, enraged.

"A simple submarine can also cause a lot of damage. We are paid to know it," added Spahr sententiously.

"They are changing course. They are coming towards us," warned Dittmer.

"Send the signal again. Twice!"

No reply. The patrol boat just continued to come towards the submarine.

"We must clarify that! Hard a-starboard. Both engines full ahead."

U-47 turned a quarter circle.

"Course north!"

The trawler backed to the right.

"Starboard 90."

The silhouette reappeared on starboard.

"Hard over to starboard! Steer o!"

The submarine was nearly level with the trawler on a parallel route.

"Both engines slow ahead! Bring up the loudspeaker! Fire a Very light!"

The two boats proceeded 500m apart.

Prien took the megaphone and yelled: "Why don't you reply?"

The door of the bridge opened and a sailor appeared, a hailer in his hand.

"I'm alone on watch!" he shouted.

Abashed, Prien remained for an instant dumb with surprise, then asked :"Where are the others?"

"They are sleeping."

Prien stifled a cry of rage and answered: "What is your identification number?"

"808."

"I order you to follow me to Wilhelmshaven! Understood?"

"Understood! Must I wake the captain?"

"No! It's not necessary. Let him sleep."

Handing over the megaphone to Spahr, Prien could not help smiling at the idea of the captain's expression when he awoke. He looked at his wrist watch: 04.47hrs.

"We have lost more than forty minutes chasing this fool," he raged. "Both engines, half ahead!"

The man had gone back on to the trawler bridge. Prien waited until his ship was half a mile ahead of the patrol boat to order:

"Course 130!"

When the submarine had finished her manoeuvre he turned round towards the escort vessel. The latter was following obediently in the coming dawn.

"I'm going down. If anything happens, warn me," he said to Spahr.

"Yes, sir," answered the officer of the watch, readily.

The latter looked at Prien going down the ladder, thinking "I hope he doesn't come up again unexpectedly before 07.00 or 08.00hrs; by then the emblem will be on the conning tower."

A little before sunrise, Endrass appeared on the bridge, a smile on his lips. Without a word, he handed the drawing to Spahr, bent down the hatch and took the pail of paint from von Varendorff. The third hand immediately came up on to the bridge.

"You hold the chart flat against the conning tower, to starboard, under the lee," said Endrass to the two men. "I'll paint it from outside."

The first lieutenant went down on the deck and critically examined the drawing held in place by Spahr and von Varendorff bending outside the bridge.

"Draw it a little higher," he shouted. "A little bit forward . . . turn the drawing so that the tail is vertical. . . . Yes, that's it. Hold on, I'm coming."

He climbed smartly on to the outside of the conning tower, taking a hold where he could. He put his right foot on the spurn water, his left on the handrail fixed above the navigation light, and clutched the flat top of the bridge railing with his left hand. Dittmer gave him the brush and he began to paint the outline of the drawing overlapping slightly on the metal of the conning tower. Once he had finished, he enjoined: "now tear off the map with a quick jerk to avoid smudges."

He examined the result and asked:

"Hand me over a small brush to give him some character."

Von Varendorff too went down on deck to find any possible fault with the necessary perspective. Endrass turned round and enquired, brush in hand, "Does he look too much like a cow?"

The third hand waited for two seconds before answering:

"No . . . the skipper wouldn't have liked that. He looks to me like a real male!"

On the bridge, the men burst out laughing. Endrass' reaction was rapid. Jumping nimbly on the deck, he joined von Varendorff, blinked, and judged his own work.

"I'll accentuate his character by making the lines thick and bold" he said mockingly.

Ten minutes later, Spahr, leaning on the bridge railing, asked:

"Well? What's happening to our wild beast?"

"I think this time, that's it. It really is 'him'," answered Endrass, with satisfaction in his voice.

The disc of the sun had emerged from the sea between two purple clouds and seemed to train its rays on the submarine, but, since the dawn, the sky was getting progressively overcast and huge grey masses of rain clouds forecast a low sky for the day. On the portside, the island of Heligoland raised her sheer cliffs towards the sky. Seagulls whirled above the foam of the wake shrieking. The two officers went back on the bridge.

"The skipper must be finishing his breakfast. This would be the right time to attract him to the deck," said Spahr.

Endrass bent down to pick up the brushes, thinking over the pretext he could put forward, when he saw the captain's white cap emerging

Painting by Jean Delpech, naval artist.

from the hatch. The first lieutenant straightened up and, his pail of paint in his hand, did not know which attitude to adopt. Prien looked surprised to see both officers on the bridge but said nothing. His eyes rested for a long while on the pail of white paint. He raised them up and wondered why the four men on watch had suddenly started scanning the sea with their binoculars as if they were in mid-Atlantic and, so doing, carefully turned their backs to him. He immediately understood that the men were trying to stifle laughter without great success.

Unfortunately von Varendorff and Spahr began to speak at the same time. The first one stopped, but the sentence of the second was unintelligible. The captain seemed more and more surprised. Spahr was, consequently, obliged to begin again:

"Sir, we wanted to give you a surprise. We . . . at least, no, it's the first lieutenant to whom all credit is due, he wanted to give personality to U-47 before her return to port, by giving her an emblem which really means what it says, after your attack in Scapa Flow,[1]" he said, developing his first sentence as well as he could.

"May I see this emblem? Where is it?" asked Prien, trying to keep a stern face.

"On the forward part of the starboard side on the conning tower, sir, but it is better to go on the deck to see it at its best," answered Spahr.

Prien went down the ladder. Four pairs of binoculars were trained at the same time, upon him, to follow his reactions.

Endrass, von Varendorff and Spahr came near the side of the bridge. They saw the captain walk up to the gun, turn on his heel, and lift up his eyes. He stared at the bull and burst out laughing loudly.

"Well, is that me? . . . What, do I look as furious?" he exclaimed, laughing heartily.

"Not furious, but resolute," rectified Endrass.

"One could not find anything better to symbolise U-47 and her valiant crew," he said, serious again.

[1] This emblem was adopted by the 7th Flotilla of U-boats.

Right; Wilhelmshaven, 17th October, 1939. Günther Prien on his return from Scapa Flow.

Below; Prien shakes hands with Admiral Boehm, Admiral of the Fleet, and Lord High Admiral Raeder, Commander in Chief of the Navy (right). / IWM

Above; Berlin, 18th October, 1939. The crew of the *U-47* arrive at Berlin. At the head is Lieutenant Prien; in the second row from left to right: Hans Wessels engineer officer, Engelbert Endrass first lieutenant and Amelung von Varendorff the third hand.

Below; Berlin 18th October, 1939. Prien and Wessels are cheered by the crowd. / Hans Wessels

Above; 23rd October, 1939. *U-47* arrives at Kiel via the Canal. / Hans Wessels

Below; 23rd October, 1939. *U-47* in the Roads at Kiel.

Kiel 23rd October, 1939. The victors of Scapa Flow are cheered by the crew of the Cruiser *Emden.* / Ferdinand Urbahns

Above; Kiel 23rd October, 1939. The
U-47 passes in front of the battlecruiser Scharnhorst, her crew lined
up on the deck. / Ferdinand
Urbahns

Below; 23rd October, 1939. U-47
moors at Kiel. / Friedrich Krupp
AG

der Betriebsgemeinschaft
Fried. Krupp Germaniawerft A.G., Kiel

| 2. Jahrgang | Kiel, 21. November 1939 | Nr. 25 |

Rolleiflexaufnahme : Dukel

Die Sieger von Scapa Flow

Left; Prien surrounded by his officers on the *U-47.* / Friedrich Krupp AG

Right; Prien surrounded by his crew on the *U-47* at Kiel. /Wilhelm Spahr

Below; The *U-47* returns to the shipyards of Friedrich Krupp Germaniawerft AG. / Friedrich Krupp AG

Above; The arrival of *U-47* at the shipyards of Friedrich Krupp Ger. to be laid up on account of damages sustained during the raid on Scapa Flow.

Left; Kiel 24th October, 1939. Prien and Wessels receive the congratulations of the builders of *U-47.* / Friedrich Krupp AG

Right; The Golden Book of the shipbuilders Friedrich Krupp Ger. AG, which relates the exploit of the *U-47* at Scapa Flow. Below the text can be seen the signatures of: Günther Prien, Lieutenant Hans Wessels, Sub Lieutenant Amelung von Varendorff, Sub-Lieutenant Engelbert Endrass, Sub-Lieutenant. / Friedrich Krupp AG

Scapa Flow

Nach der erfolgreichen Fahrt, in deren Verlauf die Torpedierung der beiden englischen Schlachtschiffe „Repulse" und „Royal Oak" am 13. Oktober 1939 in der Bucht von Scapa Flow erfolgte, traf das siegreiche Unterseeboot mit dem Kommandanten Kapitänleutnant Prien und seiner Besatzung am 24. Oktober 1939 auf der Germaniawerft ein. Die Belegschaft der Werft bereitete dem Boot einen begeisterten Empfang. Sie ist stolz darauf, das Instrument geliefert zu haben, mit dem Kommandant und Besatzung die großartige Tat vollbringen konnten.

Fried. Krupp Germaniawerft Aktiengesellschaft

Kiel-Gaarden, 24. Oktober 1939

Günther Prien.
Kapitänleutnant.

Hans Wessels
Oblt (Ing.)

Amelung v. Varendorff
Lt. zur See

Engelbert Endraß
Oberleutnant zur See

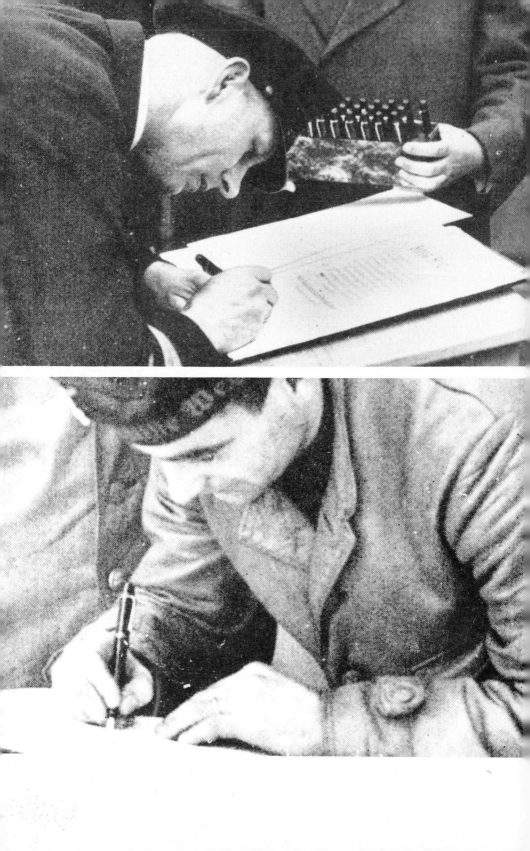

Above left; Lieutenant Hans Wessels, engineer officer of *U-47* signs the Golden Book. / Friedrich Krupp AG

Left; Leading seaman signs the / Golden Book of the shipbuilders of *U-47.* / Friedrich Krupp AG

Above; Prien seems at ease at the close of the ceremony organised in honour of the *U-47* on 24th October 1939 by the shipbuilders Friedrich Krupp Germaniawerft AG. /Friedrich Krupp AG

Right; The entire text, relating the exploit of *U-47* at Scapa Flow, from the special booklet produced by the shipbuilders Friedrich Krupp Germaniawerft AG. / Friedrich Krupp AG

Unter Kruppianern

Am 24. Oktober traf das siegreiche Unterseeboot, das in der Bucht von Scapa Flow die beiden englischen Schlachtschiffe „Repulse" und „Royal Oak" torpedierte, auf seiner Bauwerft ein. Die U-Bootsbesatzung wurde mit großer Freude von der Belegschaft der Germaniawerft begrüßt in Erinnerung der Zeit, in der sie gemeinsam mit der U-Bootsmannschaft den Bau dieses Bootes durchführte. Zum Empfang des Bootes waren die Direktion der Germaniawerft, der Vertrauensrat, die Ingenieure und Meister des U-Bootsbaues auf dem Leitwerk I versammelt. In zwangloser Gruppierung hatte die Belegschaft zu Tausenden auf den Pontons und den danebenliegenden Schiffsneubauten Aufstellung genommen. Von den hochragenden Glashellingen wehten die Flaggen des Reiches und des Hauses Krupp. Ein großartiges Bild! Von den Menschenmassen begeistert begrüßt, machte das Boot am Leitwerk I fest. Die Besatzung war an Deck angetreten. Am U-Bootsturm leuchtete das Wahrzeichen des siegreichen Unterseebootes, der „Stier von Scapa Flow", das 1. W.-O. mit gewandter Hand als Skizze in Weiß ausgeführt hatte. Der Kommandant richtete vom Kommandoturm aus herzliche Worte an die Belegschaft der Werft:

„Kameraden, wir bringen auf unsere Bauwerft, die uns unsere Waffe geschmiedet hat, auf die ganze Belegschaft, Ingenieure und Betriebsführer, ein dreifaches Hurra aus."

Der Kommandant, Kapitänleutnant Prien, begab sich dann auf das Leitwerk, wo er von dem Betriebsführer der Germaniawerft, Herrn Direktor Schrödter, mit folgenden Worten begrüßt wurde:

„Herr Kapitän! Beim Betreten der Kruppschen Germaniawerft, der Geburtsstätte des deutschen Unterseebootes, wo auch Ihr Boot das Licht der Welt erblickt hat, möchte ich Ihnen namens des Hauses Krupp, meiner Mitarbeiter und Gefolgschaft unser herzliches Willkommen, und in heller Begeisterung darüber, was Sie draußen vollbracht haben, unsere ebenso herzlichen Glückwünsche ausdrücken. Wir Werftleute verfolgen voller Spannung die Bewährung und die Taten der Boote, die hier entstanden sind. Es ist wichtig, daß wir uns um unsere Boote kümmern, weil wir dann um so grimmiger mitarbeiten und die Waffe fördern können. In Scapa Flow, dort, wo unsere ruhmreiche Flotte des Weltkrieges selbst die Flagge strich, haben Sie der jungen Marine ein Denkmal gesetzt. Der britische Löwe, der zwar nicht vom deutschen Adler, aber sonst in der Welt immer noch gefürchtet wird, hat durch Ihren Meisterschuß seine Pranken verloren. Er ist heute als Wächter des Supremats Englands in der Seeherrschaft nur noch als Invalide zu werten. Der Fangschuß wird ihm im Verlauf des vom Zaun gebrochenen Krieges erreichen. Herr Kapitän! Das deutsche Volk hat Ihnen seine Begeisterung und seine Freude kundgetan. Wer wie Sie dem Führer ins Auge gesehen hat, wer wie Sie von ihm geehrt worden ist, dem kann Größeres nicht widerfahren. Gestatten Sie aber uns Kruppianern, die wir doch an der Wiege Ihres Bootes gestanden haben, daß wir in dieser Stunde unserer überströmenden Freude, unserem übervollen Herzen Luft machen, indem wir Sie begrüßen für Ihre kühne, unvergleichliche Tat, für Ihren unvergleichlichen Erfolg. Herr Kapitän, und ich wende mich auch an Ihre Herren Offiziere und Ihre Mannschaft, nehmen Sie unseren Gruß entgegen, den wir Kruppianer darbieten wollen mit dem alten Kriegsruf der Marine. Kapitän, Offiziere und Mannschaft und das wackere Boot: Hurra!"

Herr Kapitänleutnant Prien dankte Herrn Direktor Schrödter mit den Worten: „Im Namen meiner Besatzung danke ich Ihnen allen. Unseren Dank haben wir vorhin schon zum Ausdruck gebracht durch unsere drei Hurras. Sie können versichert sein, daß wir alle stolz sind auf das Werk, das Sie uns als Waffe gegeben haben, und unsere höchste Pflicht und Freude wird es sein, diese Waffe, solange sie in unserer Hand liegt, immer erfolgreich anzuwenden für Deutschlands Ruhm und den Ruhm dieser Werft."

Anschließend trugen sich Kommandant und Besatzung des Unterseebootes in das Buch der Werft ein, deren Unterschriften in der nebenstehenden Kopie wiedergegeben sind. Unter den Klängen flotter Marinemärsche schloß die eindrucksvolle Begrüßungsfeier.

Text und Bild: Nachrichtenstelle der Krupp-Germaniawerft

Appendices

I: Crew of the *U-47*

OFFICERS

Equivalent Rank

Kommandant (Commander)
Prien, Günther,
    Kapitänleutnant   Lieutenant

Leitender Ingenieur (Chief Engineering Officer)
Wessels, Hans,
    Oberleutnant (Ing)   Lieutenant (E)

Erster Wachoffizier (First Watch Officer)
Endrass, Englebert,
    Oberleutnant zur See   Lieutenant

Zweiter Wachoffizier (Second Watch Officer)
von Varendorff, Amelung,
    Oberleutnant zur See   Lieutenant

U-Steuermann (Chief Navigator)
Spahr, Wilhelm,
    Obersteuermann   Chief Quartermaster

SEAMAN PERSONNEL

Sammann, Hans,
    Bootsmann   Chief Petty Officer
Dziallas, Ernst,
    Bootsmaat   Petty Officer
Meyer, Willy,
    Bootsmaat   Petty Officer
Dittmer, Peter,
    Matr. Gefreiter   Able Seaman

Smyczek, Rudolf,
    Matr. Obergefreiter   Leading Seaman
Schmidt, Ernst,
    Matr. Obergefreiter   Leading Seaman
Marquard, Herbert,
    Matr. Obergefreiter   Leading Seaman
Mantyk, Heini,
    Matr. Obergefreiter   Leading Seaman
Hänsel, Gerhard,
    Matr. Obergefreiter   Leading Seaman

Cooks

Walz, Friedrich,
    Matr. Obergefreiter   Leading Seaman

Wireless Operators

Blank Hans,
    Oberfunkmaat   Petty Officer Telegraphist
Hebestreit, Herbert,
    Ob. Funk. Gefreiter,   Leading Telegraphist
Steinhagen, Karl,
    Funkgefreiter   Telegraphist

Torpedo Mechanics

Bleeck, Kurt,
    Obermechanikersmaat   Petty Officer
Thewes, Peter,
    Ober. Mech. Gefreiter   Leading Seaman
Loh, Willi,
    Ob. Mech. Gefreiter   Leading Seaman
Hermann, Herbert,
    Ob. Mech. Gefreiter   Leading Seaman

TECHNICAL PERSONNEL
Central Post

Böhm, Gustav,
    Stabsmaschinist   Engine Room Artificer
                          (ERA)

Hölzer, Erwin,
    Masch. Hauptgefreiter   Leading Stoker
Sollig, Werner,
    Masch. Gefreiter   Able Stoker

Mechanics

Strunk, Otto,
    Stabsobermaschinist
	Chief Engine Room Artificer
	    (CERA)

Schmalenbach Werner, Masch, Maat	Stoker Petty Officer
Scholz, Werner Masch. Maat	Stoker Petty Officer
Sporer, Karl, Masch. Obergefreiter	Leading Stoker
Brehme, Kurt, Masch. Gefreiter,	Able Stoker
Lüddecke, Werner, Masch. Obergefreiter	Leading Stoker
Radloff, Walter, Masch. Obergefreiter	Leading Stoker
Biermann, Heinrich, Masch. Obergefreiter	Leading Stoker

Electricians

Römer, Kurt, Obermaschinist	Chief Petty Officer Electrician
Werder, Gustav, Masch. Maat	Petty Officer Electrician

Holstein, Kurt,
    Masch. Maat
    (died 13.6.62)
	Petty Officer

Winzer, Ernst, Masch. Obergefreiter	Leading Electrician's Mate
Schmidt, Friedrich, Masch. Obergefreiter	Leading Electrician's Mate
Hotzer, Gerd, Masch. Obergefreiter	Leading Electrician's Mate
Roth, Ronni, Masch. Obergefreiter	Leading Electrician's Mate

II: U-47

Technical Specifications:
Type VIIB (VIIA improved and enlarged).
1st series *U-45* to *U-55*
Shipyard: Krupp Germaniawerke, Kiel.
Order: of the 21st November 1936
Number of construction: 583
Laid down: 1st April 1937
Launched: 29th October 1938.
In service: 17th December 1938

Incorporated in the 7th U-boat Flotilla (Flotilla Wegener).

Displacement (tons): Washington: 517
      actual Surface: 753
      (Submerged): 857
Length: 66·5m
Width: 6·2/4·7m
Draught: 4·7/9·5m
Motors: 2 x 1,400hp (diesels M.A.N.)
        2 x 375hp (electric motors)
Speed: Surface: 17·2 knots
    Submerged: 8·0 knots
Range Surface: 8,850 (10 knots) 6,500 (12 knots)
    submerged: 72 (4 knots)
Diving depth: 100 (200)m
Fuel: 108 tons.
Armament: 4 torpedo tubes bow;
       1 tube stern
       12 torpedoes 533mm
       1 gun 88mm
Crew: 40 men.

III: Data concerning the tides

About tide and currents in Scapa Flow bay, Kirk Sound and Holm Sound in the night of 13th/14th October 1939. (Reproduced by permission of the French Navy Hydrographic Department.)

Hours of high and low tide at Burray point—13th October 1939.

L.T. at 17.13hrs
H.T. at 23.23hrs

14th October 1939
L.T. at 05.34hrs
H.T. at 11.45hrs

The heights at appointed hours from 13th October 1939 at 19.00hrs to 14th October at 07.00hrs (U.T.) are as follows:

13th October 1939.
19.00hrs-0·8m
20.00hrs-1·6m
21.00hrs-2·3m
22.00hrs-2·9m
23.00hrs-3·3m

14th October 1939
00.00hrs-3·2m
01.00hrs-2·8m
02.00hrs-2·1m
03.00hrs-1·3m
04.00hrs-0·4m
05.00hrs-0·0m
06.00hrs-0·0m
07.00hrs-0·4m

These hours and heights have been deduced from the data about tides in Brest for the 13th October 1939 and the shape of the mean graph of the spring tide in Aberdeen, British reference for the zone in question.

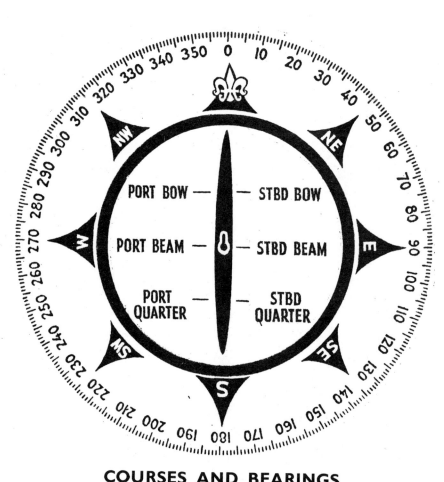

COURSES AND BEARINGS

IV: Extracts from Hydrographic Pilot

No 355 (1937 edition) pp 265 and 270

Reproduced by permission of the French Navy Hydrographic Department

The 1937 edition was in force in 1939, the reference was the tide at Dover, high tide in this port, on the 13th October 1939, was at 23.27hrs.

Orkneys: The current flows from the Atlantic to the North Sea during 06.25hrs when the tide rises at Dover and from the North Sea to the Atlantic during the same time when the tide recedes at the same place.

The speed of the currents is 10 knots or more in some parts of the Pentland Firth, and 6 knots or more in the narrow parts of the other islands' channels.

East Coast: On these coasts the tidal currents are weak and not over 1·5 knots in spring tide, except quite near the entrance of the channels leading among the islands and in the entrance of Pentland Firth. The current bearing from the Atlantic to the North Sea brings counter-currents on the east coast of some islands; they are described in the course of this book.

Scapa Flow: The tidal currents are weak in this small inland sea. No high sea except the local one which rises from shore to shore and is bad, in fact, when the wind is strong.

Holm Sound and Kirk Sound: The following information was compiled before ships were sunk in the channels to block them. The information is to be used with care.

In the Sound tidal currents bear to the east from 05.75hrs after high tide at Dover to 00.25hrs before the following high tide, then to the west for the remainder of the time.

These two currents cross Kirk Sound and Skerry Sound at a speed of 8 knots and the Weddel Sound at 6 knots. They bring strong currents in the east entrances, with the current going out, and strong currents at the western entrances with the current coming in.

This high speed diminishes rapidly when these channels widen at each of their entrances: it is 4 knots between Burray Ness and Rose Ness and 2 to 3 knots between Rose Ness and Burray Ness; it is 4 knots between Howequoy Head and Glims Holm at the western entrance of Kirk Sound and falls to 0·5 knots plus, in the west of Scapa Flow.

When the currents flow to the east they produce a counter-current under the south-east coast of Lamb Holm and in Skerry Sound this current flows to the south on Sinclair Skerry. With these currents and strong south winds, the sea breaks almost across Holm Sound and makes these channels dangerous. When the current is flowing westward and the wind is from the east, the sea is rough at the entrance of Scapa Flow.

V: War Diary of U-47[1]

Extract concerning the operation against Scapa Flow—by Commander Günther Prien. 12th-17th October 1939

12.10.39 Wind SE 7-6. overcast.

During day lay submerged off Orkneys. Surfaced in the evening and came in to the coast in order to fix exact position of ship. From 2200 to 2230 the English are kind enough to switch on all the coastal lights so that I can obtain the most exact fix. . . .

13.10.39 E of Orkney Islands. Wind NNE 3-4, light clouds, very clear night, Northern Lights on entire horizon.

At 0437 lying submerged in 90 metres of water. Rest period for crew. At 1600 general stand-to. After breakfast at 1700, preparations for attack on Scapa Flow. Two torpedoes are placed in rapid loading position before tubes 1 and 2. Explosives brought out in case of necessity of scuttling. Crew's morale splendid. Surfaced at 1915. After warm supper for entire crew, set course for Holm Sound. Everything goes according to plan until 2307, when it is necessary to submerge on sighting a merchant ship just before Rose Ness. I cannot make out the ship in either of the periscopes, in spite of the very clear night and the bright lights. At 2331, surfaced again and entered Holm Sound. Following tide. On nearer approach, the sunken blockship in Skerry Sound is clearly visible, so that at first I believe myself to be already in Kirk Sound, and prepare for work. But the navigator, by means of dead-reckoning, states that the preparations are premature, while I at the same time realise the mistake, for there is only one sunken ship in the straits. By altering course hard to starboard, the imminent danger is averted. A few minutes later, Kirk Sound is clearly visible.

It is a very eerie sight. On land everything is dark, high in the sky are the flickering Northern Lights, so that the bay, surrounded by highish mountains, is directly lit up from above. The blockships lie in the sound, ghostly as the wings of a theatre.

I am now repaid for having learnt the chart beforehand, for the penetration proceeds with unbelievable speed. In the meantime I had

[1] Extract from *Brasseys Naval Annual* 1948, William Clowes & Sons Ltd.

decided to pass the blockships on the northern side. On a course of 270 I pass the two-masted schooner, which is lying on a bearing of 315, plenty of room. In the next minute the boat is turned by the current to starboard. At the same time I recognise the cable of the northern blockship at an angle of 45° ahead. Port engine stopped, starboard engine slow ahead, and rudder hard to port, the boat slowly touches bottom. The stern still touches the cable, the boat becomes free, it is pulled round to port, and brought on to course again with difficult rapid manoeuvring, but we are in Scapa Flow.

14.10.39 *0027*
It is disgustingly light. The whole bay is lit up. To the south of Cava there is nothing. I go farther in. To port, I recognise the Hoxa Sound coastguard, to which in the next few minutes the boat must present itself as a target. In that event all would be lost; at present south of Cava no ships are to be seen, although visibility is extremely good. Hence decisions:

0055
South of Cava there is no shipping; so before staking everything on success, all possible precautions must be taken. Therefore, turn to port is made. We proceed north by the coast. Two battleships are lying there at anchor, and further inshore, destroyers. Cruisers not visible, therefore attack on the big fellows. Distance apart, 3,000 metres. Estimated depth, 7·5 metres. Impact firing.

0116 (time queried in pencil, 0058 suggested).
One torpedo fired at the northern ship, two on southern. After a good $3\frac{1}{2}$ minutes, a torpedo detonates on the northern ship; of the other two nothing is to be seen. About!

0121 (queried to 0102) (time 0123 suggested in pencil).
Torpedo fired from stern; in the bow two tubes are loaded; three torpedoes from the bow. After three tense minutes comes the detonations on the nearer ship. There is a loud explosion, roar, and rumbling. Then come columns of water, followed by columns of fire and splinters fly through the air. The harbour springs to life. Destroyers are lit up, signalling starts on every side, and on land 200 metres away from me cars roar along the roads. A battleship has been sunk, a second damaged, and the other three torpedoes have gone to blazes. All the tubes are empty. I decide to withdraw, because: (1) With my periscopes I cannot conduct night attacks while submerged. (See experience on entering.)

(2) On a bright night I cannot manoeuvre unobserved in a calm sea.

(3) I must assume that I was observed by the driver of a car which stopped opposite us, turned around, and drove off towards Scapa at top speed. (4) Nor can I go farther north for there, well hidden from my sight, lie the destroyers which were previously dimly distinguishable.

0128
At high speed both engines we withdraw. Everything is simple until we reach Skaildaquoy Point. Then we have more trouble. It is now low tide, the current is against us. Engines at slow and dead slow, I attempt to get away. I must leave by the south through the narrows, because of the depth of the water. Things are again difficult. Course, 058, slow—10 knots. I make no progress. At high I pass the southern blockship with nothing to spare. The helmsman does magnificently. High speed ahead both, finally ¾ speed and full ahead all out. Free of the blockships—ahead a mole! Hard over and again about, and at 0215 we are once more outside. A pity that only one was destroyed. The torpedo misses I explain as due to faults of course, speed, and drift. In tube 4 , a misfire. The crew behaved splendidly throughout the operation. . . .

0215
Set SE course for base. I still have 5 torpedoes for possible attacks on merchantmen.

0630 57° 58′ N. 01° 03′ W.
Lay submerged. The glow from Scapa is still visible for a long time. Apparently they are still dropping depth charges.

1935 ENE 3–4, light clouds, occasional rain, visibility bad towards land, otherwise good.
Off again, course 180°. This course was chosen in the hope that we might perhaps catch a ship inshore, and to avoid *U-20*.

15.10.39 *0600* 56° 20′ N. 0° 40′ W.
Submerged and lay at 72 metres. From 1000 onwards, depth charges were dropped from time to time in the distance. Thirty-two depth charges were definitely counted. So I lie low, submerged, until dusk.

1823 Wind NE 5, sea 4, swell from E, cloudy, visibility good.
Surfaced. On surfacing, Norwegian steamer *Meteor* lies ahead. W/T traffic from the steamer is reported in error from the W/T office; I therefore fire a shot far ahead of the steamer which is already stopped. The steamer is destined for Newcastle-on-Tyne, with 238 passengers. Steamer immediately allowed to proceed. It is reported by the W/T office that the steamer did not make any signals.

16.10.39   *0702* 54° 57′ N. 2° 58′ E. Wind NNW 2-2, visibility good. General course, 180°. Submerged on the Dogger Bank. Three drifting mines sighted, 54° 58′ N. 2° 56′ E. No measures taken, owing to the proximity of fishing vessels. Proceeded submerged throughout the day. *1856* 54° 51′ N. 3° 21′ E. Wind NW 2, light clouds, visibility good. Surfaced, Course 128°. Steered course of 128° into Channel 1.

17.10.39   *0404*

Channel 1 passed. From 0404 chased fishing vessel escort ship No. 808; gave recognition signal eight times—no reply received. This fool did not react until V/S was used at a distance of 500–600 metres. With such guardships an incident such as my operation could occur in our waters also.

1100   Entered port Wilhelmshaven III.

1144   Made fast.

1530   Crew flown to Kiel and Berlin.

VI: Memoirs of Grand Admiral Dönitz

Conception of the Operation

Some operations against the enemy's warships fall into the category of those carried out near land. The most famous is the penetration by *U-47* under Lieutenant Prien, into the bay of Scapa Flow. Because of the particular circumstances in which it was prepared and the boldness of its execution it deserves to be reported in detail.

The idea of taking action against Scapa Flow came to me at the beginning of the war. However, I first abandoned it because of the extraordinary technical difficulties and also because of the memory of the two unfortunate attempts made during the first world war by Commander von Hennig and Lieutenant Emsmann.

These difficulties derived mainly from the very strong sea currents which flow in this area. In the Pentland Firth, for example, they reach a speed of 10 knots. One of our submarines, unable to reach more than 7 knots, submerged, and only for a very brief period, would be at the mercy of these currents. Moreover, it was necessary to assume, naturally, that nets, mines, boom defences as well as sunken wrecks and patrol boats barred the access to Scapa, the most important base of the British Fleet. The Admiralty, very experienced in these matters, and the commander in chief of the Home Fleet, must have taken the greatest care to make these obstructions impassable.

Such an operation, therefore, appeared more than bold. I remember having sat down one day, before a map of Scapa, thinking about the question. My eye fell on Lt Commander Oern belonging to my operations department, a man capable of exceptional concentration of thought. Spontaneously, in his manner, so serious and convincing, he told me:

"I believe we will eventually manage to find the means of getting in."

This reflection from an officer, in whose judgment I had the greatest confidence, determined me to study the question really in depth, to decide my course of action according to the result of that study.

From the beginning of hostilities. I had asked the High Command for a report on Scapa, established according to all the information they possessed. The attached map showed the obstacles they thought in existence at every access. On 11th September 1939 I received an aerial photograph showing the presence of heavy and light vessels to the north of Flotta and in the channel between Switha and Risa. Moreover, Lt Commander Wellner, commanding *U-16* who was already operating in the Orkneys, gave me valuable information about the surveillance, the lighthouses and the conditions of the currents. He thought it possible to enter Scapa by Hoxa Sound, if the barrage was open by chance. I asked the 2nd Air Fleet to let me have photographs as detailed as possible of the various obstructions lying in each possible passage. I received them on the 26th September and arrived at the following conclusion.

(a) "I think that entrance is almost impossible by Hoxa Sound and quite impossible by Switha Sound and Clestrom Sound because of the obstructions there."

(b) "In Holm Sound, there are only two steamers which seem to be sunk across Kirk Sound and another on the north side. To the south of the latter and up to Lamb Holm there are: a first gap 17m wide at low tide mark, where the depth reaches 7m; and a second, smaller, to the north. On both sides the shore is almost uninhabited. I think it is possible to pass there during the night and on the surface at flood tide. The greatest difficulty remains the navigation."

I decided to have an attempt carried out. My choice fell on Lieutenant Prien, Commander of *U-47*, who, in my view, possessed all the qualities of leadership and all the necessary nautical knowledge. I gave him the papers leaving him free to accept or refuse, after forty-eight hours for reflection. He made a very thorough study of it and accepted.

I then personally advised the Head of the Navy in Berlin. The operation, to succeed, demanded the greatest secrecy. I saw that the most favourable opportunity would be during the night of 13th to 14th October because the two slacks at high tide and low tide would take place in darkness and because there was no moon. Prien set off from Kiel on 8th October. I had decided to give him G7e torpedoes but no mines, for he would have to attack targets directly, on the presence of which one could count with certainty.

On the 14th at 11.00hrs the British radio announced that the battleship *Royal Oak* had been sunk, probably by a submarine. On the 17th Prien arrived at Wilhelmshaven and reported to me as follows:

"Have been able to enter and leave by Holm Sound, not without great difficulties. Very little room between the sunk ships, very strong undertow, current 10 knots full ahead at the exit. No watch in front of Holm Sound. *Repulse* and *Royal Oak* present alone at Scapa. On the first attempt a direct hit on the forward part of *Repulse*. On the second, shortly afterwards (two torpedoes were fired in the interval), three direct hits on *Royal Oak*. The battleship blew up in a few seconds. Manoeuvred immediately to get out. Having crossed Holm Sound, noticed very active searches on the bay of Scapa, with launching of depth charges. Very strong Aurora Borealis rising to the zenith, giving a very dangerous light."

Prien had carried out his mission with the greatest boldness, showing proof of the most remarkable qualities and an exemplary prudence.

After this event, the British very naturally had to check and close with extreme care, all the means of access to the bay, causing the latter to be evacuated by the Home Fleet. Where would she go? Loch Ewe, the Firth of Forth and the Firth of Clyde seemed to me the most likely answers.

In consequence I sent towards these places submarines, this time armed mainly with mines, because we could no longer count with certainty on the presence of ships.

In the course of these operations *U-31* (Lt V Habekost) laid mines in front of Loch Ewe. The battleship *Nelson* hit them and suffered very serious damage. At the same time, immediately after similar mine laying had been carried out by *U-21* (Lt V Frauenheim) in the Firth of Forth, we learned that the cruiser *Belfast* had struck one of these mines. The operation in the Firth of Clyde unfortunately brought about the loss of *U-33* and all her crew.

The official British History[1] is expressed as follows. On the subject of Prien's operation and those which followed it: "One must pay tribute to the courage and the resolution with which Lieutenant Commander Prien carried out Dönitz's plan . . .

Doubts existed naturally on the route which he had actually taken. Perhaps it was through one of the passages at the extremities of the barrages guarded by the few patrol boats available, or by one of the entrances from the east imperfectly obstructed. One thing was certain:

[1] *The War at Sea* Vol I, Captain S. W. Roskill, DSC. RN. See Appendix VIII.

it was necessary in every way humanly possible to make these entrances impassable with the least delay. But this required time and meanwhile, the Home Fleet found itself unable to use the most favourable base. Ironically enough, the hull intended to be sunk in the channel used so effectively by Prien, arrived in Scapa the day after the *Royal Oak* was torpedoed."

VII: War Diary of Grand Admiral Dönitz

Extracts concerning Prien's mission
Diary of the Operations of the B.D.U.

15.10.39 *18.oohrs*
Receipt of the news that *Royal Oak* was sunk by a submarine—no indication of place. About 370 survivors. It must be caused by *U-47* (Ref at 23.oohrs)

15.10.39 *23.oohrs*
Received from *U-47* the following message: "Operation carried out as planned. *Royal Oak* sunk: *Repulse* damaged. Please send particulars about route back to base for 16.10 evening, for I no longer have data on this subject."

Consequently, have sent radio (come back to Wilhelmshaven). This message confirms the happy result of an operation planned a long time beforehand: the penetration of a submarine in the bay of Scapa Flow. It is a remarkable feat on the part of Lieutenant Prien, Commander of the *U-47*, and of his crew. The execution was preceded by the following considerations and preparations:

1. Since the beginning of the war the possibility of having a submarine entering Scapa Flow has been studied. The meaning of a success was obvious.

2. As a first stage, we got the information possessed by the Skl [Seekriegsleitung] on the barrages which were thought to exist in Scapa Flow. But we needed details, for they did not allow one to see if an entrance was possible.

3. On the 8th September I learnt that an aircraft of the meteorological reconnaissance from the 2nd Air Fleet had taken a photograph above Scapa on 6th September. I asked for it. It showed the presence of heavy and light units to the north of Flotta and also in the channel between Switha and Risa.

4. *U-14* was sent to the Orkneys (13-29.9) and brought back from this expedition valuable observations on the surveillance, the lighthouses, beacons, currents, etc. . . . The commander thought it possible to enter by Hoxa Sound if the net was open.

5. At my request, the 2nd Air Fleet on the 26/9 at 15.00hrs had excellent photographs taken of Clestrom Sound through Risa up to Switha, of Hoxa Sound and (in part) of Holm Sound of the bay before Scapa Flow and Kirkwall—on studying them I arrived at the following conclusions:

(a) I think it almost impossible to make a penetration across the barrages of Hoxa Sound and completely impossible by Switha and Clestrom Sounds because of obstructions.

(b) Holm Sound is barred only by two steamers apparently sunk across the channel of Kirk Sound and by another a little more to the north. To the south of them, up to Lamb Holm, there exists a gap of 170m wide with a depth of water of 7m up to the shallows. North of these wrecks there is also a gap but narrower. On the two shores, the coast is almost uninhabited. I think it possible to enter through there, on the surface, at the slack of high tide. Navigation will constitute the main difficulty.

6. A new photograph of Hoxa Sound confirmed me in the opinion that a penetration was impossible there.

7. I decided to undertake the operation and I obtained the personal agreement of the Commander in Chief of the Navy whom I went to see at the Skl. To carry it out, Lt Cdr Prien seemed to me particularly suitable. He accepted with enthusiasm.

8. It was decided that the submarine would carry out the operation in the night of 13th/14th October for, on that date, the two slacks took place at night and it was new moon. The submarine, therefore, left Kiel on the 8th October. Before her departure, I personally brought the commander up to date with the information given by the latest aerial photographs.

9. The ship possessed only G7e torpedoes. It was queried whether it was not preferable to employ mines but it was decided to use torpedoes, for, in the case of a hit, success would be more certain.

10. Group A (Colonel Werder), received the order to carry out a reconnaissance with photographs of the situation at Scapa Flow on 12th October, a little before the operation, so that the submarine could be advised of the result in time.

11. *U-10*, *U-18*, *U-20*, and *U-23* were withdrawn from the Orkneys on the 4th October so as not to arouse the attention of the British. One must use all the trump cards.

12. 11th October. Without having received orders, an aircraft of the 2nd Air Fleet flew over Scapa Flow at low altitude. On the 12th

October at 15.00hrs an aircraft of group A (S/Lt Newe, with Warrant Officers Böhme and Wolff) carried out an excellent reconnaissance which showed the exact position of an aircraft carrier, five heavy ships and ten cruisers. This reconnaissance was commented upon verbally, during the night, by S/Lt Newe at Wilhelmshaven. A message was sent to *U-47* who did not receive it, for the submarine was, at that moment, lying on the bottom.

13. According to the observations of the listening service a large number of the ships got under way It is possible that they did so because the appearance, on two occasions, of aircraft above Scapa Flow, made them begin to fear an air attack on the base. These flights would seem to have had a regrettable result. The return of the submarine to Wilhelmshaven is expected on the 17th in the morning.

Finished for the 15.10.1939   Signed: *Dönitz.*

17.10.39   10.30hrs
    U-47 arrives in Wilhelmshaven. The commander in chief of the Navy comes to welcome her. Her commander makes his report. The entrance and exit by Holm Sound have been possible under great difficulty. The sunken ships left little room. The current was very strong: 10 knots ahead at the exit. No watch in Holm Sound.
    Of the Fleet, there remained only *Repulse* and *Royal Oak* in front of Scapa.
1st attack: a hit on *Repulse* (forward)
2nd attack: later—(reloading of two torpedoes)
3rd attack: hits on *Royal Oak*. She blows up in a few seconds.
    Taken immediately the way out. Having left Holm Sound, noted a very active searching operation (with depth charges) in Scapa Flow.
    Strong aurora borealis, up to the zenith, causing dangerous light.
    It is obvious, from the report, that the operation had been carried out with enormous courage and competence.
    [See details in the War Diary of *U-47*.]
    Today an aerial reconnaissance, accompanied by bombers, will take place over Scapa Flow. I do not delete Scapa Flow from my objectives but I think it necessary to undertake a permanent reconnaissance (with photographs) to see what changes will have been made in the obstructions and surveillance.

Signed: *Dönitz*

VIII: Account of Captain S. W. Roskill

Extract from *The War at Sea*, Official Publication of the British Government (HMSO) (Volume I, edition of February 1961)

"After the last fleet operations (8th to 11th October) the battleship *Royal Oak* had returned to Scapa. There in the early hours of the morning of the 14th she was torpedoed and sunk by *U-47* (Lieutenant Prien) which had made a daring entrance to the Flow through Kirk Sound, the northernmost of the eastern passages, encumbered though it was by sunken ships. At about midnight on a clear moonless night, while the northern lights flickered overhead, Lieutenant Prien, who remained throughout on the surface and had chosen a time near the top of high water, passed between the blockships and the northern shore. Though she touched bottom and also fouled the blockship's cable with her stem the U-boat got clear without damage and, at twenty-seven minutes past midnight, entered the Flow.

To the south-west the big ship anchorage was seen to be empty, but when Prien turned back again to the north he sighted what he believed to be two battleships close to the north-east shore. In fact, these were the *Royal Oak* and the old seaplane carrier *Pegasus*, then used for transporting aircraft. At 12.58am Prien closed to 4,000yd and fired three torpedoes (the fourth tube missed fire), and one of these hit the *Royal Oak* right up in her bows or possibly on the anchor cable. The explosion was so slight and the damage so small that on board the battleship the Captain and other officers who went forward to investigate believed the explosion to have been internal. Meanwhile Prien turned to the south, fired his stern tube at the same target without effect, and then withdrew to reload his bow tubes. At 1.16am he returned and fired three more torpedoes at the *Royal Oak*, this time with immediate effect. Two of the salvo hit and, thirteen minutes later, the battleship rolled over on her side and capsized. Twenty-four officers and 809 men of her complement perished. *U-47* now withdrew at high speed and retraced her passage through Kirk Sound, passing this time between the southern blockship and Lamb Holm. With the tide falling and a strong current flowing, this was the most hazardous part of the whole operation, but she passed through safely, and by 2.15am was out in the open sea again. Meanwhile inside the Flow it was realised that a U-boat had probably penetrated the defences, but a search by every available vessel revealed no trace of her. Such doubts as might still remain were dispelled a few days later when the enemy announced Prien's success; but Admiral Forbes had not waited for this to take such remedial steps as lay within his power. The few fleet cruisers at Scapa were sent to Loch Ewe while the Northern Patrol cruisers were ordered to use Sullom Voc, in the Shetlands, as their base temporarily—in spite of that harbour being protected only by nets.

It is now known that this operation was planned with great care by Admiral Dönitz, who was correctly informed of the weak state of the defences of the eastern entrances. Full credit must also be given to Lieutenant Prien for the nerve and determination with which he put Dönitz's plan into execution."

IX: Memoirs of
Sir Winston Churchill
Account of the Operation of *U-47*
at Scapa Flow[1]

Amidst all these preoccupations there burst upon us suddenly an event which touched the Admiralty in a most sensitive spot.

I have mentioned the alarm that a U-boat was inside Scapa Flow, which had driven the Grand Fleet to sea on the night of October 17, 1914. That alarm was premature. Now, after exactly a quarter of a century almost to a day, it came true. At 1.30am on October 14, 1939, a German U-boat braved the tides and currents, penetrated our defences, and sank the battleship *Royal Oak* as she lay at anchor. At first, out of a salvo of torpedoes, only one hit the bow and caused a muffled explosion. So incredible was it to the Admiral and Captain on board that a torpedo could have struck them, safe in Scapa Flow, that they attributed the explosion to some internal cause. Twenty minutes passed before the U-boat, for such she was, had reloaded her tubes and fired a second salvo. Then three or four torpedoes striking in quick succession ripped the bottom out of the ship. In less than two minutes, she capsized and sank. Most of the men were at action stations, but the rate at which the ship turned over made it almost impossible for anyone below to escape.

An account based on a German report written at the time may be recorded:

At 01.30 on October 14, 1939, HMS *Royal Oak*, lying at anchor in Scapa Flow, was torpedoed by *U-47* (Lieutenant Prien). The operation had been carefully planned by Admiral Dönitz himself, the Flag Officer (Submarines). Prien left Kiel on October 8, a clear bright autumn day, and passed through Kiel Canal—course NNW Scapa Flow. On October 13th, at 4am, the boat was lying off the Orkneys. At 7pm—Surface; a fresh breeze blowing, nothing in sight; looming in the half darkness the line of the distant coast; long streamers of Northern Lights flashing blue wisps across the sky. Course West. The boat crept steadily closer to Holm Sound, the eastern approach to Scapa Flow. Unfortunate it was that these channels had

[1] From *The Gathering Storm* Cassell & Company Ltd.

not been completely blocked. A narrow passage lay open between two sunken ships. With great skill Prien steered through the swirling waters. The shore was close. A man on a bicycle could be seen going home along the coast road. Then suddenly the whole bay opened out. Kirk Sound was passed. They were in. There under the land to the north could be seen the great shadow of a battleship lying on the water with the great mast rising above it like a piece of filigree on a black cloth. Near, nearer—all tubes clear—no alarm, no sound by the lap of the water, the low hiss of air pressure and the sharp click of a tube leaver. *Los!* (Fire)—five seconds—ten seconds—twenty seconds. Then came a shattering explosion, and a great pillar of water rose in the darkness. Prien waited some minutes to fire another salvo. Tubes ready. Fire. The torpedoes hit amidships, and there followed a series of crashing explosions. HMS *Royal Oak* sank, with the loss of 786 officers and men, including Rear Admiral H. E. C. Blagrove (Rear-Admiral Second Battle Squadron). *U-47* crept quietly away back through the gap. A blockship arrived twenty-four hours later.

This episode, which must be regarded as a feat of arms on the part of the German U-boat commander, gave a shock to public opinion.

X (a): *Royal Oak*

Technical Specifications:
Class: 'Royal Sovereign'
Programme: 1913 to 1914
Naval Dockyard: Devonport
Laid down: January 1914
Launched: 17th November 1914
Put in service: May 1916
Displacement: 29,150 unladen: 35,000 tons fully loaded
Length: 189·10m
Breadth: 31·8m
Draught: 10·10m
Power: 40,000hp
Speed: 22 knots
Engines: Parsons turbines—4 propellers
Boilers: 18 Yarrow
Fuel Oil: 3,400 tons
Range of action: 4,200 miles at 15 knots
Complement: 1,198 men
Armament: VIII 381/42, XII 152/50
VIII 102 AA (II x 4)
XVI 40 AA (VIII x 2)
Number of AA machine guns
1 catapult   2 aircraft.
Observations: She differs from the 'Queen Elizabeth' class in the disposition of the secondary guns, lower speed and heavier protection.
Latest refitting: 1934–36
Modernisation included reinforcement of the armour plating of the decks, an increase in anti-aircraft guns and the installation of a catapult on the 'X' turret. Torpedo tubes in course of removal.

X (b): *Iron Duke*

Technical Specifications:
Gunnery School ship
Class: 'Iron Duke'
Programme: 1911
Naval Dockyard: Portsmouth
Laid down: 1911
Launched: 1912
Put in Service: 1913
Displacement: 26,671 unladen
                28,450 tons fully loaded
Length: 190m
Breadth: 27·40m
Draught: 9·80m
Power: 29,000hp (designed): max: 32,000hp
Speed: 21·5 knots
Engines: Parsons turbines, 4 propellers
Boilers: 18 Babcock
Coal: 3,700 tons
Fuel Oil: 1,600 tons
Complement: 1,200 men
Armament: X 343, XII 152AA, IV 47
XV machine guns
IV torpedo tubes 533
Observations: Refitted 1928–29. Used from June 1929 as a sea gunnery school. Declassified by the Treaty of London 1931–32. Two 343mm gun turrets, torpedo tubes, lateral armour plating and part of the boilers were removed. The speed was reduced to 18 knots. At the battle of Jutland, the battleship *Iron Duke* was the flag ship of Admiral Jellicoe.

X (c): *Repulse* and *Renown*

Technical Specifications:
Battlecruisers
Programme 1914–1915
Shipyard: Brown, Clydebank (*Repulse*)
          Fairfield, Govan (*Renown*)
Laid down: January 1915
Launched: January 1916 (*Repulse*)
          March 1916 (*Renown*)
Put in Service: August 1916 (*Repulse*)
          September 1916 (*Renown*)
Displacement: 32,000 tons unladen
          37,000 tons (fully loaded)
Length: 242m
Breadth: 31·3m
Draught: 9·60m
Power: 112,000hp (*Repulse*) 120,000hp (*Renown*)
Speed: 28·5 knots fully loaded
Engines: geared turbines Brown Curtiss. 4 propellers
       Boilers 42 Babcock (*Repulse*)
       8 Admiralty (*Renown*) at 21 Kg
Fuel Oil: 4,250 tons
Range: 3,600 miles
Armament: VI 381/42, XII 102/40, VIII 102 AA
       (XX 102 AA on *Renown*).
       XVI or XXIV 40 AA. Numerous AA machine guns
       Repulse VIII Torpedo tubes 533m
       1 catapult—four aircraft
Complement: 1,181 to 1,205 men
Note: Planned as battleships then transformed into battlecruisers after the Battle of Falkland Islands.

Refits:
Repulse 1919–1922
     1932–1936 cost of modernisation: £1,475,000
Renown 1923–1926
     1937–1939 Completely rebuilt
     Rearmed for tests in June 1939

X (d): *Hood*

Technical Specifications:
Battlecruiser
Shipyard: J. Brown, Clydebank
Laid down: September 1916
Launched: 22nd August 1918
Put in Service: March 1920
Displacement: 42,100 tons : 46,200 tons (fully loaded)
Length: 262·3m
Breadth: 32·1m
Draught: 9·6m
Power: 144,000hp
Speed: 31 knots
Engines: Geared turbines Brown-Curtiss—4 propellers
Boilers: 24 Yarrow
Fuel Oil: 4,000 tons
Range: 4,000 miles at 10 knots
Armament: VIII 381/42, XII 140/50, VIII 102/45 AA,
　　　　　IV 47, XVI 40 AA (VIII X2), IV T533,
　　　　　　1 catapult on the quarter deck
　　　　　　1 seaplane
Complement: 1,341 men
Refitting: 1930
Sunk in the North Atlantic on 24th May 1941 during an action with the German battleship *Bismarck* (3 survivors).

X (e): *Pegasus*

Technical Specifications:
Seaplane carrier
Shipyard: Blyth ship building Company
Launched: 1914
Put in Service: End of 1914
Displacement: 6,900 tons
Length: 111·60m
Breadth: 15·40m
Draught: 5·40m
Power: 3,000hp
Speed: 11 knots
Engines: alternating triple expansion—1 propeller
Boiler: cylindrical
Fuel oil: 500 tons
Complement: 136 men
Armament: XIV AA machine guns
Notes: ex *Ark Royal*—cargo ship in construction in 1914, bought by the Navy to be transformed to a seaplane carrier.

In 1939 used by the School of Naval Co-operation for the trials of catapult launching and sea landing ramp. She is not to be confused with the aircraft carrier *Ark Royal*.

XI: The sinking of the *Royal Oak*
Account by R. F. Nichols RN

When the *Royal Oak* steamed into Scapa Flow in August 1939 I noticed the sea defences did not appear to be as secure as those in World War I but I was much too busy to go into that, and in any case it was not my job. Local defence of a harbour is the responsibility of the Senior Naval Officer in Charge of the Base, who is responsible in turn to the Commander in Chief.

Our job was to teach the ship's company (many of whom were reserves) how to live in a ship, and fight her, under modern conditions. The threat of attack from the air, night or day, in harbour and at sea, was new to many and therefore one of our main concerns. Radar was in its infancy and not fitted in the *Royal Oak*.

On the 13th October 1939, the *Royal Oak* was at anchor half a mile from the eastern shore of the Flow, because the high land provided protection from air attack from that direction. The old aircraft transport *Pegasus* was anchored about 7 cables (1,400yd) 340° from us; the *Iron Duke*, a few destroyers, a depot ship, etc: were anchored in the western end of the Flow, some eight miles, and the far side of the islands of Cava and Fara, from us. The *Repulse* had been anchored quite close to us for a day or two but she sailed at about 16.00hrs on the 13th and the *Pegasus* anchored in her stead.

That night, as usual, we darkened ship and were alert to air attack. I turned in at about 22.30hrs and at four minutes past one was awakened by a heavy shaking of the ship. Throwing on a coat, I went on deck but no one could tell me what had happened. I gave orders for the *Daisy II* to raise steam and for the picket boat and launch's crews (both of which boats were lying at the ship's lower boom) to man their boats.

There was a faint aurora by which I could see the outline of the land against the sky and men moving about the deck, but not distinctly enough to recognise them. Proceeding forward I reached the forecastle and saw that the Blake slip stopper on the starboard cable had parted so the cable had evidently run out to a 'clinch'. Manifestly the trouble was below in or near the cable locker flat where I found the captain and engineer commander. It seemed that an explosion had occurred in the inflammable store and a man was going down in a smoke helmet to investigate.

Then, just thirteen minutes after the first explosion, came three terrific, shattering thuds abaft us on the starboard side. Each explosion shook the ship severely, all lights went out and she at once took a list of about twenty-five degrees. There was no doubt in my mind what had happened this time, nor what was going to happen shortly. But how on earth had a submarine got through the defences? In addition to the heavy damage done by the torpedoes there was a large number of portholes open, fitted with light-excluding ventilators. (We had the commander in chief's approval for this.) I knew that every one of these on the starboard side must now be submerged and it would be impossible to close them against the incoming rush of water.

There was no power to hoist out the larger boats and, because of the ever increasing list, the smaller boats became more and more difficult to handle, especially in the darkness. The drifter *Daisy II* lying alongside the port aft, was a consolation as her life saving capacity was large.

In almost complete darkness the captain and I, assisted by a number of the ship's company, released as much life-saving material as we could find and then, just eight minutes after the second salvo of torpedoes had hit her, the *Royal Oak* capsized and sank.

About an hour and a half later we, who had been supported by a Carley raft, were picked up by one of the *Pegasus*'s boats and taken back to the luxury of a hot bath where we could rid ourselves of the oil fuel and get into clean clothes (and outside a good drink!) which our rescuers so generously provided.

I wish to state emphatically that no ship in Scapa Flow was damaged by Prien's torpedoes except the *Royal Oak*. Further, there were no battlecruisers in the Flow on the night of 13th-14th October 1939.

XII: The Scapa Flow Mystery

What really happened at Scapa Flow during the nights of 13th/14th October 1939? Much has been written and deduced on this subject. It has been said among other things that:

(a) Prien never penetrated Scapa Flow; *Royal Oak* was blown up accidentally or maybe by sabotage.

(b) Prien entered Scapa Flow, sank the *Royal Oak* and damaged the battlecruiser *Repulse*.

(c) Prien entered Scapa Flow, sank the *Royal Oak* but did not damage any other ship.

(d) Prien entered Scapa Flow, sank the *Royal Oak* and damaged the old aircraft transport *Pegasus*.

(e) Prien entered Scapa Flow, thanks to a German spy installed in the Orkneys who may have guided him up to the anchorage of the *Royal Oak*.

Rarely has a feat of war been the subject of so much controversy. The absolute secrecy with which the British continue to surround the event does not help to clarify it.

(a) Prien never penetrated Scapa Flow.

The theory of sabotage or accidental explosion has numerous supporters especially among those who escaped from the *Royal Oak*.

In October 1967, on the occasion of the 28th anniversary of the loss of the *Royal Oak*, four members of the crew of *U-47*[1] went to Portsmouth on the invitation of one of the British survivors, Mr Vincent Marchant, and the controversy started more than ever.

A hundred of the survivors of *Royal Oak* took part in a funeral ceremony at Southsea War Memorial; some of them then took part in a frank discussion with the four German submariners. However, certain former sailors from *Royal Oak* remain convinced that no submarine had ever penetrated Scapa Flow. Expressing the opinion of

---

[1] Wilhelm Spahr, Ernst Dziallas, Kurt Römer, Herbert Herrmann. The latter, a naturalised British subject, lives in Scotland.

HMS *Royal Oak.*

numerous comrades, Mr Arthur W. Scarff declared to journalists his conviction that the ship had not been torpedoed. Mr Ellis Clarke stated that he would maintain, for his part, to the end of his days, that the battleship had been blown up by sabotage. The theory of sabotage entails astonishing consequences, not to say unbelievable.

The passages concerning the operation in the war diary of Grand Admiral Dönitz would have been made up for purposes of convenience. The war diary of *U-47* would be a falsification. Prien would be an impostor and the thirty-nine men of his crew, his accomplices.

The official British announcement, as for example, the reply of Winston Churchill, then first Lord of the Admiralty, to a question asked on 17th October 1939 by Mr A. V. Alexander, would have been made only to support a non-existent feat of arms of the enemy.

The paragraphs describing the operation in the Memoirs of Grand Admiral Dönitz, those of Sir Winston Churchill and the History of the War published by the British Government would only be humbug.

Why this humbug? Quite simply because in the psychosis of the 5th Column, sabotage is infinitely more demoralising than the shock caused by a naval exploit of the enemy. It is possible to reinforce the defences of a base and make it impenetrable; it is much longer and more difficult to destroy the 5th column. To discover sabotage in time is chancey.

Then any ship can blow up unexpectedly, as well at sea as in the shelter of a base. This explanation, possible on the surface, is not valid when applied to a warship and, more particularly, a battleship.

There was a total of five explosions, according to some, and four, according to others. The first one happened a few minutes after 01.00hrs. It came from the bow. A shudder ran through the ship. The starboard anchor chain ran through the hawse hole. This explosion, stifled according to some sailors, was also described as terrifying. An acrid odour floated over the forward deck. The rumour spread that an explosion had taken place in the CO_2 compartment. The stability of the battleship was scarcely affected because of the narrowness of the forward compartments filled with water. The damage appeared insignificant. This explosion might have produced no visible sign externally. All the evidence agrees on this point. Fifteen minutes later, the time varies according to the witnesses, three explosions, this time very violent, took place, in rapid succession, on starboard. (Some witnesses only counted two of them.) On each explosion the *Royal Oak* rolled in an alarming fashion, to port. Then, immediately, she took a list of about 25° to starboard. All the lights went out, shortly afterwards.

Most of the sailors had seen a column of water reach the height of the mast at the level of the bridge superstructure. To starboard, but more towards the stern, a thick and heavy black smoke spread over the deck and superstructures. At last a final explosion occurred, which produced the most spectacular apparent results, according to several witnesses, only three or four minutes later. A tongue of fire spurted to the top of the rear mast. The flame came clearly from burning cordite. Some survivors thought of sabotage because of the approximate coincidence between the places where the explosions took place and the holds in which had been stored the supplies taken on the previous evening. This circumstance is not extraordinary in itself when you take into account the dispersal of the points of impact along all the length of the hull of the battleship. But what has really troubled the men and confirmed their conviction of sabotage was the impression of the internal origin of the explosion. However the column of water at the level of the bridge superstructure proves the contrary irrefutably. Though evidence differs on this point it is probable that the other hits had also thrown up these columns of water. Certainly, the burning of the cordite in the secondary magazines, without doubt for light arms, had clearly caused a series of more or less violent internal explosions.

After the second series of explosions there was no doubt, in the minds of many of the sailors, as to what was happening to them. The manner in which the *Royal Oak* rolled before turning over convinced Mr Davies, Corporal in the Royal Marines, that the ship had been hit from outside. At this moment, an incident which happened a few years earlier came back to his mind. This had happened when he was serving on board the *Hood* when his ship was in collision with *Renown*. The bow of the battlecruiser had struck the *Hood* starboard aft; under the shock but without sinking, the latter behaved exactly like *Royal Oak*.

However it may be, the rumour of sabotage spread like a powder trail and went from mouth to mouth after the first day following the disaster. Gossip went on magnifying it and even naming the possible author of the crime as the 'Saboteur of Lyness'.[1]

To blow up a battleship by sabotage is a practically impossible task. There are no known examples in the past. Sabotage requires a network of complicity inside the ship herself. This was certainly not the case in the Royal Navy. The hypothetical saboteur would have had to bring in explosive, and lots of it, with the supplies. Normally, supply is contained in small standard parcels and barrels where a considerable

---

[1] Naval base in the south of the island of Hoy.

change in the nature of the content or the weight is easily recognisable. One of the major difficulties of sabotage would have been the bulk of the explosive to hide. A torpedo contains on average 300kg of explosive. It is difficult to see how the saboteur could have brought in 1,200kg of explosives in packets of 300kg without attracting attention.

There remains the theory of the accidental explosion. There was a previous case of such an accident at Scapa Flow itself where the battleship *Vanguard* blew up in the night of 9th July 1917, almost certainly because of a spontaneous combustion of the cordite in one of the magazines. At the time, the rumour of sabotage had also been spread and the Admiralty had willingly allowed this rumour to get about. At the time, sabotage affected the morale much less than an uncontrolled ignition of the powder which could strike blindly at any ship. At this period there was no knowledge of how to preserve cordite with safety and five other disasters had happened for the same reason, among them the loss of the battleship *Bulwark* at Sheerness and of the cruiser *Natal* at Invergordon. These ships had literally been blown to bits. A whole turret of *Vanguard* had been found on Flotta island. The main powder magazines of *Royal Oak* did not explode. The battleship turned over in eight to ten minutes under the weight of water which poured in by the holes due to the explosion and through the portholes opened for ventilation.

The doubt about a submarine attack is no longer even possible when you know that divers have recovered, in the vicinity of the wreck, the remains of at least two foreign torpedoes among which two tails and an engine plate marked 'Siemens-Schuckert' were found.

In 1939 the presence of a U-boat inside the base was so unthinkable that, after the first explosion, the men were not even called to their action stations: there was no alert and the battleship remained without defence. Supposing that an aircraft had dropped a bomb, gliding, so as not to attract the attention of the AA, men on watch had begun to scan the sky. Mr Davies still remembers some sailors going to their anti-aircraft shelters under the armoured deck, the last place to go with a U-boat at Scapa Flow. As this former sailor of the *Royal Oak* has properly pointed out, the base enjoyed a solid reputation for inviolability among the sailors.

"When we got into Scapa Flow," he added, "we were, so we thought, safe from everything except an air attack and the idea of a submarine attacking inside the base was as unlikely as an attack by men from Mars."

This state of mind explains, to some degree, the disarray which followed the first salvo of the *U-47*.

The German observations confirm the British confusion with an air attack which everyone expected. The two survivors of the crew on duty on the U-boat bridge corroborate this fact.

"After the battleship had sunk, when we were on our way out of Scapa Flow, most of the searchlights were not sweeping the sea, but the sky. Hearing the noise of engines—not aircraft but of the *U-47*—and still not believing in the presence of a submarine, the crew manning the searchlights aimed the beam directly above us. We proceeded, for some time, under a luminous vault of beams criss-crossing above our heads. It was for this reason that our commander thought that the destroyers, seen behind us when getting out of Scapa Flow, had not spotted us."

Still if the evidence of the former enemies are in accordance on the principle of the error, they differ totally on the material facts.

Asked again precisely about the searchlights, Mr Davies gives a plain answer, even a slightly irritated one: "once more, I affirm there were no searchlights, signals, or alerts of any kind on the Flow after the *Royal Oak* was sunk. Outside the survivors in the boats and in the sea, the whole region, for miles around, remained dark and silent as a tomb. It is true that men fighting for their lives in the sea could not have seen anything at any distance, even if there had been something to see, for their only worry was to survive. But on the MFV *Daisy*, fifty to a hundred pairs of eyes looked and searched in all directions for comrades in the water and for help which was not coming. Some, myself included, sure as we were that we had been torpedoed, opened our eyes too, in case the submarine should attack again. Only one searchlight was lit, that of the *Daisy*, to help the rescue operations but it did not turn to explore the Flow. The MFV remained stationary so that men could swim to it without running the danger of being caught by the propeller.

Two hours, at least, elapsed before any help did come, and it came from *Pegasus*. One thing is sure, definite, absolute. There was no attempt to answer, no chase by any kind of ship, destroyer or any other one, between the moment *Royal Oak* was sunk at 01.30hrs and the time when we arrived alongside the *Pegasus*, that is towards 04.00hrs. On this, there cannot be any question, any doubt."

This testimony is confirmed by many other survivors. The differences in statements by the Germans and the English in what concerns the minor fact of the searchlights is only one of the numerous contradictions, trying because of their very number.

Whatever the moment when they realised it at Scapa Flow, they had to acknowledge the fact that everything was in favour of admitting that a submarine had succeeded in penetrating the base. If the Navy had not been sure of it, the base of Scapa Flow would not have been abandoned, even temporarily, for secondary and still more vulnerable bases. Commodore Dönitz, guessing correctly the movements of the Home Fleet, had the approaches of the possible secondary bases mined. The *U-31* (Lt Cdr Habekost) placed mines in front of Loch Ewe and the *U-21* (Lt Cdr Frauenheim) in the Firth of Forth. If the *U-33* (Lt Cdr Dresky) was sunk with all her crew in the Firth of Clyde by the mine-sweeper *Gleaner* on the 12th February 1940, the result had already been felt.

Here follows what Captain S. W. Roskill, official British historian, says on this subject.

"On the 18th October, after the loss of *Royal Oak*, the First Lord told the Cabinet that he thought Scapa Flow quite unfit to serve as a base for the Fleet.

"After a long debate, it was decided to continue to use Loch Ewe as temporary base while the defence of Scapa Flow was improved. But the enemy rightly thought that we would take this measure and Loch Ewe being less well defended than Scapa, it is no wonder that the *Nelson*, Flagship of Admiral Forbes, was severely damaged there on the 4th December by striking one of the mines placed at the entrance by a submarine 5 weeks before. On the 21st November, the newly built cruiser *Belfast* also struck a mine in the Firth of Forth and her keel was broken. The facts proved that Admiral Forbes's fears about the vulnerability to mines of the long approach to Rosyth were very well founded indeed.

"We had to wait till the 4th January, by which time five more of the eighteen mines placed in the channel had been destroyed, to think it possible to send her (*Nelson*) without danger, to Portsmouth to be repaired. The secret was cleverly kept from the enemy but the implications were none the less extremely serious, for it was obvious that, as long as no way of nullifying the magnetic mine had been found, any one of our main ports or any of our bases could be blocked for weeks. . . .

"It remains certain that this inability to defend Scapa adequately against an air or submarine attack caused not only the loss of a

countries. The German tonnage wa
tonnage for all categories of surfa
characteristics or displacement. So
proportion was fixed at 45 per cer
parity—attaching without doubt
British no longer believed in the
Admiralty addressed in 1937, to
Committee a report according to w
again be able to give us the same pr

The Germans had not waited for
laying down small coastal submar
cruisers in reply to the French ba
Despite the treaty of Versailles w
constructions and fixed their maxii
these two battlecruisers were plan
reached, in reality, 32,000 tons. L
Deutschland and *Admiral Scheer*, laid
for 10,000 tons displaced 14,000. . . .

Having their hands freed, within
June 1935, the Germans did not lau
an important programme of Naval
marked time. Awaiting the elaborat
set up a transitional programme
heavy cruisers, torpedo boats, subr
size. Apart from the budgetary
difference of opinion broke out be
Submarines, Commodore Dönitz
favoured long range submarines o
relating to the new installation crea
of torpedo boats.

In May 1938, Hitler, not beli
imminent, the High Command se
gramme Plan Z, which provided for
of 1948 of a homogeneous and wel
destruction of British Trade. Hitler
forward the term from ten to six yea

The declaration of war, on 3rd
consternation by the superior office

[1] Initials of Allied Submarine Detection In
the apparatus conceived under the auspices of
water by ultra-sonic echoes.

battleship and damage to another and to a precious new cruiser, but
handicapped the execution of her assignments by the Fleet."

To appreciate the facts, it is proper to consider them in the context
of the first weeks of the war. The account of the full details which
caused the decisions of the War Cabinet is outside the limits of this
book. Sir Winston Churchill explains them in detail in his memoirs
and Roskill in a precise and concise way in the first volume of his work
The War at Sea. Summing up to excess, you could say that the
commander in chief of the Home Fleet, Admiral Sir Charles M.
Forbes, was handicapped by the consequences of the policy of the
Government between the two wars and by the errors of the intelligence services. The successive British cabinets had neglected the
armed forces. Scapa Flow, the main strategical base of the Royal
Navy, had been abandoned and the defences cancelled.

In 1938, the year of Munich, when Sir Charles Forbes took the
Home Fleet to Scapa Flow, he found the base in an alarming state and
quite out of date. Soldiers from the marines were carrying out the
breaking up of the last gun dating from the first world war while layers
of nets were prepared for anti-submarine barrages for the second.

In fact, up to 1938, the Admiralty had foreseen that in case of war
with Germany, the Home Fleet would be based at Rosyth, in the Firth
of Forth, as in the course of the last phase of the 1914–1918 war. Going

Scapa Flow after Prien's attack. This aerial picture taken at Scapa in July
1940 shows the secret Fleet Tenders—Merchant ships camouflaged with
wood and canvas to represent 'R' class battleships and the aircraft carrier
Hermes. Dummy 'R' class battleships (foreground) and left background the
dummy carrier Hermes. / IWM

through the problem again the
Backhouse, and the Command
that Rosyth presented too m
Scapa. In April 1939, six mor
took the decision to transfer
Unhappily, the death in May
and that of the General Co
Henderson entailed a change
Council and brought about una

In spite of the growing
Government refused all measu
Scapa Flow for fear of alarm
Hitler and nothing serious v
hostilities.

Admiral Forbes did his best,
Stromness a cement barge for £

The anti-aircraft defences di
few pieces in existence were situ

On 7th September, the Adm
report heavily exaggerating the
north-west Germany, ready t
estimate brought the number o
total effective strength of the Lu
In consequence, the Admiralty
Chief of the Home Fleet to prep
of Scotland. Sir Charles Forbes
ment, for he considered second
and submarine attacks. If the I
on 1st October, on the 12th a
graphed it in its entirety at
examined, the same evening,
U-boats. The movements of th
notice of the German informat
date on the use of Loch Ewe or
based on the one hand on air r
on the interception and decodin

On the German side, in Aug
war. The young German Navy,
with Great Britain, on 18th Ju
agreement permitted Germany
proportionally to the Royal I

caught short, began the war with forces inferior to the limits allowed by the naval treaty of 1935.

The submarine arm entered the fight with a force of 56 U-boats,[1] of which only 22 were capable of operating in the Atlantic.

"But with these 22 ships, the average of those which would be at the same time on operations had to be from 5 to 7. Harsh reality showed, however, that this figure could fall to two," explains Grand Admiral Dönitz in his *Memoirs*.

At the beginning of hostilities, the commanders were bound by a series of restrictions relating to attacks on merchant shipping. These restrictions were only lifted progressively.

During the first weeks of World War II, as at the beginning of World War I, operations were mounted above all, against warships. It is in this framework that the raid on Scapa Flow was carried out. The great success of this operation, master-minded by Dönitz and brilliantly executed by Prien, affected the whole submarine arm.

(b) *Prien penetrated Scapa Flow, sunk* Royal Oak *and damaged the battle-cruiser* Repulse.

It is the official German version. Thirty years after the event the survivors of *U-47* are still sure that such was the result of their mission.

Prien does not seem to have worried too much about the identity of the enemy. This question certainly did not take much of his attention during the operation. In his war diary[2] he does not quote any name and simply lists the category of the targets.

"00.55hrs

Two battleships are lying there at anchor, and further inshore, destroyers. Cruisers not visible, therefore attack on the big fellows. Distance apart, 3,000 metres. Estimated depth, 7·5 metres. Impact firing.

0116 (time queried in pencil, 0058 suggested).

One torpedo fixed on the northern ship, two on southern. After a good $3\frac{1}{2}$ minutes, a torpedo detonates on the northern ship; of the other two nothing is to be seen. About!"

---

[1] At the declaration of war, Britain possessed 57 submarines with a displacement superior to the U-boats, the global tonnage of which did not exceed the 45 per cent permitted by the Naval Treaty of 18th June 1935. France disposed of 78 submarines, the USA of 92 of which 62 were out of date; Italy of 69, of which 27 were out of date, and Japan of 69 also.

[2] See Appendix V.

It is very difficult to establish the exact identity of a ship in the course of a night attack and what is more, from a conning tower. The Germans had no chance to determine the names of the two ships of the line in front of them. The ship to the south could be any of five battleships of the class 'Royal Sovereign'.[1] In what concerns the ship to the north, two-thirds of which were hidden, it was still more difficult to identify her with accuracy. According to the experts in submarine warfare, the two ships were moored in alternate lines and the visual angle of *U-47* allowed them to see only the forward deck of the ship to the north which was visible behind the bow of the one to the south. Two or three kilometres away, the superstructures of the two units were merging into each other in the darkness. This ship to the north was identified by all the officers as a battlecruiser.

Leading Seaman Hänsel, who was on the bridge behind Prien, heard him say that *Renown* being on operation elsewhere, it could only be *Repulse*. Later on, in the course of interviews by the Press and radio, Prien stated he had identified *Repulse* by her two funnels while *Royal Oak* had but one.

In fact, it was the BBC who identified the battleship sunk in Scapa as being *Royal Oak* as soon as the 14th October, in the news bulletin at 11 o'clock in the morning. The British radio did not mention any other ship.

[1] *Royal Oak, Revenge, Royal Sovereign, Resolution* and *Ramillies.*

When *U-47* returned to Wilhelmshaven, on the 17th October, after Prien had made his report on the action, the second ship was definitely identified as *Repulse* from the excellent aerial photographs taken on the 12th by Lieutenant Newe. These photographs showed a battlecruiser with two funnels, at anchor next to *Royal Oak*. The commodore of submarines endorsed the torpedoing of *Repulse* and quoted Prien's report in his war diary.[1]

(*c*) *Prien entered Scapa Flow, sank* Royal Oak, *but did not damage any other ship.*

It is the official British version. The loss of the battleship was impossible to conceal. Her wreck was sunk, her keel just at water level, could be photographed at any time. It would not have been the same if she had simply been damaged. So the British informed the whole world about the destruction of *Royal Oak* ten hours after the event. Then, when the German official statement announced triumphantly that a U-boat had entered Scapa Flow, sunk *Royal Oak* and damaged *Repulse*, the Admiralty answered without any more comments that in the night of 13th/14th October 1939 the battlecruiser was at sea. Everybody maintained their positions and things stopped there until the end of the war.

In the meantime the men of *U-47* were sent to other submarines and went on serving with different fortunes. Some of them died in the war, others survived.

After the war, historians, writers and journalists took up the subject and each of them gave their version. Prien and his two deck officers, Endrass and von Varendorff, were dead. They died at sea and could no longer testify.

According to the official British history, the ships Prien had taken for ships of the line were, in fact, *Royal Oak* and the old aircraft carrier *Pegasus*. The latter was not hit. Post Captain S. W. Roskill writes on page 73 of the *War at Sea* Vol I, that one of the three torpedoes of the first salvo had struck the bow of *Royal Oak* or possibly one of her anchor chains. (The two other torpedoes had been lost.) On board the battleship, the explosion was only lightly felt and the damage seeming unimportant, the commanding officer and the other officers who had come up on deck, before realising what the situation really was, concluded it was an accidental explosion, internally.[2]

How is one to believe that a commander of a submarine and his

1 See Appendix VI and VII.
2 See Appendix VIII.

The transport carrier HMS *Pegasus* / Wright & Logan

officers could have confused a battlecruiser of 32,000 tons, having a length of 242m, that is to say one of the biggest ships of the British Navy, with this ancient cargo ship of 6,900 tons transformed into an aircraft carrier? Besides, *Pegasus* measured only 111m, less than half of *Repulse* and, above all, was distinctive because of one of the most characteristic silhouettes of the Royal Navy, with a flat deck and a funnel like a stove pipe right aft. This official version is difficult to accept.

Sir Winston Churchill, who had access to all the documents, does not mention *Pegasus*. In his memoirs, he makes Prien aware of only one battleship silhouette, that of *Royal Oak*.[1] However, if you accept the official British version according to which the German torpedoes had struck only *Royal Oak*, the second silhouette becomes only a superfluous detail in Sir Winston's memoirs and then it is understandable that no mention was made of her. Confirming in every way the official version the officer in command of *Royal Oak*, Commander R. F. Nichols thinks, too, that Prien would have confused, in the darkness and in the excitement of the moment, a battlecruiser with an aircraft carrier. He does not doubt in any way that one of the three torpedoes of the first salvo had struck the starboard chain which ensured the mooring of the battleship and caused a leak in the hold containing inflammable material. This is how he reports on it immediately after the explosion.

"I immediately went forward from my cabin situated aft to try to discover what had happened. I quickly reached the forward deck

[1] See Appendix IX.

where I saw that the starboard cable had come out of the Blake stopper which held it, and run out completely. (The sixteen lengths [1 length = 30 metres] had left the chain altogether.) Going below, I found the captain and the chief engineer already there; a man wearing a smoke mask was going down to examine the hold of inflammable material from where it seemed fumes were rising."

Several witnesses speak of a movement of ships which may have taken place after the departure during the day of the 13th towards 16.00hrs, some say the battlecruiser *Repulse*, others assert it was *Renown*. Would *Pegasus* be at anchor on the mooring left free by the battle-cruiser?

To the exact question put in writing "where was *Pegasus* moored?" the War Ministry replied evasively: "to the north of *Royal Oak*." "7 cables or a little less than 1,400m, 340° true from *Royal Oak*," states Commander Nichols. "About two miles to the west of *Royal Oak*," say other British witnesses with no less conviction. "Yes, we saw *Pegasus* in the north-west, that is to say to the west of *Royal Oak*," affirm the two German eyewitnesses. Who is right, who is wrong? One contradicts the other on the least little fact of this mission apparently fertile in events. It is disconcerting. Why all this mystery?

(d) *Prien entered Scapa Flow, sank* Royal Oak *and damaged the old aircraft transport* Pegasus.

This theory contradicts the official declarations of each of the two former enemies. Its supporters, visibly impressed by the British official history, compromise. They accept that Prien made a mistake in

HMS *Repulse.* / IWM

identifying the second ship but give him the credit of having scored a hit on *Pegasus*. This point of view has been adopted by serious German writers. Of course, the survivors of *U-47* protest and, with some surprise, at their having made such a mistake. Questioned on this point, the eyewitness Hänsel declares: "besides *Royal Oak* I saw the silhouette of a second battleship. She was behind *Royal Oak* and from our position when attacking we could see only her bow."

The captain declared it was *Repulse* but Hans Herlin, in his book *Verdammter Atlantik* page 44, writes in a note that it was the old seaplane transport *Pegasus*. However, the British Admiralty would not have confirmed that the latter was hit. There were only two ships of the same type as the first one: *Repulse* and *Renown*. The captain says that *Renown* was on operations elsewhere, consequently it seems to have been *Repulse* and only this ship. It was hit forward and a huge column of water rose up. Hänsel adds that this silhouette could not have been *Pegasus* since he had seen the latter in the north west, far enough from *Royal Oak*, about a mile and a half to two miles away. Dziallas, the second German eyewitness, states that the battlecruiser was moored a short distance away from *Royal Oak* and seemed to be longer than the latter.

(e) *Prien entered Scapa Flow thanks to a German spy settled in the Orkneys who would have guided him to the mooring of* Royal Oak.

This version, close to the realm of fancy is amusing to mention because of its folkloric quality. Nevertheless, this story went all around the world in the Press, with such success that Captain Roskill

himself thought fit to give it the lie categorically.[1] This version was
mentioned in a publication in Zurich in 1946, by the *Falken Verlag*
under the title *Spione und Verräter des Zweiten Weltkrieges* by Kurt Singer.
On the 24th December 1947 the Berlin newspaper under French
control *Der Kurier* published on page 5 an article entitled *Der Mann die
der* Royal Oak *versenkte* (The man who sank the *Royal Oak*). The hero is
a naval officer. It is not Prien. His name is Alfred Wehring, one of the
youngest and most brilliant officers of the battleship *Admiral Hipper* of
the Imperial Navy.

In 1923 Wehring joined the Intelligence Service of the Navy. In order
to have a 'cover', he was sent to Switzerland to learn watchmaking. He
remained there for three years. In 1927 he arrived in England with
Swiss papers in the name of Alfred Örtel. Where was he going to
settle? In the Orkneys, of course, for there was the most important
base of the British Navy. In Kirkwall, Örtel opened a small watchmaking and jewellery shop.

This modest craftsman led a quiet and peaceful life. He repaired
watches to perfection and gained the esteem of everyone around. Who
on earth could suspect that this little clockmaker was really a hero of
the battle of Jutland? As a good dutiful son, Örtel sent, every month, a
letter to his old father, still living in Zurich, the father of a large family
indeed, for papa Örtel was no other than the head of German
Intelligence.

These letters would certainly have proved of great interest to the
British counter-espionage service. They might have found funny the
relation between clockmaking and the details about coastal and anti-
submarine defences.

About a month after the declaration of war, Örtel learned about the
existence of a gap in the east defences of Scapa Flow. On an October
afternoon, having completed all his information, he shut his shop early
and went home. Opening a sideboard, he put on the earphones of an
old-fashioned looking radio which hid a short wave transmitter of an
ultra modern type. The message received by the naval attaché in The
Hague, Captain Baron von Bulow, was decoded: "Gap in the most
northern defence east of Scapa Flow stop Heavy units moored
here...."

All the U-boats cruising in the Channel and in the North Sea were
alerted. Günther Prien, commanding the submarine *B-06*, received the
order to head for the Orkneys.

13th October 1939. In the ink black night the mass of the islands,

1 *The Navy at War 1939–1945* Collins, London, in a note on page 50.

darker than sky and sea, emerges from a thick fog. In this damp cotton like atmosphere, Prien, his binoculars trained on the shore, makes out the light signals agreed upon: short — short — long . . . a rubber dinghy is put to sea. Shortly afterwards Örtel, a chart rolled under his arm, gets on board.

Finding himself, at last, in his own element, Örtel pilots the submarine with brilliant ease, among the wrecks blocking Kirk Sound and suddenly: here they are in Scapa Flow.

Örtel has a last look through the periscope. The powerful silhouette of the abhorred *Royal Oak* which he fought against in the battle of Jutland shows itself in the sights. The motors are stopped. "Fire!" — the departure of the two torpedoes slightly shake the submarine. The battleship is blown to bits.

The *B-o6* brings Örtel back to Germany. After a short stay at the hotel of the Golden Lion in Kiel he flies to Berlin to report to his 'father', Admiral Canaris, in charge of the German Intelligence service and since that time nobody heard any more about Alfred Wehring-Örtel.

The article was not signed but bore the copyright of *Falken Verlag* Zurich. The reading of this 'paper' first amused the naval officers. Still, this story was blown up in a disproportionate way and ended by being condemned by people in the Navy. The officers who had something to do directly or indirectly with the mission of *U-47* were irritated. All those who had access to the official or confidential documents, such as Wolfgang Frank, War Correspondent attached to the press service of the submarine force were incredulous. The officers of the former HQ of Grand Admiral Dönitz received a lot of letters from naval officers requesting information. The affair was taking an unpleasant turn. To end this unfortunate situation, Rear Admiral Godt, former Chief of the General Staff of Grand Admiral Dönitz, wrote on the 1st January 1948 a corrective letter on five points to the Editor of the paper but *Der Kurier* did not condescend to answer.

In the beginning of January 1949 the *Saturday Evening Post* published a long article *The U-Boat mystery of Scapa Flow* under the name of Burke Wilkinson.

This second version tried to present a more credible explanation with photographs, maps and plans. The author possessed some ideas about the Navy and, from all evidence, had read Prien's own work: *Mein Weg nach Scapa Flow* (my way towards Scapa Flow)[1] and the war

1 Published in Germany in 1940—The English translation *I sank the Royal Oak* appeared in 1954.

diary of *U-47* published by Brassey's Naval Annual 1948. In fact, besides Wehring-Örtel, you find this article again contains sentences taken from Prien's book and war diary.

Wilkinson had made a curious mixture of truth and fiction. The publication of the *Saturday Evening Post* brought this affair to life again. German newspapers seized the opportunity, adding sensational headlines.

In July 1949 Wilkinson's article appeared in No 15 of the French Review *Constellation*. 'The mysterious submarine of Scapa Flow' had left for a long course throughout the world's Press. Almost ten years later, in 1958, she is found again in England.

Need one add that journalists and writers such as Wolfgang Frank and Alexander McKee carried out thorough research,[1] the first in Germany and the second in Great Britain, and that their results have clearly confirmed the 'mythical character' as Roskill so well names it, of the watchmaker of Kirkwall.

The night of Friday, 13th October 1939

Except for the brief British Communiqué announcing on the morning of the 14th that *Royal Oak* had been destroyed, "it seems by U-boat attack", for fifteen years the only sources of information remained of German origin. The Admiralty remained silent until the publication in 1954 of the official history of the war. Sir Winston Churchill had devoted a whole page of his memoirs to the torpedoing of the *Royal Oak* but he did not use the British information. He based his account on a German document, as he himself states. The night of 13th October remained shrouded in the most absolute secrecy, even after the war.

As early as the 14th October the Admiralty had given strict orders to all naval personnel present at Scapa Flow to avoid the Press and, in all cases, not to reply to questions; more precisely to ignore certain of them. These instructions were followed to the letter. Journalists paid the expenses of rounds of drinks in the pubs of Kirkwall, but no information filtered through the chatter. Everything was secret: the position of *Royal Oak*, the number and strength of the explosions, the position of *Pegasus*, of the old battleship *Iron Duke*, partly disarmed, of the auxiliary cruiser ss *Voltaire*,[2] destroyers and minesweepers, to mention only these.

---

[1] *Der Stier von Scapa Flow* by Wolfgang Frank, Stalling Verlag Oldenburg 1958. *Black Saturday* by Alexander McKee, Souvenir Press Ltd, London 1959.
[2] Former steamship of the Lamport and Holt Line.

Official correspondents had no other option than to base themselves on the very brief statement put out by the Admiralty on 14th October. However, numerous survivors of the *Royal Oak* maintained that the battleship had been sabotaged and they did not hide their opinion. It was whispered that the saboteurs came from Lyness. The most contradictory rumours began to circulate. The mystery was born. And, in the course of thirty years that were to follow, it was to deepen considerably. The Navy lost no time in undertaking its enquiry on the exact causes of the destruction of the battleship. Nobody was sure of anything—on the day after the drama, arrangements were made with a view to having the wreck examined by divers. At the same time they started to look actively for possible torpedoes which had not exploded. Through fear of the Fifth Column, an abundance of precautions assured the utmost discretion about the operation. Once more, secrecy was respected. Some three months later the Admiralty thought it advisable not to hide the fact that the remains of foreign torpedoes, of which an electric motor plate bore a name of German manufacture, had been recovered near the wreck.

In spite of these substantial and irrefutable proofs, the partisans of the theory of sabotage did not acknowledge defeat. Even today, some survivors of the *Royal Oak* remain convinced that Prien never entered Scapa Flow. They must believe that these proofs have been 'fabricated' to give credence to the submarine attack.

In 1947, articles on Alfred Örtel, the spy who never existed, muddled up still more a situation rendered obscure by the persistent silence of the authorities. Relying on the 'Official Secrets Act', the

HMS *Iron Duke* before her partial disarmament and declassification in accordance with the Treaty of London 1931-32. / IWM

Admiralty continued to keep all information confidential. The legal duration of secrecy has been reduced from 50 to 30 years. The label 'secret' might then have been taken off the file 'Scapa Flow' on 14th October 1969. However, nothing obliges the Ministry of Defence to divulge anything.

The official history of the *War at Sea* could not pass over this episode in silence. The text has been composed by Captain S. W. Roskill. He gives certain information, some of which contradicts Prien and others correspond to the latter's war diary but diverge from the evidence of the survivors of *Royal Oak*.

Roskill expresses some doubt on the course followed by *U-47*. Had she passed the obstructions of Kirk Sound, or had she slid along the land bypassing the submarine nets which barred incompletely another passage? The uncertainty of Roskill shows suspicion of the veracity of Prien's war diary and the German statement. But the principal interest of this report resides in the affirmation relative to the error of identification of the second ship, and that is where the shoe pinches. If one accepts the official British version according to which Prien might have confused *Repulse* with *Pegasus*, the behaviour of the authorities remains troubling. If there is nothing to hide, why all the secrecy? A layman might have, with difficulty, confused these two ships. Could Prien have committed such an error? Mr Davies, like other survivors, thinks that Prien never saw a second ship:

"I think that he never even saw *Pegasus* and if he had seen her he could never have confused her with another, especially not with *Repulse*."

In any case, it would be interesting to know the exact position of *Pegasus*. The majority of the evidence places her to the north-west of *Royal Oak*. In this case, *U-47* attacking from the south, turning from port to starboard, would have had to fire first on *Pegasus*. But all the German evidence confirms entirely the war diary. The first two torpedoes were destined for *Royal Oak*. The distance must also be taken into account. If the aircraft transport was moored at some two miles to the north of the battleship, there was little chance that Prien attacked both ships simultaneously. If he thought he was dealing with *Repulse* at anchor there, where *Pegasus* was lying, the true target being much smaller than the assumed target, he would, of necessity, have overestimated the real distance by about 5,000m. In this case, he could not be unaware that the chances of a direct hit were insignificant. He would certainly not have risked firing blindly one of the three precious torpedoes of the first salvo, all the more as he could not reply on the lack of reaction of the British which permitted him to resume the attack. On the other hand, if one of the torpedoes of the first salvo had hit the starboard chain of *Royal Oak*, of which ship did this column of water hide the bow? No sailor of the battleship seems to have seen this column of water. This is what gives belief to an internal explosion. Was *Pegasus* lying more to the east? Unfortunately the British witnesses situate her without hesitation between positions diametrically opposite, from west-north-west to east-south-east.

Each one confidently gives a different point of view, and not only concerning *Pegasus*. On the least little fact arising in the course of that night, the witnesses often diverge, sometimes oppose one another, and rarely agree. One wonders whether all these witnesses have not sworn on oath never to divulge anything. Certainly, thirty years do not pass without blurring the memory and time alone explains most of the gaps and errors committed in perfect good faith. Alexander McKee questioned a number of witnesses, more than 10 years ago, before writing his book on the destruction of the *Royal Oak*[1]. He had arrived at the conclusion that *Pegasus* was lying moored near the north coast of Mainland somewhere between the west and north-west of the battleship, at a distance of about two miles. Hänsel and Dziallas assert having seen the aircraft transport far in the north west. Mr Davies also places her in this direction, again at a large distance; moreover he states that nobody on board *Pegasus* had realised anything.

"Two hours, at least, elapsed before any kind of help came and that help came from *Pegasus* (. . . .) On arriving on *Pegasus* I spoke to the corporal on the gangway, whom I knew and he assured me that nobody on board *Pegasus* had the least suspicion of what had happened to us until the arrival of the first survivor."

On the other hand, Mr R. A. Rowley of *Pegasus* says that the crew were awakened hurriedly about 01.20hrs by two violent explosions. He saw enormous sparks spring suddenly from fore and aft of the *Royal Oak*, then three explosions reverberated over the bay.[2] Mr Rowley makes no mention of the distance between the two vessels.

Mr Rowley noted the silhouette of *Royal Oak* standing out against the sky. This fact would indicate a position of the *Pegasus* more to the north, the battleship being anchored near land, at about half a mile from the east coast of Mainland and at a distance less than two miles because of the proximity of the north shore. The Ministry of Defence

[1] *Black Saturday* Souvenir Press, London 1959.
[2] *Scapa Flow* by Malcolm Brown and Patricia Meehan. Allen Lane, The Penguin Press, London 1968.

referring to the official history gives a position exactly north, in other words places the *Pegasus* in the position where Prien noted the presence of the *Repulse*. Commander R. F. Nichols says so without ambiguity.

"The *Repulse* got under way and then *Pegasus* was moored practically in the same place." (At 1,400 yards in 340° true from the *Royal Oak*.)

In this case, why did the survivors not try to reach the *Pegasus*? And why is it that they waited two hours for the arrival of lifeboats? Only one sailor, Petty Officer G. R. Kerr, told Alexander McKee that he had swum in the icy water for three hours to reach the *Pegasus*. Mr Kerr had this courage despite serious burns and no other person is known to have reached the *Pegasus* by swimming. All are not of the same opinion and situate the *Pegasus* in quite a different direction. For his part, Mr Herbert Johnston remembers clearly having been rescued by the *Daisy II*, then taken with other survivors on board the *Pegasus*, moored a little to the east of the south of the *Royal Oak*, roughly between two and three miles, in Sandoyne bay.

He had already said so to the authors of *Scapa Flow*[1] and he confirms it with a small sketch to support his account. Mr Johnston knows Sandoyne bay especially well because he lived in the small neighbouring village of St Mary. From this position you could also see the *Royal Oak* standing out against the sky. Could she be the small tanker spotted by the watch of *U-47*? Hänsel does not think so because of the superstructure placed clearly more to the centre of the ship. Questioned on this point, Mr Johnston cannot remember the presence of any tanker in Scapa Flow. The German and the Briton have seen two different ships at the same time and in the same place. It is disconcerting to note that the statement of Mr Johnston on the position of the *Pegasus* differs by 180° or more from those collected by Alexander McKee, especially that of John Gatt, skipper of *Daisy II*, as well as the indications supplied by the Ministry of Defence, Commander Nichols and Mr Davies. On the other hand, Mr Johnston, like Mr Davies, but in contradiction to Mr Rowley "never heard it said that anyone on board the *Pegasus* had realised that *Royal Oak* had just been torpedoed."

Mr Johnston's sketch contains two indications which complicate the problem a little more. You see on it two auxiliary cruisers, the *Rawalpindi*[2] of which nobody has spoken, and the *Voltaire* at anchor on

---

[1] Page 147.
[2] Former liner of the P & O Company, the *Rawalpindi* (Commander H. C. Kennedy) was sunk on 25th November 1939 during an unequal battle with the battlecruisers *Scharnhorst* and *Gneisenau*.

the main mooring place of the Fleet, respectively to right and left of the axis of Hoxa Sound. The first of these ships is placed on the course taken by *U-47* after her entry into Scapa Flow. If Mr Johnston's information is correct, either Prien never came to the Orkneys or his war diary is a fake. It is inconceivable that he had not seen these two

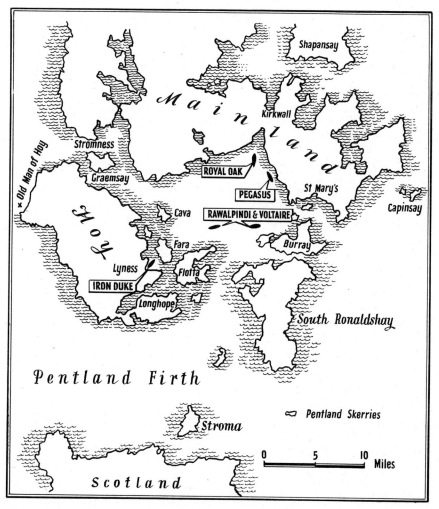

This sketch by Herbert R. Johnston (surviving British eye witness of the sinking of the *Royal Oak*), shows the respective positions of *Pegasus* and the other ships at Scapa Flow during the night of the drama.

liners high in the water or confused one of them with the little patrol boat guarding Hoxa Sound. But if, by chance, the cruiser on the right had been anchored two or three miles more to the south, Prien could not see her effectively behind the land when the submarine was in a south-west course.

In fact, after the torpedoing of *Royal Oak* while *U-47* was steering towards the exit of Scapa Flow sailing along the east coast of Mainland, the Germans on watch had spotted ships getting under way from the direction of Hoxa Sound. The cruiser on the left, moored two or three miles farther north, could be confused, in the darkness, with a cargo ship or a tanker (the tankers 'sleeping at anchor' mentioned in Prien's book). Mr Johnston's sketch intended to give an idea of the respective positions of the ships present at Scapa Flow does not claim to be an accurate map.

The position of *Royal Oak* during the attack also gives rise to divergences. The direction varies according to the statements by 360°. Mr Johnston shows the *Royal Oak* and *Pegasus* anchored parallel to the east coast of Mainland. It is the opinion of a certain number of witnesses both British and German, at least in what concerns the battleship and with the difference that some situate her with her bow to the north and others to the south. According to Commander Nichols the bow was approximately north, the starboard side parallel to the shore. This statement implies that Prien might not have fired from the south and at 3,000m, as he writes in his war diary, but from the east and from much nearer, perhaps from 500 or 600m since the battleship was moored half a mile from Mainland.

The commander of *Royal Oak* explains the two failures of the first salvo and of the stern torpedo precisely because Prien might have attacked from too short a distance. Effectively, when leaving the submarine, the torpedo dives first for some distance before reaching the depth for which it has been regulated. The three torpedoes would have passed under their targets. The war diary mentions that the torpedoes were not magnetic ones (built to explode under the keel of the target). Then the professional error would be obvious and it is difficult to believe that Prien, an experienced submarine officer, could have behaved like a beginner. You would also have to admit either that the crew of *U-47* had completely lost their sense of direction or that Prien took the risk of faking his war diary and presented an imaginary report to his superiors. It would be very surprising, in this case, that the men of the crew had not talked about it and continued to keep silent and the respect the survivors have for Prien's memory gives the lie to such an assumption.

Nobody respects an incompetent and untruthful officer. From the bridge of *U-47* Mr Dziallas had estimated the position of the battleship as being between east and north-east. It is also the opinion of Mr Davies who expresses it with a convincing sincerity.

"It is a question on which opinions differ. Officially I believe, it is thought that the bow of *Royal Oak* was near enough the true north, at the time of sinking: I was only a humble and very insignificant corporal of the Royal Marines at the time and to dispute the fact is without doubt an impertinence on my part. But I was to port of the upper deck when the ship began to sink and I remember very clearly that I saw cliffs well behind the stern because I thought for a moment of the possibility of reaching them by swimming. If the prow had really been to the north I would not have seen the cliffs at all and certainly not in the position where I *know* I *did* see them. I think therefore, that the bow must have been somewhat east of north—about north-east quarter-east, which, naturally, exposed the starboard side to an attack from the south."

The modesty of Mr Davies is much in his favour and he never tried to boast. All the witnesses do not possess this quality. Whatever the reason, the map of Scapa Flow published by the Admiralty under No 35 confirms Mr Davies's statement. The wreck of the *Royal Oak* is shown on it with its bow slightly east of north-east. There is no chance that the battleship might have changed direction appreciably when sinking in the course of the eight to ten minutes after the three hits of Prien's second attack. It is surprising that the hydrographic service of the British Navy has published such a map for the one in the official history marks the wreck with the conventional sign without any indication of direction; without doubt it is a question of lack of co-ordination between the interested services.

The second German eyewitness, Mr Hänsel, has kept a picture of the battleship head on to south-east, the port side parallel to the cliffs (and that of the *Repulse* moored between the *Royal Oak* and the land).

"The *Royal Oak* and the *Repulse* had their bows to the south-east, which is understandable because of the current prevailing at the time of the attack. It is well known that every ship avoids being head on to the current, and, if there is none, head on to the wind. At the time of the attack we were head on to the north-east and were therefore coming from south-west. The second attack came also from south-west but we approached from the east before taking up firing position. At the time of this second attack the distance from *Royal Oak* was very small."

U-47 entered Scapa Flow with the current and there is nothing to say about that. But how to explain the north-east position of the wreck if it were not that the battleship had veered 90° between the moment when her starboard chain ran through its hawse hole and the instant of the hits from the second salvo? The contradictions of the witnesses are only apparent. If, for some the bow was to the north and for others to

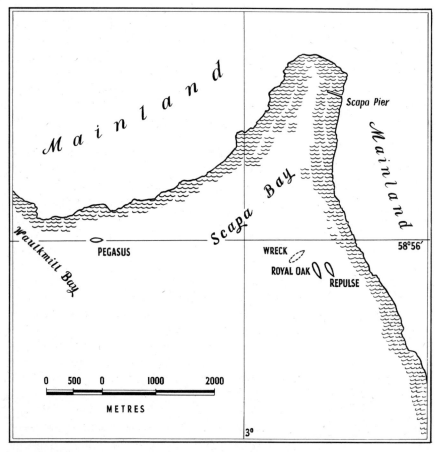

Positions of the *Royal Oak*, *Repulse* and *Pegasus*, reconstructed by Leading Seaman Gerhard Hänsel, one of the two German eye witnesses still living, who was on watch on the bridge during the attack.

224

the south, Nichols, Johnston and Hänsel place the *Royal Oak* parallel to the coast which must have been the case.

Davies and Dziallas place the ship with her bow to the north-east remember the final phase and are equally in the right.

It is interesting to know that Prien had approached much nearer the *Royal Oak* when returning to the attack, very likely less than a mile. The two German eyewitnesses confirm this. This fact reduces still further the possibilities of confusion with *Pegasus*.

Other events or circumstances, having no direct connection with the results obtained by Prien, also lend themselves to different interpretations. For example, was the aurora borealis shining above Scapa Flow as the Germans describe it? The night was so dark that on the deck of *Pegasus* the men were knocking against one another according to Mr Rowley.[1] The adjectives used by the survivors of the *Royal Oak* vary from 'pitch-black' to 'starry'. Some survivors state that they heard men speaking without making them out, in the darkness. In view of the avalanche of statements in favour of complete darkness, it would have been tempting to conclude that Prien had invented the aurora borealis if Commander Nichols had not also noted its lights twinkling in the sky. These subjective appreciations on the darkness of the night illustrate very well the frailty of the evidence.

One should not be too circumspect, especially when it is a question of reconstituting a past event. Memory distorts images; time disembodies and effaces them. Another secondary question: had the British reacted after the destruction of *Royal Oak*? Is it true that the base was hurriedly wakened as Prien says? "And how!" exclaims Hänsel, who adds; "naturally everything livened up enormously. All the ships which were near the coast got under way."

"Yes," confirms Roskill: "even before *U-47* had regained the open sea, about 02.15hrs they had realised at Scapa Flow that a U-boat had probably penetrated the defences and all the available ships took up the hunt."

"No," assures Mr Davies, "nobody except the survivors had realised anything between 01.30hrs and 2.15hrs. For at least two hours nobody carried out any search. On none of the ships was it understood before this time, that we had sunk, and it took even longer for them to begin to react."

Mr Davies expresses the general opinion of some 200 survivors of the battleship. In fact, the latter must have seen nothing. At sea level, they were in bad conditions to observe what could be happening miles

[1] *Scapa Flow*, p 148.

away. The men were moreover, too busy saving their lives to attend to anything but getting themselves out of this mess. The north-east corner of Scapa Flow is a cul-de-sac and no ship would have come there to hunt the attacking submarine. It was logical to suppose that the U-boat had immediately left the scene of her exploits and was trying to escape by one of the passages. We must not forget that Roskill has the decisive advantage of having access to documents such as the log books.

Although the British do not mention it, the presence of the destroyer seen by *U-47* near the entrance of Kirk Sound is probable and it is not surprising that the shipwrecked men struggling in the icy sea four miles away did not see her. It is even less surprising that numerous survivors admit not having made out the *Pegasus* in the night though it was nearer to them and bigger than the destroyer. The two German eyewitnesses assert that they saw the destroyer clearly. Leading Seaman Hänsel distinctly remembers this encounter because of the British signals.

"The destroyer first explored the surface with her large projector, but we were already near the exit. It was only then that she made light signals in our direction. I asked the captain if it was necessary to reply. The destroyer quickly turned away. Probably she had not seen us for, from her position, we were in the shade of the boats sunk in the fairway and she must have taken our wake for an eddy, the current being, then, very strong. We remained in the same position although both our motors were full ahead. We did not manage to progress until after adding the power of our electric motors."

Obviously no British document refers to this encounter and for a good reason; clearly the destroyer had not spotted the submarine otherwise she would not have turned away.

Some British writers blame Prien for having exaggerated the effect produced by the torpedoes. The battleship did not blow up in a few seconds, they argue. However, it does not seem that Prien claimed that the ship was blown to bits by the explosion as would have been the case if the powder magazines had blown up. According to the majority of the British witnesses, a few seconds after the explosion of the three torpedoes of the second salvo, two huge showers of sparks burst on the deck and an intense flame leapt to the height of the mast, that is to say 15m high. Then a very violent explosion shook the ship, letting off thick black smoke, the battleship took a list of 25°.

In three sentences Hänsel describes the impression that the end of *Royal Oak* left on him. "At first, the projectors were trained on the sky, we had already turned about and were making for the exit. The *Royal Oak* sank very quickly after having been hit forward, centre and aft. In the light we saw bits of the ship fly in the air."

This is roughly what Prien writes in his war diary: "Severe explosion, a roar and rumblings. Then columns of water, followed by columns of flames. Debris flying all around."[1]

Paradoxically the torpedoes produced a much more spectacular effect on the crews of *Pegasus* and *U-47* than on that of *Royal Oak*. If in his report to Grand Admiral Dönitz[2] Prien dramatised the end of the ship in summing it up in a brief sentence. "The battleship blew up in a few seconds" it is nonetheless true that *Royal Oak* was definitely out of action a few seconds after the hits.[3]

Some also reproach Prien with writing that he had seen, after the torpedoing, cars 200m away, when the nearest road was a kilometre or more from the shore. They ascribe to Prien what he never said. In fact, he writes in his war diary that cars were running noisily on land 200m away. (Without doubt the south west point of Mainland.) In other words, he does not say that he saw the cars, but heard the throbbing of the engines; in the silence of the night sounds carry far, particularly over water.

Who is Right?

In spite of their contradictions, the British are remarkably unanimous on one point. Prien did not torpedo *Repulse*; the second ship of the line existed only in his imagination. They all say so. The eyewitnesses and the official spokesmen. Who to believe—the Germans or the British? Both are equally positive.

Can you explain the German attack on a 'ship which did not exist' for the British otherwise than by confusion with *Pegasus*? Many English writers and many sailors after them, too British to use the word 'lie' prefer to see in it an hallucination.

For them, Prien 'saw' what he expected to see: *Royal Oak* and *Repulse* moored side by side as they had been photographed on the 12th at about 15.00hrs by Lieutenant Newe. Luckily for *Repulse*, Prien was a little more than twenty-four hours late, for the battlecruiser had got under way at the end of the afternoon on the 12th. How would Prien have had knowledge of this photograph? By radio, quite simply.

---

[1] See Appendix V.
[2] See Appendix VII.
[3] *Royal Oak* sank in: two minutes according to Churchill; eight minutes according to Nichols and thirteen minutes according to Roskill. This last estimate is probably excessive by five to seven minutes at least.

If you accept this theory, you must admit that the hallucination was collective. Prien, Endrass, von Varendorff, Sammann, Dziallas and Hänsel had the same vision of two ships of the line. On the other hand, the Germans assert that Prien received no message. Here is their version of the facts. On the evening of 12th October, Lt Newe was summoned to Wilhelmshaven to comment, in the presence of the commodore of submarines, on the photographs showing heavy and light ships. In effect, the news of the presence of the Home Fleet was the subject of a radio message, in the course of the night, but *U-47* lying at the bottom of the sea never acknowledged receipt[1] of it. The following day, the German listening services intercepted an unusual amount of British radio messages. The decoding service deciphered the meaning of these. The Fleet had left Scapa Flow. As soon as he learned this, the commodore of submarines immediately cancelled the order to transmit his message of the day before.

In any case, the identification of the *Repulse* poses a problem. If, in reality, *U-47* did not receive the message, how could Prien identify a ship which was not there but which was lying precisely at that spot a short time before? Could it have been another battlecruiser, the *Hood* or the *Renown*? The two German eyewitnesses Hänsel and Dziallas have no doubts; they saw the *Repulse*. For the British the only plausible explanation lies in the receipt of the messages.

But could not events have been different? Might not Prien have torpedoed without knowing it the only other battleship present at Scapa Flow?

Witnesses, also British, some of whom are naval officers, recognise it. Moreover the old *Iron Duke* had two funnels, like the *Repulse* and in the night, nothing is more alike than the foredecks of ships of the line. The theory is not improbable and the explanation is logical.

At the beginning of the war the main fear was air attacks. The *Iron Duke* had been partly disarmed and served as a training ship for naval cadets. In the evening of 13th October, the battleship left the badly defended naval base for the anchorage left vacant by the *Repulse* in the shadow of the sheer cliffs on the north-east shore of the bay. At least the bombers could not attack from this direction. Moreover, since the departure of the Fleet, the anti-aircraft guns of the *Royal Oak* constituted the best protection against the Luftwaffe.

The ship to the north was none other than *Iron Duke*. The confusion between the *Repulse* and the former flagship of Jellicoe is more under-

---

[1] See Appendix VI.

standable than the mistake in confusing it with the ex-cargo ship of 6,900 tons.

As it cannot be compressed, water is a good conductor of explosions. This property is used for anti-submarine warfare. A depth charge exploding in the vicinity staves in by pressure the plates of the

Below; Battlecruiser HMS *Repulse* on 23rd April 1938. / Marius Bar

Bottom; HMS *Iron Duke* transformed into a gunnery training ship, photographed in 1939 after her declassification. The two principal 343mm gun turrets have been removed as has her lateral armoured plating, and her speed has been reduced to 18 knots. *Iron Duke* was the flagship of Admiral Jellicoe at the Battle of Jutland. / Wright & Logan

submarine being pursued. The explosion of the torpedo on the *Iron Duke* was clearly felt on board the *Royal Oak* but in a manner sufficiently deadened to make them believe in an internal accident especially as nobody had noticed any column of water. Had the shock wave broken the starboard chain? No witness heard a second explosion, neither on the British side nor on the German.

On board the *Iron Duke* they immediately realised the danger. The explosion could not have escaped the watch of the *Royal Oak* and would not fail to cause an alert, they thought. Still disposing of the necessary pressure, *Iron Duke* let out her anchor chain to gain time and headed for the naval base from which she had come a few hours before. On the one hand, the battleship no longer offered an immobile target for torpedoes and on the other hand, if the watertight doors gave way, the shallow waters around the south-east of the island of Hoy would allow her to go aground without difficulty. At dawn, the personnel of the naval base found the *Iron Duke* again at her anchorage of the evening before. Seen from outside, the battleship appeared intact.

Three days later, on 17th October, four light Ju-88 bombers attacked Scapa Flow. The small group under command of Captain Doench, discovered the principal anchorage deserted. A single large warship, the *Iron Duke* was spotted near the naval base with the auxiliary cruiser *Voltaire*, the hospital ship *Saint Abba* and some small units. The battleship served as a target. Despite the weakness of the anti-aircraft defence, the Germans did not succeed in hitting the target; however, two 500kg bombs exploded very near the battleship, sending up huge columns of water. The pressure caused by one of them blew up the main steam drum. The pipes burst with a din, letting loose a burning cloud. The *Iron Duke* took on a list which went on increasing. Fearing the worst, the crew was allowed to abandon ship. Meanwhile on the foredeck, sailors had let out the hawse to cast off from the buoy to which the battleship was moored. The boats which surrounded the wounded ship to beach her, if it was needed, began to push and pull her 26,000 tons towards the shore. A small tug boat belonging to a private company came to the rescue. The deck of the giant stopped listing as if by a miracle. The *Iron Duke* came to rest for ever on a sandbank in the bay of Ore.

What are the arguments of those who favour the identification of the 'north ship' with the *Iron Duke*? The former flagship of Admiral Jellicoe also served as a floating post-office. The mail was centralised there before being distributed among the different ships. On the morning of the 13th the MFV *Daisy II* had been sent, as usual, to collect the mail bags on board the *Iron Duke* moored near the naval base, ten miles away, and, in the evening, towards 21.00hrs in complete darkness, a motor boat from the *Royal Oak* is ordered to bring back the mail. Can this choice be explained otherwise than by the proximity of the *Iron Duke*?

The Ju-88s used to attack Scapa Flow, were light bombers. This aircraft could only carry two bombs of 500kg on the distance between northern Germany and back. Against ships at anchor the Luftwaffe used armour piercing bombs with delayed fuses containing only 125kg of explosive. This type of bomb had been chosen the day before for the raid on the warships anchored in the Firth of Forth. Efficient in direct hits, those bombs were not so when they burst in the sand or mud at the bottom of the sea. Admitting that the Germans had let off ordinary bombs containing 250kg of explosive, could one or two near misses inflict mortal damage on an intact battleship? Even considering the fact that the lateral armoured plating had been removed, a battleship is intended to withstand even more important hits. It took three torpedoes and internal explosions to sink the *Royal Oak*. Nothing similar happened on the *Iron Duke*. The battlecruiser *Repulse* withstood 18 Japanese aerial torpedoes before sinking. If two explosions of bombs of medium calibre, in the vicinity, had been sufficient to put out of action an undamaged ship of the line, it is inexplicable that the Admiralty, after this experience, would have sent the battleship *Prince of Wales* and the battlecruiser *Repulse* without any air protection within range of the Japanese bombers.

On the other hand, if the *Iron Duke* had been seriously damaged by a torpedo from *U-47*, the underwater explosions of the bombs could have finished off the battleship: watertight doors stove in, pumps stopped by the bursting of the steam drum. Incidentally, the *Iron Duke* might have received Prien's torpedo on the foredeck, according to some, and on the afterdeck, according to others. As for the *Royal Oak*, opinions differ on the direction from the *Iron Duke* when she was torpedoed.

Finally and above all, the *Iron Duke*, if intact, would have had no reason to be surrounded by small boats ready to beach her. If they had not been already alongside, these boats would never have been able to arrive in time to pull and push the battleship during an air attack. They had no reason to come to the rescue of the battleship before she began to list and the experience of the *Royal Oak* had shown that the ship could sink in a few minutes. That is really why they gave permission to abandon ship.

U-47 had put out of action the only two ships of the line present at Scapa Flow, and Prien, without knowing it, avenged the honour of the High Seas Fleet on the very spot of its sacrifice.

On their side the British, only partially recognising Prien's success, and surrounding the operation with the most absolute secrecy, succeeded adroitly in limiting the disaster. They deprived Dr Goebbels of a wonderful propaganda potential which would have aroused the enthusiasm of the Nazi crowds. The *Iron Duke*, partly disarmed and at the end of her days, was only good for scrap. But she had been the flagship of Jellicoe at Jutland, and the flag of Admiral Sir Wilfrid French, commanding the Orkneys and Shetlands, floated at her mast at the moment of her torpedoing.

The story could be true, the arguments appear convincing. But a reply from the Ministry of Defence, dated 18th August 1969, puts everything back in doubt. Here is the text of this official letter:

"In reply to your letter asking for information relative to the destruction of HMS *Royal Oak*: on 12th October 1939, HMS *Renown* was at Freetown, having left the United Kingdom on 2nd October for this destination. No other large ship was in the vicinity when the *Royal Oak* was sunk in the early hours of 14th October 1939. HMS *Hood* was at Loch Ewe, HMS *Repulse* at Rosyth. The sea planes transport HMS *Pegasus* was moored to the north of *Royal Oak* in the bay of Scapa, HMS *Iron Duke* was at the naval base situated on the east coast of Hoy, opposite Switha Sound."

This question of the 'ship to the north'—one of the most important concerning the operational details—is it so important? Grand Admiral Dönitz does not think so. For the former commodore of submarines the main thing was that Prien had carried out his mission brilliantly. The tactical and strategic success of the operation was complete.

Notes

In order not to overload the text with names, three eyewitnesses have been chosen to represent the principal shades of opinion of the survivors of the *Royal Oak*. These are Commander R. F. Nichols, Mr Norman Davies, Royal Marines Corporal, and Mr Herbert Johnston, Stoker.

The crew of the *Royal Oak* cannot be blamed for the loss of their ship. The battleship was anchored in one of the principal bases of the Navy, the security of which depended exclusively on the sedentary services. The naval personnel could only trust in the efficiency of the defences put in place to bar the entrances. The only danger was air attacks and in any case, the old anti-aircraft defences of the *Royal Oak* had been reinforced.

A buoy marks the position of the wreck of the *Royal Oak*. From the air you can see a discoloration of the water caused by the fuel oil which escapes little by little from the hull. The *Royal Oak* lies on her starboard side at an angle of 120° from the vertical, her superstructure embedded in the sand. Only her twisted mast sticks out. The wreck is covered by a dozen metres of water. In 1951, on the occasion of an examination of the wreck, it was noticed that the anchor chain had been cut off with a blow lamp. By whom?

In 1957, the plan to demolish the wreck raised a wave of protest. The Admiralty, respecting the feelings of the relatives of the dead, gave up their plan. The *Royal Oak* covered over with a thick coat of seaweed will remain for a long time the tomb of 833 sailors.

It was on Saturday 21st October 1939 that the ss *Lake Neuchatel* was sunk in Kirk Sound to make it impracticable for navigation. To avoid any possibility of a new disaster, Churchill decided to close the eastern passages by a sea wall in reinforced concrete. The construction cost £2,000,000, took four years and 500 British and Irish workmen and 1,200 Italian prisoners of war to finish this gigantic work baptized 'Churchill's barriers'. On the sea wall, a road joins the north shore of Kirk Sound to South Ronaldsay island passing by Lamb and Glims islets and Burray Island.

On 16th October 1939, in the presence of General Jodl, Grand Admiral Raeder reported on the operation of *U-47* to Hitler. Commander and Commodore Dönitz was promoted Rear Admiral commanding submarines. The captain of *U-47* was decorated with the Iron Cross First Class and the rest of the crew with the Iron Cross Second Class.

Hitler decided to invite the entire crew of *U-47* to the Chancellery. On 18th October, Prien made his report and received from the hands of Hitler the Iron Cross First Class. Prien's two deck officers, Endrass and von Varendorff and his navigator Spahr promoted to officer rank, each received a command.

Lieutenant Commander Spahr carried merchandise from Bordeaux to Penang with *U-178* (type IX D2).

On 24th May 1944, he returned to Bordeaux after an absence of 424 days. He now lives in Hamburg.

Endrass distinguished himself with *U-46* from April 1940 to August 1941: twenty-three ships destroyed, totalling 215,241 tons, among them the auxiliary cruisers *Carintha* and *Dunvegan Castle*. In October

Intense activité des sous-marins allemands

110.000 tonnes de navires coulées

BERLIN, 23 mai. — *Le Grand Quartier Général allemand communique :*

Des sous-marins ont coulé dans un convoi destiné à l'Angleterre neuf navires de commerce ennemis, jaugeant au total 70.900 tonnes brut. Au nombre de ceux-ci se trouvaient trois bateaux-citernes de 8.000, 10.000 et 13.000 tonnes, ainsi qu'un vapeur de 7.000 tonnes lourdement chargé de munitions. 18.000 autres tonnes ont été coulées par des sous-marins agissant isolément.

Au large de l'Afrique occidentale, des sous-marins ont coulé 21.400 tonnes. L'arme sous-marine allemande a donc coulé, au cours de ces derniers jours, un total de 110.300 tonnes brut de navires de commerce ennemis.

Le sous-marin commandé par le capitaine de corvette Günther Prien n'est pas revenu de sa dernière croisière. Ce submersible doit être considéré comme perdu. Le capitaine de corvette Günther Prien, le héros de Scapa Flow, qui a été décoré par le Führer d'une palme à sa croix de chevalier de la Croix de fer, survivra, ainsi que son vaillant équipage, dans le cœur de tous les Allemands.

Comme l'a annoncé un communiqué spécial, l'armée de l'air a infligé hier de très lourdes pertes à des forces navales britanniques opérant en Méditerranée orientale.

French communiqué from the German Supreme Headquarters announcing the death of Prien.

1941 he received command of *U-567*. The submarine disappeared with all hands during her second cruise, in December 1941.

Von Vardendorff commanded *U-213* for a year, when the submarine was destroyed on 31st August 1942, south-east of the Azores. There were no survivors.

Prien died very probably in March 1941. 'Probably' for since the end of the war and up to the present, rumour has it that he is alive. Many persons have seen him throughout Germany, in a prisoner of war camp, in hospital, or in the streets. Madmen, hoaxers, but also witnesses of good faith such as a minister, claim to have passed by him. However, nobody has succeeded in finding him again and for a good reason: Prien perished with the *U-47*, sunk in the early hours of 8th

March 1941 by the escort vessel *Wolverine* (Commander J. M. Rowland) in the course of an attack on convoy OB-293.

Finally, quite recently, in September 1969, the presence of Wehring-Örtel, the spy of Kirkwall, has been announced in southern Germany. But the man who 'knows' does not wish to give either his name, or his address.